Finding Balance

About the author

Helene Lerner-Robbins is the author of *Embrace Change*, *My Timing Is Always Right*, *Stress Breakers*, and *Creativity*. She leads seminars on balancing career and family issues and reducing stress, and conducts networking and mentoring workshops for women. Lerner-Robbins also hosts and produces a popular New York cable television show on wellness and health issues and writes a column for a national magazine. Lerner-Robbins is available for consultation and seminars regarding these topics.

Finding Balance

Helene Lerner-Robbins

 HAZELDEN

Hazelden Educational Materials
Center City, Minnesota 55012-0176

ISBN: 0-89486-901-9

Editor's note:
Hazelden Educational Materials offers a variety of
information on chemical dependency and related areas.
Our publications do not necessarily represent Hazelden's
programs, nor do they officially speak for any Twelve Step
organization.

Some of the names of the people in these meditations
who have shared their experiences have been changed;
some have not been changed and are used with their
permission. These meditations also include some
experiences that are composites taken from a group of
people who have had similar experiences. In the last case,
any resemblance to specific people or specific situations is
coincidental.

INTRODUCTION

Most of us lead hectic life-styles, and juggling our many roles as family members, workers, friends, and community members is often challenging. Tapping into our intuition can help us find balance and prioritize our responsibilities. Over the past twenty years, I have found that one of the greatest gifts of recovery is that I have discovered my intuitive self.

As I have grown, my life has gotten fuller and fuller. I am now a wife, mother, and owner of a business. There are many demands on my time. I have learned not to let stressors in my life determine my actions. Most of the time now, I can pull back from apparent crises and let my intuition guide the actions I take. When I have my off moments, they don't last as long as they used to, and I reach out and get the support I need.

I've been fortunate to know many wonderful people over the years who have also transformed their lives. Their stories are shared in these meditations to offer you hope and courage to press on. You'll probably relate to many of their relationship and work issues and find their solutions applicable in your life.

These practical meditations can be used throughout your day; consult the index at the back of the book to find appropriate topics. You can also use this book in the morning, starting your day with a few minutes of quiet time, then opening the book to see what meditation you're guided to. You're likely to find that its theme is exactly what you need to focus on that day.

As you read this book, know that you have the power to transform your life. Open your heart as you speak one of the closing affirmations out loud. Say it three times. Each time, allow it to penetrate deeper and deeper into your being.

Balance brings up many issues, such as slowing down, giving up being superman or superwoman, handling stress, managing time, living in the moment, and establishing priorities. I've explored many issues that hold us back on our journeys, but I've also explored more comforting aspects of life that are always available to us as we continue to find ways to balance our lives and tap into our intuitive resources.

Today I face my challenges with ease.

As adults, we find that our lives are filled with responsibilities. It's common for many of us to take ourselves too seriously, forgetting to schedule time during the day for recharging our batteries when they start to run down.

A friend of mine, a top corporate executive, says, "I've learned to view crises on the job as challenges, and I take a time-out when I'm faced with a challenge. I've been known to leave the office mid-morning, take a walk around the block, and then come back to work. Removing myself for a short time from a stressful environment helps me see problems from a fresh perspective when I return."

Shelving our problems temporarily and doing something that pleases us is a way to balance our perspective. It ultimately leads to new insights into our challenges.

Help me manage my impulse to figure things out,
and help me take time out to put things into
perspective.

*Today I take an action
to recharge my batteries.*

Many of us give to our co-workers, friends, and loved ones to the point of neglecting ourselves. By not taking time to replenish, we may find ourselves running on empty. Like a long-distance train that needs to refuel midway before it reaches its destination, we need to refuel emotionally, physically, and spiritually. Why is it so hard for us to give to ourselves? Colleen, an acquaintance of mine, put it this way: "My job is very demanding, and by the end of the week, I just want to hibernate. My social life suffers because I don't have the energy to see my friends. My therapist suggested that I take actions during the week to recharge: 'Get a manicure during lunch. Go for a massage a few times a month after work.' She's right. I have to start taking more time for myself."

Many of us don't know how to nurture our-selves, and starting to do so may feel uncom-fortable. But if we persist, it will get easier to act in healthier ways.

> *Grant me the willingness*
> *to replenish myself when*
> *I am drained.*

*Today I take the time
to evaluate my priorities.*

Many of us go from one thing to the next, taking little time for ourselves. Karen worked from seven in the morning to nine at night, until she had a mild heart attack and was forced to make changes.

She says, "I denied that I was overtired and depleted by working such long hours. I was only forty-two when I had the attack. I never thought that it could happen to me. In a way, my illness was a gift because I was forced to look at myself. While I was recovering at home, I read a lot, took long walks, and went to concerts—things I haven't done in years."

Now, Karen's back at work, but she doesn't spend as much time in the office, and to her amazement, she's more efficient. She has learned that there's a cut-off point at the end of the work day, and she has other interests that she wants to pursue.

Each day, we need to take some personal time for ourselves. And when we do, there seems to be enough time to accomplish the things we have to do. What doesn't get done today can wait until tomorrow.

Help me get off the treadmill,
just for today.

*Today I experience my growth
even when setbacks occur.*

When we are perfectionistic, our expectations about ourselves are often unreasonable and leave us frustrated. Mike, a friend of mine, told me about his first acting coach, who helped him keep a balanced perspective about the auditioning process.

"The nature of the entertainment industry is extremely competitive," Mike says, "and every actor experiences lots of setbacks. It's easy for an actor to get perfectionistic.

"One night in class, our coach pointed to an entrance door and said, 'You see this door. You can see that I'm ten steps away from it. Now, I'm going to take three small steps toward it. People in the business will point out how far you are from the door. There's always something you may be lacking—a certain look, a better acting technique, etc. Don't measure yourself as they do. Measure yourself by the progress you make. You are three steps closer to the door, aren't you? And as you grow as actors, you'll be ten steps closer to the door. If you measure your success on how much you've grown, rather than on how close you are to a result, you'll rarely get frustrated.' "

Our perfectionism keeps us from expanding. But when we lower our expectations of ourselves and allow for mistakes, we take giant steps in our growth process.

*Grant me the willingness
to be less perfectionistic
with myself and others.*

*Today I experience a benevolent force
looking after me.*

We may hold on to our challenges with a tight grip, not wanting to let go of them. But when we believe that the universe is governed by a benevolent force that is looking out for our best interests, it's easier to loosen up.

Rhonda, an acquaintance, told me that she was able to go through surgery to have a growth removed, trusting that she would be taken care of: "I was able to remain calm because I knew that I had done everything I could do. I got the best doctor and was at the best treatment center. I let only my closest friends visit me. I didn't want to see anyone who would be nervous and worried about my condition.

"I trusted that the success or failure of the operation was in my Higher Power's hands. Right before I went in for the surgery, I met another patient who was having a similar operation. We wished each other luck and I felt her genuine concern for me. Our momentary connection was so reassuring."

As we give support to and receive support from others, we become centered in our true selves.

Help me know
that I need not face
my challenges alone.

Today I use the right amount of energy on a given task.

Why do many of us feel exhausted throughout the day? Well, for one thing, we expend too much energy on simple tasks that could be done with relative ease. For each activity we undertake, we need only put out what's needed to complete it, nothing more or less. If we pay attention to the task before us, we'll know what measure of effort is appropriate.

Carole explains it this way: "When I'm sitting and writing a letter to a client, I do that, nothing else. I used to write the letter, listen to office gossip, and answer the phone when it rang. Working this way only gave me stress headaches. I've learned to tackle one activity at a time. And when I do this, I am more efficient and calm."

When we get pulled in different directions, we need to *stop* and prioritize our tasks. In this way, we can give our full attention to the most important task before us.

Help me do one thing at a time and not feel scattered.

Today I understand the value of having a backup plan.

When we put all our energy into anticipating that things will go one way, we are caught off balance when our plans don't work out. A great stress reducer is to have a Plan B so we can easily shift from one course of action to another.

Michael has learned the value of planning for a variety of outcomes in business: "I used to count on specific clients to buy my products. Inevitably, some of them wouldn't come through, and I'd fail to meet my sales quota. Now, I've learned to make a second group of calls, no matter what accounts I think will come through."

There's a difference between projecting and planning: planning helps situations work out smoothly; worrying or projecting whether things will work out creates added stress and confusion.

Help me plan adequately for the things
that I want in my life.

*Today I focus on myself
and don't get sidetracked.*

It's so easy to get off balance by *reacting* to angry people who push our buttons. That's a sure way to drain our energy and lose our perspective.

My friend Cheryl has learned how to avoid reacting: "I've always had a terrible problem blowing up at people who were angry with me, and I exhausted myself fighting with them. I joined a support group to learn a different way. The members in my group suggested that I learn to *detach* from angry people. I learned that I could separate myself from them and keep the focus on my needs. I didn't cause their anger, I can't control their anger, and I can't cure their anger. I'm finding that I don't have to rise to the bait anymore."

If we realize that the people who attack us are crying out for help, we need not react with our anger. Even though they are off center, they do *not* have the power to change the way we feel about ourselves.

Help me realize that people
who try to hurt me are really hurting
themselves.

13

*Today I share in the abundance
around me.*

Very often, we create imbalance by trying to
make things happen, instead of *letting* them un-
fold. Rosalie, a colleague of mine, has learned
to make her sales calls, do the follow-up, and
then let go. As a result, she's become very successful over the past two years.

Rosalie says, "I used to push too hard to get
the accounts I wanted; I was afraid that they
wouldn't come my way. What ended up happening is that I alienated my prospects. I was labeled a pest. Instead of looking forward to my
calls, my customers dreaded them. I was desperate for business, and people felt it.

"My manager gave me some advice, which I
took. It turned things around for me. He said,
'Just be of service to your customers. You have a
product, and they need it. Focus on that, and
more business will come your way.' He was

right. I do the legwork, and the people who need my services continue to be drawn to me."

When we serve others, we create abundance in our lives. We need only let people know what we are offering, and wait until they are ready to receive it.

Help me trust that as I offer my services,
I will receive my fair share
of prosperity.

*Today I will take time out
to do the unexpected.*

How often do we get so caught up in activities that we can't take advantage of the unexpected gifts that come our way? When we get too busy to smile back at a caring neighbor, or chuckle with a child who is tugging at our coat, or lend a hand to an elderly person who is walking across the street, we are out of sync with what's really important in our lives.

We can get back in balance if we bring ourselves into the moment, pause, and take a look at what's around us, really *see* the people in front of us and *listen* to what they are saying. If we put our full attention on them, we'll be surprised by the gifts that come our way.

Sally's recent experience illustrates this point. She says, "I was busy working at home, and my two-year-old daughter came running over to me. I asked my baby-sitter to take her away. I kept trying to get through to my client but was unable to. My daughter was also persistent and kept calling, 'Mommy, come in here,' from the next room.

"It dawned on me that maybe I should take a break. Left to my own devices, I wouldn't have realized that I needed one. But my daughter knew better. We spent a lovely half hour rolling around on the floor and playing with her favorite ball."

Balance happens when we take time out to play. When we do, we find that we have renewed enthusiasm to tackle our projects again.

Grant me the willingness to play
in the midst of a busy schedule.

*Today I let go of my expectations
of people around me.*

Expecting the people around me to act as I would like them to gets me off track. Through the years, I've learned that the only person I have any control over is myself. My friend Barbara has guided me in this area.

"If I keep on *demanding* something from my husband," Barbara says, "he never does it. And if I'm on my son's back, I don't get his cooperation, I get a tantrum instead. Demanding things from people never works.

"What works is to *ask* for something and then let go. Asking and demanding are two different things. In asking, we give people the option of saying yes or no, while demanding puts pressure on them to do what we want."

Having expectations of others can drain our energy. There's a metaphor I use to describe my potential energy: I think of my body as being composed of sugar cubes. When I demand that my husband go shopping for groceries and he doesn't, I get upset. As a result, I've used up about fifteen sugar cubes, the same amount I would have needed to do the job myself.

When we let go of our expectations, we take care of our needs, and we empower ourselves.

Help me keep the focus on myself
and channel my energy
productively.

*Today I pull back and reassess the situations
in my life that cause me stress.*

Most of us are so used to feeling under pressure
that we believe excessive stress is a normal part
of everyday life. But the truth is, *we are stressed
because we are "stressable."* It's not the situations
in our lives that cause us stress but our reactions
to them.

Jim, a friend of mine, has learned this the
hard way. He says, "I've always been a hyper
person and filled my life with lots of stress. At
work, if something went wrong—and it always
did—I felt compelled to try to fix the problem."

About six months ago, Jim's doctor warned
him that he was getting an ulcer and had to
slow down. At his doctor's suggestion, Jim
started to ask himself before reacting to a crisis,
Do I need to get involved?

"I've gotten much better because I don't
have to handle *everything* these days," says Jim.
"Last week, my boss asked me to reconcile an

accounting error that had been made. In the past, I would have had to find out who made it and why it happened. This time, I adjusted the error and went on to the next assignment."

When the repercussions of stress overload creep up on us, we need to look for new ways of dealing with situations. We can diffuse our stress if we learn to pull back from a potential crisis and sort out what we need to do about it.

Help me learn to be discriminating about
what my fair share of the responsibility is
and take appropriate actions.

*Today I take a step forward, even if it means
giving up something or someone
I've known for a long time.*

Sometimes, in order to grow, we need to let go
of someone or something that is no longer appropriate for us. Often we stay with a person,
place, or thing too long because we are afraid to
experience the pain of letting go. But when our
heart counsels separation, we cannot deny its
guidance.

Karen was debating whether to stay married
to her husband. The two of them had had a
stormy marriage from the start and had been
seeing a therapist for a year trying to work things
out. She says, "I have a five-year-old girl and
thought it best to give the marriage one last
chance for my daughter's sake. Unfortunately, it
was becoming apparent that no matter how
much I worked on myself, my husband and I
were incompatible. There was constant fighting,
which wasn't good for any of us. I hesitated to
leave because my new business was just getting

off the ground, and I didn't make enough money to support my daughter and myself yet.

"I called a close friend who is like a spiritual adviser to me, and I asked her if she thought it was the right time to leave. 'Relationships should be empowering,' she counseled. 'Change doesn't happen when it's convenient for us. Keep taking actions to grow your income, and trust in the goodness of the universe. Know that you and your daughter will be taken care of.' "

Many of us stay in situations that we've outgrown, feeling drained and off balance because we haven't worked out all the details of leaving yet. If we choose to separate, we can find support to do so from caring friends who'll help us to move on.

Help me find the courage to follow
what my heart counsels.

Today I refuse to worry.

What drains our energy more than anything else? *Worry!*

We worry about events that have not happened to us yet. We worry about things that have already occurred. Our worries are often not logical, they just seem to appear in our consciousness.

A friend of mine named Gabrielle has shared some insights with me: "I think of worrying as an energy-drainer, and I just don't have that much energy to let drain away. So when I catch myself starting to worry, I focus my attention on something that's productive.

"For example, on Friday night, I found it difficult to put my work problems to rest. I caught myself thinking about a situation that had no solution yet. I told myself, *Thinking these thoughts will not change anything. What you really need is a distraction. Go to the movies.* And I did.

I was able to relax with friends and enjoy the rest of my weekend."

Worrying about a worry never makes it go away! Worrying is a choice. You can either let it consume your energy, or you can focus on being centered. When a worry strikes, let go of it by focusing on something totally unrelated.

Help me understand that there
is no productive value
in worrying.

Today I accept the reactions of people in my life.

When we try to manipulate people to make them act as we would like them to, we create imbalance in our lives. Despite what we might think, we can't *make* co-workers, friends, or lovers do things unless they want to.

Once we understand this, we begin to know that the people, places, and things in our lives are exactly as they are supposed to be. This realization frees us to spend our energy more productively.

Help me understand that I can not control the uncontrollable.

Today I take nurturing actions for myself.

Many of us have encouraged others to grow and flourish but have neglected ourselves in the process. Nurturing ourselves is as necessary to our well-being as the air we breathe and the food we eat. By giving ourselves little gifts each day, we begin to fulfill our needs. These things can include fresh flowers, long walks, warm baths, and regular conversations with loving friends.

As we give these things to ourselves, we feel recharged and better able to tackle the challenges before us.

Grant me the willingness to do
nice things for myself.

*Today it's okay to take
the slower track.*

I feel stressed and off balance when I give my attention to more than one thing at a time . . . when I am with a client and thinking about what I have to do next . . . when I overload myself with too many things on my "to do" list.

Our culture rewards action, and many of us feel that if we are not doing something, we are wasting our time. Eastern philosophies teach us that this isn't so. Being still and listening to the sounds around us are some of the most productive things we can "do."

A colleague of mine, Bee, makes a conscious effort each day to have her children pitch in and do some of the housework. She says, "I've learned that when I take on too much, I'm less efficient. Each of my boys now has two chores to do each day. In that way, I give my full attention to what is in front of me, and I don't burn myself out."

Many of us are beginning to understand the wisdom in the adage "Less is more." Once we understand the value in downscaling, it becomes more acceptable to say no to some of the demands on our time.

Help me let go
of the things in my day
that are not essential to do.

Today I will start one thing that I have been putting off.

Procrastination keeps us off balance and depletes our energy. Rather than achieving our desired goals, we hold on to the guilt of never starting a project. Why do we procrastinate? Many of us are afraid of failing or not getting something we really want. When we come to understand that there's a Divine Guidance overseeing all that we do, we realize that there is no such thing as failure, because each experience offers us the lessons we need for growth.

A friend, Kathleen, handles procrastination by just doing *one* task to move a project along. She says, "If I do some little thing, like getting out a folder and labeling it, that's a beginning."

Procrastination stops when we make a small start. Taking *one* action propels us in the right direction.

Let me divide challenging projects into simple tasks and begin by doing one of them.

Today I take actions and let go of the results.

We need to take actions and go for our visions, and then leave the results up to our Higher Power. When we try to manipulate things into going our way, our lives become imbalanced. My friend Leslie has a wonderful analogy about taking action: "A bird can't fly unless it has two wings; just using one won't get it off the ground. I think of one of its wings as *effort* and the other wing as *grace*. When grace and effort are combined, the bird soars through the sky."

It's the same with taking actions to achieve our desires. We can put forth the effort, but we need God's grace to make them happen.

*Help me take actions to achieve my desires
and understand that if my goals don't materialize,
something better is in store for me.*

*Today I give up
needing to be all things
to all people.*

It's comforting to know that other people can care for our loved ones and that we don't need to do everything ourselves. My friend Alisha learned this the hard way. "I am a doctor in a cancer care unit and love my job," she says. "I took three months' leave when I had my first child, and I felt very conflicted about returning to work. I felt guilty about leaving my son, Alan, with someone else.

"I hired a wonderful woman to take care of him, but that didn't make me feel any less guilty. One day, I dropped in on them unexpectedly, and they were reading together. Alan seemed happy, and I realized that he was doing just fine without me. Also, I've come to understand that it's not the *quantity* of time I spend with my son that's important, but the *quality* of time we have together that makes the difference."

Giving up the need to be all things to all people is hard for many of us, because we've acted this way for so long. But if we take baby steps and just do *one* thing a little bit differently, we'll begin to make changes.

Help me let go
of the need to be superman
or superwoman.

Today my body is in perfect health.

Are we keeping ourselves in good shape? Are we getting enough rest? Do we exercise? Are we eating the right foods? When we don't take the time to care for our health, we become vulnerable to emotional mood swings and physical diseases.

A colleague of mine, Mel, has gained fifty pounds in the last year. "I don't know how the extra weight crept up on me," he says. "One day, I looked in the mirror and I was the same person, but I looked blown up. It's really hard to take weight off once you've gained it. When I was thinner, I could never get myself to exercise. But because I'm heavier and vulnerable to heart disease, I'm finding the time to go to the gym."

Unfortunately, for many of us, pain is the touchstone of growth. And like Mel, we learn to care for our bodies out of necessity and not until then.

Grant me the willingness to take care of my body by eating well and getting enough rest and exercise.

Today I will choose my priorities and act accordingly.

We often get sidetracked by making a fuss over petty issues. Instead, we need to set our priorities and choose the matters that are worth fighting for. Norman, an acquaintance, learned this the hard way. He says, "I was labeled the office troublemaker because I just blurted out what I felt on any issue, big or small. I could sense my co-workers and boss distancing themselves from me, but I couldn't seem to change my behavior. One of the guys took me aside after work and confirmed what I felt. He suggested that I try to focus on the important issues at hand and listen more to other people, rather than say what was on my mind."

As Norman found out, if we want to have a positive impact on the people we work with, it's best to offer our opinions only on issues of great concern to us.

Grant me the willingness to let go
of my self-centeredness.

*Today I do one task
at a time.*

Many of us try to cram too much into our days
and become used to doing several things at
once, which is a great source of stress and
strain. Trying to tackle more than one thing at
a time not only depletes our energy but creates
undesirable results. Tasks get done haphazardly
when we don't give them our full attention.

Marie always does too much. If you call her
at home, she's usually making a dress for her
daughter and taking care of the roast in the
oven as she's talking to you.

She says, "I've always had a lot of energy, so I
do a lot during the day. One evening, I was trying to fix my daughter's bike, and I keeled over
with violent cramps. They didn't go away, so I
went to see my doctor in the morning. He took
some preliminary tests, and a week later, I found
out that I have an ulcer. Now I have to learn to

slow down. I find myself saying no more often, which has always been hard for me to do."

When we find ourselves overcommitted, we need to lessen our load by saying no to requests that will create added stress and strain.

Grant me the willingness
to slow down and not
take on too much.

Today I look for new ways to reduce my stress load.

When we are stressed and *reacting* to situations, we are off balance and not using our energy productively. If we take a moment to pull back from the approaching challenge, we will be better able to see what needs to be done. Vicky did just that. She says, "I used to waste a lot of time and energy trying to get back to vendors who'd call me. Often it would take three phone calls before we'd talk to each other. That left all of us frustrated. One day, it dawned on me that my secretary could set up telephone appointments with these people. This system really works. I end up saving time, energy, and money, and I speak to them within a week of their original call."

So often we spin our wheels because we get caught up in the stress around us. At these times, it's best to pull back as Vicky did and evaluate the situations.

Help me take creative actions to
diffuse the stress around me.

The solutions to my challenges are here for me now.

Often when we are faced with challenges, we keep our minds on the problem instead of leaving ourselves open to possible solutions that may present themselves. A wise friend of mine named Jack told me what he does to let go of worrying: "When I find myself worrying, I take a deep breath. I say to myself, *There will be a solution in God's time.* I take a few more deep breaths, and by this time, I can feel myself starting to relax. As I calm down, an option that I hadn't thought about usually pops into mind. Or sometimes a friend shares a story that gives me insight into my problem."

As Jack realized, our answers will come to us when we take the time to be still and quiet our racing minds.

Help me understand that worrying serves
no useful purpose.

*Today I open myself up
to the suggestions of people
around me.*

Often our friends, colleagues, and acquaintances provide us with answers to meet our challenges. We need to be open enough to hear them and humble enough to receive their help.

A friend of mine, Madeline, told me how a parent at her daughter's school had the solution to a problem she was facing: "I work at home so I can be around my daughter, Michelle, who is two years old," Madeline says. "Sometimes, when I'm working and she's playing in her room, I feel that I don't give her the attention she needs.

"I'm on a limited budget, so I can't hire a baby-sitter full time. One mother suggested that I make play dates for Michelle. She said, 'The other children have sitters, and they'll watch the children as you work. And when you have time, you'll do the same.' It was a great idea, and I've already started doing it."

There are always answers to our concerns, if we are open to receiving them. And as Madeline found out, they sometimes come to us from unexpected sources.

Let me rest in the awareness
that everything I need to know
is available to me now.

Today I take time to pause in between activities.

Many of us get overly caught up in daily responsibilities and chores. Under stress, we lose perspective and think these tasks have to get done, or else. We become so attached to the outcomes of our actions that if we don't "make" something happen the way we desire it, we become panicked and fearful.

How can we get back on track? By simply taking time to pause in between activities. Most of us go from one activity to the next without taking a break. We need to stop, pause, and gain perspective before we go on to our next task.

The practice of pausing between activities can change our lives. Don't take my word for it. Try it and see.

Help me get off the treadmill by pausing
throughout my day.

Today I look forward to exercising.

Finding a balanced exercise regimen can be both centering and exhilarating. Unfortunately, when it comes to exercising, some of us go to extremes, doing too much of it or too little.

Tara started to exercise again after not working out for a while. She says, "It was so hard to get back into a routine. But people at the gym kept on encouraging me to keep it up. They said it would get easier the more I did it. It's been about two months now. I do twenty minutes of aerobics before I go to work. I feel energized by my routine, ready to face the challenges ahead of me."

As Tara found out, when we take care of our bodies better, our whole psyche is transformed. Our friends can support us in getting started and keeping up a disciplined routine until we become aware of the benefits that result.

Help me take a step toward bringing
my body and mind into balance.

*Today I can accept the things
I cannot change.*

Being overly concerned with our loved ones creates imbalance in our lives. My friend Paula was spending a lot of time trying to get her recently widowed mother to become more social.

Paula says, "I love my mother and was concerned that she was spending too much time alone. I'd take her out to dinner and suggest that she go to movies and concerts with friends, but she never did. I was obsessed with trying to make my mother happy.

"My husband's friend Tom recently lost his father, and I called him up to see how he was doing. We talked at great length, and I told him how concerned I was about my mother. I really felt that he understood what I was going through. He told me that all I can do is love Mom. She's going to do whatever she does, and there's nothing I can do to change that.

Paula began to realize that the best thing she could do for her mother was to pray for her well-being. By taking this action, she felt more peaceful.

As we give up trying to control our loved ones, we find the Serenity Prayer a great source of comfort: "God, grant me the serenity to accept the things I cannot change, the courage to change the things I can, and the wisdom to know the difference."

Help me release my concerns
for my loved ones.

Today I challenge myself by doing something new.

Our fears can hold us back from achieving our heartfelt desires, but if we learn to accept them, not suppress or deny them, we can take actions to move our lives forward.

Marla just came back from a dream vacation. She says, "I had always wanted to go to the island of St. Thomas but never got farther than the next state because I was terrified to travel so far away. I've been working hard in therapy to take more risks, despite my fears, and I decided to go to the Caribbean. Although I was afraid at times during the trip, I had the time of my life."

Our fears can keep us from growing, if we let them. Instead, we need to become observant of what we are afraid of and, with support, challenge ourselves to break through and take actions anyway. When we do, we are often given gifts beyond our expectations.

Help me move beyond my fears by taking small steps to accomplish my heartfelt desires.

Today I listen to my heart and act accordingly.

Often we get complacent and stay with the status quo, ignoring the yearnings of our hearts. My friend Henry is a lawyer who has recently been unhappy because he didn't feel challenged by his work. One evening, while we were out to dinner, he started to draw on a paper tablecloth. I was very surprised because I wasn't aware that he had artistic talent. He said, "I've always loved to sketch but never got around to doing it. I was too busy building my career and raising my family. I've yearned to make time to paint." I suggested he enroll in an evening course, especially now that his children were grown and out of the house. He smiled, and I knew I had given him something valuable to think about.

We need to balance our lives with activities that nourish our spirit. Despite what we sometimes think, there is always a way of doing this. We just need to create it for ourselves.

*Grant me the willingness to take an action
to nourish my soul.*

Today I share quality time with my family.

It's so easy to get distracted by work matters, and when we do, it can take away from quality time we could be spending with our families and friends. My friend Nora sells clothing out of her home and found herself spending little time with her family.

She says, "My daughter, Katie, is unhappy because I don't play with her much. The whole purpose of running a business out of my home was to spend more time with her. And I'm letting administrative chores get in the way of spending important time with Katie. I need to do something about this."

We can all benefit by reevaluating our priorities. As we do this, we are better able to change the things that need changing.

Help me re-prioritize and spend more time with those I love.

48

Today I enjoy the people around me.

Do we laugh with our friends? Do we do silly things, just for the fun of it? Are we able to sing, dance, go to the movies, or go on outings with people we like? If the answer is no to more than one of these questions, we need to stop and reevaluate how we spend our time. And we can profit by making a commitment to put *fun* back into our lives.

Let me create more "joy time"
with my friends and loved ones.

Today I greet other people,
knowing that we are
all united.

We get off balance when we become defensive, seeing those around us as separate from ourselves. Our gender, hair, eye color, and personality may be different, but our makeup as people is the same.

Our true nature is to love and deeply care about other beings. When we do, we feel unified with all creatures on the planet. On a spiritual level, there is only one Self. When we forget this, we feel isolated from the people closest to us.

Maxine has told me how her perception of her husband shifted within the course of an evening. She says, "My husband blurted out something that was insensitive. He thought that I had gained weight, and let me know it in a crude way. I was hurt by his remark and pulled away from him until bedtime. Lying there on the bed, I felt so lonely. So I decided to tell him how upset I was. He apologized, and I felt my heart opening up to him again."

When others hurt or wrong us, we usually become defensive and push them away. But when we hold on to their wrongdoings, we are the ones who truly hurt, because we close them out of our hearts and deny our loving natures. It is by loving that we come to know the truth—that there is only one Self.

Help me know that we are
of one mind,
one heart,
and one soul.

*Today I can handle
whatever challenges
are presented to me.*

Life can become overwhelming when we are consumed by our challenges. That happened to my friend Jane, who was concerned about whether her company would survive tight financial times: "I worried constantly about whether I'd make my office rent and used up a lot of valuable time that could have been better spent making sales calls.

"One night, I called a colleague I've always looked up to. He's a spiritual man and a good listener. I told him how traumatized I felt, and he responded, 'Jane, you're never given more than you can handle.' I reflected on what he said, and it was true. Any previous challenge I'd been faced with had ultimately worked out for the good. That simple statement and his confidence in my ability to turn things around helped me. The next day, when my worrying started, I was able to stop it by thinking, *I am never given more than I can handle.*"

Grant me the willingness
to accept the loving guidance
of friends.

*Today I take care
of my physical health.*

We all know that it's important to keep ourselves in good health, but do we take the time to do this? Because of our hectic life-styles, we may forget to have our annual checkup at the doctor's or go to the dentist regularly.

Some of us have grown up with poor role models. An acquaintance of mine, Alice, talks about her mother's self-neglect: "My mother was busy doing for us, but she didn't take very good care of herself. When I was about ten, she was taken to the hospital. She was overweight, and she had had a mild heart attack, but that didn't stop her from eating chocolate cake.

"I've picked up some of her bad habits. Sometimes I have a candy bar instead of lunch. I know that I shouldn't be doing that."

Taking care of our bodies is a prerequisite for taking care of our emotional and spiritual well-being. When we let ourselves go, we create imbalance in all areas of our lives.

Help me do what's needed
to keep myself
in good health.

As I serve people in my life,
I keep a balanced perspective.

Sometimes when we start a new venture, we put all our energy into it, to the exclusion of spending time with our family and friends. Ralph, a friend of mine who started a business eight months ago, has learned what helps him keep his equilibrium.

He says, "My business is growing, and I'm very excited. I've been working long hours, but somehow I know that when I close the door on my shop, my business day ends. I've purposely scheduled dinner engagements with friends at least twice a week and have been open to receiving calls from a volunteer organization that I belong to. I could have told them that I was too busy now, but I knew that it was good for me to get out of myself and support others."

It's important that we lead well-rounded lives. We can work hard, but we also need time to relax and share ourselves with friends and loved ones. Living this way replenishes our energy and creates a balanced perspective on work, family, and civic responsibilities.

*Help me to remember that giving
service to others is a great
equalizer.*

Today I give myself the gift of time.

Many of us feel that there isn't enough time in the day to do the things we need and want to do. Yet, if we learn to prioritize our tasks, we find that the important things get done.

My friend Sheila has learned to organize her day. She says, "I used to be all over the place at work, never feeling that I accomplished what I needed to. My boss suggested that I order my tasks, which I started doing. I actually labeled them, from the most important A's to the least important C's."

By using our time effectively and setting priorities, we can always do what's important to us.

Help me organize my day so I can accomplish my work with relative ease.

Today I stop rehashing worst-case scenarios.

How often do we take an action, then scrutinize what we have done, wondering if we have done the right thing? Rehashing whether we would have been better off doing something else is unproductive. If we have made a mistake, we'll know soon enough, and there's probably nothing we can do about it.

Kate has practiced letting go of her negative thinking for many years now. She says, "When I second-guess what I've done, I know from many painful experiences that I drain my energy, and frankly, I'd rather put it to better use."

Breaking old habit patterns, especially that of negative thinking, is not an easy task. But if we persist, we can make headway, and the reward is great: we live more vital, exciting lives.

Help me become aware of my negative thinking and focus my attention on something more productive.

*Today I find joy
in doing simple things.*

Many of us think that by achieving power and fame, we'll feel whole and complete. However, for some of us, the price of succeeding is such long hours and fierce competition that we lose sight of our loving nature.

A friend of mine, Greg, says, "When I was in my thirties, I wanted to be the president of a large financial institution. My life was about work and nothing else. I was always striving for one thing or another.

"Now that I'm in my early fifties, I'm much more content with living a simple life. I live at the beach with my family and teach tennis classes to vacationers. I have the time to enjoy simple pleasures. I've eliminated all the frills. I no longer have an apartment in the richest part of town or dine in fancy restaurants. I don't miss any of it, because I never want to go back to the crazy pace I kept to afford those extravagances."

As Greg found out, we can all benefit by simplifying our lives, and the gifts we get by slowing down are priceless.

Grant me the willingness
to simplify my life.

*Today I don't allow myself to get
too hungry, angry, lonely, or tired.*

There's a slogan in the Twelve Step programs: "HALT—Never get too **h**ungry, **a**ngry, **l**onely, or **t**ired." When we are in any one of these states, we are extremely vulnerable to reacting inappropriately.

If we feel hungry, we need to stop what we are doing and have a meal. If we are angry, we need to share our irritability with those who can listen. If we spend too much time alone, we need to reach out to friends. And if we are tired, we need to rest instead of pushing ourselves to do more.

Being aware of our needs and taking actions to get them met constructively can help us live more harmonious lives.

*Help me stop and take appropriate actions when I
get too hungry, angry, lonely, or tired.*

Today I use humor in all my affairs.

Humor is the great equalizer. It can diffuse stress and make us look on the brighter side. We need to get into the habit of using it when we start taking ourselves too seriously.

Ben has a wonderful sense of humor. He says, "My father was always joking around. Even when times were tough, he found time to smile. I really admired his light touch and have tried to follow his example. After all, when you've done everything you can do about a challenging situation, why cry about it? It's much more fun to laugh and get on with your life."

Like Ben, we can all benefit by looking on the brighter side of the challenges we face.

Help me become aware of when
I am taking myself too seriously.

*Today I will contribute appropriately
to the people around me.*

Many of us have a tendency to give too much of
our time and energy to others. We have to learn
to define our boundaries in relationships, saying
yes when we're comfortable with requests and
no when we're uncomfortable.

Yvonne is learning to give in new ways. She
says, "As a child, I was expected to be like a
mother to my mother, so caretaking has been a
problem for me. As I've been able to sort out
my past, I've started to establish new types of
relationships.

"I recently volunteered at a local library.
They asked me to come twice a week, but I
knew that would be too much for my schedule.
We agreed upon once a week. I read to the children, and I am really enjoying my time with
them."

We are in sync with our spirituality when we find the balance between giving too little or too much.

Help me discern
what I truly want to give,
then let me give
with a full heart.

*I will slow down and take care
of myself.*

When we take on too much, we often feel exhausted and don't listen to our bodies when they tell us to slow down. And when we don't listen, we are prone to sickness.

Nathan told me how he's slowing himself down: "I'm used to pushing and getting myself worked up over nothing. I recently started to get bad headaches, which I thought were stress-related, so I enrolled myself in a stress-reduction class at my gym. The instructor taught us how to breathe from the diaphragm and said we should do this when we find ourselves becoming agitated."

If we are stressed and feeling at the mercy of people and situations, we need to stop whatever we are doing. By taking a few deep breaths, we can find some distance from our problems.

Then we can better think about our options
and chart a course of action.

When I'm troubled, grant me the willingness
to take a few deep
breaths.

Today I allow myself to rest.

Most of us feel that we are only productive when we take actions. But it is equally productive to rest during the day and replenish our energy. Lunch hours, coffee breaks, walking to the gym before or after work—all are quiet periods when we can slow down. As we take these quiet times, we begin to feel revitalized and once again find ourselves in sync with the flow of the universe.

Help me take rest periods throughout the day.

*Today I make sure not to overload myself
with activity.*

Sometimes we run ourselves ragged trying to jam all the activities that we think we "should" be doing into our day. At night when we hit the pillow to rest, we may be so burned out that we can't sleep, perpetuating a cycle of frenetic activity and exhaustion. Realizing this, it's important to pace ourselves, cut back on the number of things we undertake each day—selecting the ones that are important to do—and let the rest go until another time.

*Let me be content with doing
my fair share each day.*

*Today I understand the importance
of quality time.*

The family of the nineties is truly a collaborative effort. Men and women, moms and dads, shoulder many responsibilities. It takes negotiation to juggle it all.

Today's couples find out almost immediately that there's no such thing as perfectionism. It's impossible to clean the house, take care of the kids, show up at the office on time and clearheaded, and do it all perfectly. "Supermom" or "Superpop" just doesn't exist.

Terry has given up trying to be the perfect mother. She says, "I used to feel guilty because I was at work when my children really needed me after school. My husband pointed out that I have breakfast with them, I get home at a reasonable hour, and we spend our weekends together. I had been looking at what I wasn't doing for them instead of how much we shared as a family."

Our society puts a premium on "doing more." But that's misleading, because many of us are doing enough. It's not the quantity but the quality of time we spend with our families and friends that makes the difference.

Help me make the most
of the time that I spend
with people close
to me.

*Today I lessen my expectations of myself
and others close to me.*

When we expect too much of ourselves and
others, we can't appreciate our lives. We are
usually looking at what we don't have instead of
what we *do* have. But if we begin to shift our
perceptions and look at how much we have accomplished, or what people are giving to us, our
lives will become rich and enjoyable.

Marnie told me how disappointed she had
been with her husband and how her attitude
had changed: "I kept on looking at what my
husband wasn't doing to contribute to our
household. He didn't make enough money, and
he wasn't pitching in with the chores. I felt that
I was expected to do everything.

"I kept on insisting that he change, but he
never did. I was so distraught that I went to see
my minister and confided in him. He suggested
that I try to see what my husband *was* doing.

'Even if you feel like criticizing him, try not to, and see what happens.'

"I did this for a month, and our relationship began to change. I realized that, in his own way, he was pitching in. And, financially, he was doing the best that he could. My life circumstances haven't changed any, but I'm happier because I've changed the way I see things."

It is possible to create equanimity in our lives by shifting our perceptions. When we do this, we can transform even the most frustrating situations.

Grant me the willingness to change
the things I can.

Today I value the moments
I spend with my family
and friends.

It's the small, day-to-day incidents that make our lives meaningful. Yet, we look to our major accomplishments to bring us a sense of well-being. We say, "When I get that new job . . ." or "When I earn a certain amount of income . . ." Nevertheless, attaining goals often leaves us feeling empty because we expect too much from them.

Fred shared just this dilemma with me, saying, "I seem to be spending a lot of my time at the office. I have a wonderful wife and two beautiful children, but I'm not seeing much of them. I was recently made a partner at the firm, but at what cost? I've paid a great price for it."

Many Americans are reaffirming the importance of spending time with their families and friends. In fact, some people like Fred are decreasing their business commitments so they can enrich their personal lives.

Help me restructure my time
in order to spend more of it
with those
I love.

Today I have enough time and energy to do what's needed with grace and ease.

When we put too much on our "to do" list, we often go through our days in desperation, never knowing when we'll get the time to do everything. When we handle our tasks this way, we take away from our effectiveness. It's useful to stop when we find ourselves getting worked up, take a deep breath, and tell ourselves to relax. If we affirm, "I have the right and perfect time and energy to do the task in front of me," it will get done with grace and ease, instead of stress and strain.

Grant me the willingness to stop what I am doing when I feel stressed.

Today I do things in moderation.

It's often easier to deal in extremes. We either like someone or we don't. Things are either black or white. When we maintain an extreme point of view, we lose out on many of life's simple joys and blessings. My friend Nancy is dating Joe, who she knows isn't the marrying type. She says, "In the past, when I knew it wasn't going to be a permanent relationship, I'd break up with the man, so it was a long time in between dating the 'loves' of my life. I'm trying to do things differently now. I'd like to see if I can have a friendship with Joe."

Taking moderate actions is new behavior for many of us and will feel uncomfortable at first. But if we stick it out, our lives become fuller because we have more options available to us.

Grant me the willingness to let go
of my extreme behavior.

Today I use my financial resources creatively.

Some of the greatest sources of stress are our concerns about money. We ask, "How can I make more of it?" or "Do I have enough of it to pay the bills?" Many of us are forced to make do with less.

Don and Joan have actually been able to create *more* with less. They are moving into a new apartment that is twice as large as the one they've had, but they'll be paying the same rent.

Don says, "Joan and I like our current place, but we need more space. We decided to take a drive one Sunday, not really seriously looking for anything else. We just wanted to see the cost of apartment units out of the city.

"We stumbled onto a beautiful development, right on the water. And when we asked the real estate agent to show us a unit, we fell in love with it. The apartment had four large rooms with two fireplaces, and both bedrooms faced

78

the water—for exactly the rent we were paying in the city."

We often think that in order to live comfortably, we have to make more money. But if we creatively use the same resources, we can add to the quality of our lives without undue strain.

Help me look for new ways
to use the resources
that I already have.

Today I can admit
when I'm wrong
and start my day
all over again.

Admitting our mistakes is truly liberating. Instead of blaming others for our shortcomings or defending ourselves for our wrongdoings, we can take responsibility for our actions.

A friend of mine, Neal, makes his amends with the help of his Higher Power. He says "If I do something that I later regret, I can say 'I'm sorry' and mean it. And if I'm afraid to approach the person I've harmed, I have faith that my Higher Power is watching out for me. I have a real sense that I am not alone."

Taking responsibility for our lives is really all that we can do, because we have the power to change only ourselves. So when we make mis-

takes, we need to forgive ourselves, take appropriate actions to amend them, and move on.

Grant me the willingness
to take responsibility
for my shortcomings.

*Today I look forward
to slowing down.*

Too many of us spread ourselves thin. We jam our lives with continuous activity and accomplishments, but at what price? Stress, strain, and poor health.

A colleague of mine, Beatrice, told me about her brother-in-law, who took an early retirement and is doing just fine: "My brother-in-law was sent to Portugal with his family to complete a project for his company. When it was over, he was fifty-five and decided to take early retirement.

"He had worked all his life but had a deep desire to live in Portugal and do nothing. Well, he's been doing nothing for about ten years now and loves his life. He reads when he wants to, takes long walks on the beach, and never wears a watch."

When we slow down, we find that we don't have less of ourselves; in fact, we have *more*, because we get in touch with a peace that transcends all our accomplishments.

*Help me slow down
and get in touch with
my true Self.*

Today I set boundaries
with the people
around me.

We often get off balance when we say yes when we really want to say no. The first step in learning to set new boundaries is to become aware of how much we want to give in any situation. A friend of mine, Jill, is beginning to do this.

She says, "The other day, clients asked me to work late on Saturday. I was clear that I didn't want to work past five. They insisted that I do so, and I maintained my position and said no. When they showed up, they were a half hour late, and of course, they asked me to stay an extra half hour. I again told them I couldn't."

Taking positive actions for ourselves and setting boundaries sometimes feels uncomfortable. Not everyone likes our assertiveness, and we may even begin to question whether we've done the right thing. However, if we coura-

geously persist, our self-esteem will increase,
and we will grow more confident with our new
behavior.

Help me to say no
when that is what
I truly want
to do.

*Today I reach out
to other people
around me.*

It's easy to isolate ourselves from other people, and when we do, we feel depressed and disconnected from the world around us. One way to get out of this isolation is to reach out to other people.

A friend of mine, Alex, described how he recently did this. He says, "I stayed in my house all morning preoccupied about the work I had to accomplish, but I started feeling uncomfortable. I decided to take myself for a walk. As I was walking by the river, I forced myself to say hello to some people who were passing by. I even ran into a neighbor, and we chatted awhile. Taking these small actions made me feel better."

When we feel isolated, it is important to do something different from what we've been doing. If we've been in the house, it's useful to go out for a walk. If we've been working long hours, it's often productive to take a break. When we make these simple changes, we feel more connected to the world around us.

Grant me the willingness
to reach out
when I feel
isolated.

I listen to my inner guidance and set my priorities.

Many of the so-called crises in our lives are nothing of the sort. They are simply situations that evoke our *fear*, and when we feel fear, we cannot see situations clearly.

Paula shared how she's able to discriminate between situations that are important and need her attention, and those that do not. She says, "Instead of reacting when I'm faced with a challenge, I've learned to take a deep breath and ask myself, *How important is this?* Taking a moment to reflect on this question helps me see situations as they really are."

Remember that 80 percent of the situations we worry about will resolve themselves if we leave them alone. If we know this, we are free to concentrate our energy on the other 20 percent that require our attention.

Let me take a step back and reflect
on the challenges I face.

INDEX

Other titles from Helene Lerner-Robbins…

Creativity
Turn your weaknesses into strengths through the creative process. These practical meditations can be used throughout your day to tap into your intuitive resources. Learn how to silence your critical mind, trust the creative process, bring spontaneity in your life, and live each day with gratitude. 4" x 6", 96 pp.

Order No. 1492

My Timing Is Always Right
Discover why people, places, and things are as they should be right now in your life. Learn about synchronicity—the powerful sense of spiritual coincidence—that can help you overcome worry, anxiety, and frustration in your daily situations. 4" x 6", 96 pp.

Order No. 5471

Embrace Change
These affirmations and meditations can help you make the most of each day so you can focus on the future. Find renewed courage for making changes in your attitudes, ideas, projects, and relationships. 4" x 6", 96 pp.

Order No. 5470

For price and order information, or a free catalog,
please call our Telephone Representatives.

HAZELDEN EDUCATIONAL MATERIALS
Pleasant Valley Road • P.O. Box 176
Center City, MN 55012-0176
1-800-328-9000 (Toll Free. U.S., Canada, & the Virgin Islands)
1-612-257-4010 (Outside the U.S. Canada)
1-612-257-1331 (24-Hour FAX)
Hazelden Europe • P.O. Box 616 • Cork, Ireland
Int'l Code+353+21+314318
FAX: Int'l Code+353+21+961269

Words
of Life

THE BIBLE DAY BY DAY

EASTER EDITION JANUARY–APRIL 2006

Hodder & Stoughton

LONDON SYDNEY AUCKLAND

AND THE SALVATION ARMY

Written at International Headquarters, 101 Queen Victoria Street,
London EC4P 4EP, England

First published in Great Britain in 2006

1

British Library Cataloguing in Publication Data
A record for this book is available from the British Library

ISBN 0 340 86379 X

Typeset in NorfretBQ–Regular by AvonDataSet Ltd,
Bidford on Avon, Warwickshire

Printed and bound in Great Britain by
Bookmarque Ltd, Croydon, Surrey

The paper and board used in this paperback are natural
recyclable products made from wood grown in sustainable forests.
The manufacturing processes conform to the environmental
regulations of the country of origin.

Hodder & Stoughton
A Division of Hodder Headline Ltd
338 Euston Road
London NW1 3BH
www.madaboutbooks.com
www.hodderbibles.com

FORGIVENESS

Forgiveness opened the cage
and set the trapped bird free
but as she spread her gentle wings
Unforgiveness reminded me
of the sweet cool taste of revenge
symmetry of an even score

I grabbed her tiny foot
and squashed her spreading wings
shoved her back into the cage
then slammed shut tight the door
Unforgiveness would not set her free
but the one locked up inside was me

Barbara Sampson
New Zealand

CONTENTS

Major Barbara Sampson writes...

MAJOR BARBARA SAMPSON WRITES...

'Diamonds are forever' has been dubbed the world's most memorable advertising slogan. A devout Christian woman who worked in the diamond industry in America reportedly said her prayers one evening before going to bed, then woke up during the night with those words on her mind. Twenty words would say a lot more about diamonds but those three words say it all.

In this day of catchy slogans, advertising jingles and mission statements, the key seems to be brevity, conciseness and impact. It works like a mathematical formula – as few words as possible, regularly repeated, results in an unforgettable concept.

If you were to capture the essence of the Christian life in just a few words, what would those words be? Massive tomes have been written on the subject but in the hunt for fewer words rather than more, how would you sum it up?

- A life worth living
- Jesus is Lord
- I am a new creation

Hymnwriter Henry Francis Lyte says it this way – 'Ransomed, healed, restored, forgiven'. For me those four words are the neon lights of the Christian life. Strong, action-packed verbs, they describe both the saving work of God and the blessed state of the Christian believer. They take but a moment to say or sing but a lifetime to experience and live out.

May this edition of *Words of Life* with its particular focus on forgiveness help us all to walk tall as the ransomed, healed, restored, forgiven people of God.

ABBREVIATIONS USED

AV	Authorised (King James) Version
Amplified Bible	The Amplified Bible, Zondervan, 1965.
GNB	Good News Bible
JB	The Jerusalem Bible
JFM	James Moffatt, *A New Translation of the Bible*, Hodder & Stoughton, 1925.
Living Bible	The Living Bible
The Message	Eugene H. Peterson, *The Message*. Scripture taken from *The Message* copyright © 1993, 1994, 1995, 1996, 2000, 2001, 2002 by Eugene H. Peterson. Used by permission of NavPress Publishing Group.
NIV	New International Version, copyright © 1973, 1978, 1984 by International Bible Society. Used by permission of Hodder & Stoughton. All rights reserved. 'NIV' is a registered trademark of International Bible Society. UK trademark number 1448790.
NRSV	New Revised Standard Version
SASB	*The Song Book of The Salvation Army*, 1986

SUNDAY 1 JANUARY

An Armful of Blessings

Exodus 33:12–23

'My Presence will go with you, and I will give you rest' (v. 14, NIV).

Welcome to the first day of the new year – 2006!

A turn of the calendar brings with it both the fresh potential of a new beginning and the frightening prospect of an unknown future. What will this new year hold? How will we cope personally, nationally, globally with all the challenges and conflicts that this year will inevitably bring?

Like squirrels who store up food for winter, we need a supply of spiritual food to keep us going through the darkest moments of this year. A chapter towards the end of Exodus provides us with just such a resource.

Moses has come down from the mountain with the Ten Commandments, only to find the people of God worshipping idols. Both he and God are angry. God tells Moses to take the people on into Canaan, the promised land. God will send an angel to accompany them but he himself will not go with them.

Aghast at the prospect of going on ahead without God, Moses begs the Lord to reconsider. 'Do not let us go on alone. We need your presence. We are only a people because

you have made us so. If you do not come with us we are nothing.'

Unable to be anything other than compassionate, God answers Moses with an amazing cluster of promises. 'My Presence will go with you. I will give you rest. I will do the very thing you have asked. I will cause all my goodness to pass in front of you. I will proclaim my name, the LORD, in your presence. I will have mercy on whom I will have mercy. I will have compassion on whom I will have compassion. I will put you in a cleft in the rock and cover you with my hand.'

These wonderful promises are like an armful of blessings to carry with us into this new year. Tuck them into your wallet. Stick them up on your office wall. Paste them on your bathroom mirror. Above all, write them on your heart. Let them be God's special storehouse of grace for you this year.

MONDAY 2 JANUARY
Wise Men Worshipped

Matthew 2:1–12

'On coming to the house, they saw the child with his mother Mary, and they bowed down and worshipped him. Then they opened their treasures and presented him with gifts of gold and of incense and of myrrh' (v. 11, NIV).

The account of the coming of the Magi moves the church year from Advent to Epiphany (meaning 'manifestation'). The verbs surrounding these dignified figures from the East are full of majesty and reverence. 'They came, they saw, they bowed down and worshipped. They opened their treasures and presented gifts.' Joseph is not even mentioned and Mary is simply seen. The full focus of their attention is the infant Jesus who is probably about two years old by now.

Tradition teaches that these worshippers were important religious leaders from Parthia, near the site of ancient Babylon. In seeking after truth and knowledge they had probably studied ancient manuscripts from all around the world, as well as copies of the Old Testament Scriptures left in their land after the Jewish exile centuries before.

They would have been familiar with Balaam's prophecy, 'A star will come out of Jacob; a sceptre will rise out of Israel' (*Num 24:17*). They may have travelled up to a thousand miles on a journey that would have taken months. Eastern tradition sets their number at twelve but Western tradition puts it at three – based on the three gifts they bring.

They have one goal in mind – to find the One who has been born king of the Jews. The people of Israel had long waited for God's Messiah but it is through these Gentile Magi that the announcement of his arrival is made. Attentive and educated, they arrive in Jerusalem and report, 'We saw his star in the east and have come to worship him.'

They may not understand that Jesus is God in the flesh. They may not understand the deep significance of their gifts as gold for a king, frankincense for a god, myrrh for one who is going to die. They may not understand the alarmed reaction of Herod 'and all Jerusalem with him' at their arrival. But with gentle, sincere hearts they seek out the child and bring the offering of their worship.

Bow down
Bend low
Bring your gift to the One who is God's gift to you.

TUESDAY 3 JANUARY
The Family Escaped

Matthew 2:13–15

'When they had gone, an angel of the Lord appeared to Joseph in a dream. "Get up," he said, "take the child and his mother and escape to Egypt. Stay there until I tell you, for Herod is going to search for the child to kill him"' (v. 13, NIV).

If the shepherds' visit on the night of Jesus' birth was a surprise to Mary and Joseph, the visit of the Magi must have been incomprehensible. No conversation is recorded, no explanation given as to why these regal figures from the East have made such a long, tortuous journey simply to come and see a child. Worship is the only language they speak. Their precious gifts must look incongruous against the humble backdrop of the house where Mary and Joseph are staying.

Those gifts will soon be needed, however. The Magi have no sooner gone than there is another angelic appearance to Joseph, another disturbing dream. 'Get up . . . take the child . . . escape to Egypt.' The warning is urgent, the instruction clear, the reason horrifying. 'Herod is going to search for the child to kill him.' Once more Mary and Joseph must realise they are caught up in a drama far greater than themselves.

Like Abram summoned out of Haran (*Gen 12*), Joseph takes charge, gathers up the child and his mother, and they leave under cover of darkness. There is no reason to debate, no time to delay. They would need to travel about eighty miles from Bethlehem to the border of Egypt and then from the border a further distance to one of the many communities of Jewish people scattered throughout Egypt. But there they would be safe, as Egypt was a Roman province outside Herod's jurisdiction and beyond his murderous reach.

According to Luke's record the angel who first appeared to Mary declared that the child she would bear would 'be great and will be called the Son of the Most High. The Lord God will give him the throne of his father David, and he will reign over the house of Jacob for ever; his kingdom will never end' (*Luke 1:32,33*). This child, now a toddler, flees with his parents from their homeland. His earliest memories will be not of being royalty, but of being a refugee.

Child, you need to run
Find the place that is safe
Come shelter here in my heart.

3

WEDNESDAY 4 JANUARY
Herod Schemed and Slaughtered

Matthew 2:16

'When Herod realised that he had been outwitted by the Magi, he was furious, and he gave orders to kill all the boys in Bethlehem and its vicinity who were two years old and under, in accordance with the time he had learned from the Magi' (v. 16, NIV).

Dark and deadly threads weave through the account of the Magi's visit to the infant Jesus. The name of Herod is like the first rumbling of a thunderstorm on an otherwise cloudless day. His name is like a sudden body chill that sends us off to bed with a hot-water bottle.

Herod was King of Judea from 37 to 4 BC. He was only part-Jewish and was not from the Davidic family line. His title, King of the Jews, was conferred on him by Rome but never accepted by the Jewish people. He made lavish efforts to repair the temple in Jerusalem but he also built various pagan temples. He treated people with intimidation, suspicion and jealousy, and even had several of his own children and at least one of his wives put to death. Herod's only loyalty was to himself.

When the seekers from the East first arrive in Jerusalem, Herod is reported as being 'disturbed' (v. 3). When he finds out that they have come to worship one who has been born king of the Jews, the shadows darken around him. He calls the Magi 'secretly' to pinpoint the exact time of the child's birth, then sends them on to Bethlehem with the instruction that they report back to him, 'so that I too may go and worship him' (v. 8).

Just how threatening is the news of a child born to be a king is shown by Herod's response when he discovers that the Magi have not obeyed his instructions. Rather than return to Jerusalem and report their findings to the king, the Magi, warned in a dream, give him a wide berth as they return to their home by another route.

When Herod eventually hears that he has been outwitted he is furious, enraged. In a fit of senseless brutality he orders the slaughter of all the boys in Bethlehem and its vicinity who are two years old and under. By killing them all Herod must imagine that he will wipe out the one who poses such a great threat to his throne.

THURSDAY 5 JANUARY

Rachel Wept

Matthew 2:17–18

'A voice is heard in Ramah, weeping and great mourning,
Rachel weeping for her children and refusing to be comforted,
because they are no more' (v. 18, NIV).

Herod schemed and slaughtered. Bethlehem mourned. Matthew spares us the tragic details by simply telling us of Rachel and Ramah.

Rachel was Jacob's favourite wife (see *Gen 29:30*), the mother of his favourite son, Joseph, and the grandmother of Ephraim and Manasseh, the two most prominent and powerful tribes in the northern kingdom of Israel. Rachel's name in this context is used to personify the whole kingdom of Israel.

Matthew could have said, 'The male children of Bethlehem were killed and all Israel mourned.' But by saying, 'Rachel [is] weeping for her children . . . because they are no more', he is reminding the Jewish people of their history and of one greatly loved mother from the past who weeps again now for her children in Bethlehem's present moment of anguish.

The mention of Ramah would likewise take them back to a significant moment in their history. Centuries earlier, Nebuchadnezzar's army had gathered the captives from Judah in the town of Ramah before they were taken off into exile in Babylon. Forcibly removed from their own land, cut off from all that was familiar, they felt they were no longer a nation. They were as good as dead.

Matthew's mention of Ramah in this present context is like saying, 'Remember how the exiles felt as they moved from Ramah into exile? That is how Bethlehem felt on that day when the children were slaughtered.' Once Rachel and Ramah are mentioned Matthew does not need to say anything more. These two names alone paint a picture of raw anguish.

Tragically, the slaughter of innocents still happens today. We do not need to review the grisly details, for the very mention of Dunblane, Columbine High School or Beslan is enough to take us to the spot, to recall the horrific sights and the needless bloodshed. Rachel still weeps today for her children.

But God's power is greater than the power of the forces that cause sorrow. Miraculously, God's Son was spared Herod's slaughter. The child who escaped is the Christ who returned to atone for Rachel's tears for the innocent children of every age.

FRIDAY 6 JANUARY
The Family Returned

Matthew 2:19–23

'He went and lived in a town called Nazareth. So was fulfilled what was said through the prophets: "He will be called a Narazene"' (v. 23, NIV).

When King Herod dies, the angel appears once again to Joseph in a dream, instructing him to take the child and mother back to Israel. When he discovers that Herod's son Archelaus, whose reputation was even more vicious than his father's, is ruling over the region of Judea, Joseph is warned in another dream not to return to Bethlehem. The family goes to Nazareth in the region of Galilee and there they settle. Jesus, growing up in this small, out of the way village, will be known as a Nazarene.

There is a double wordplay in this name that is lost to us. Nazareth was originally settled by people from the line of David who gave the town a deliberately Messianic title as a way of expressing their hope for the coming Messiah. 'A shoot will come up from the stump of Jesse; from his roots a Branch [*neser*] will bear fruit' (Isa 11:1).

Those who believed in the coming Messiah were also known as a Branch or shoot. 'They are the shoot I have planted, the work of my hands' (Isa 60:21). So the founders of the town of Nazareth were members of a movement which was waiting for the Messianic Branch and which required them to live as God's faithful people in Israel.

But there is also another significance in Jesus being called a Nazarene. When Nathanael asked, 'Nazareth! Can anything good come from there?' (John 1:46), he was expressing popular opinion that Nazareth was not only obscure but objectionable. People despised the place and anyone who came from there.

Jesus is therefore the fulfilment of the hope for a Messianic *neser* – the Branch from the line of David – but, at the same time, his association with lowly Nazareth declares that his coming is not in glory but in humility. Those who follow Jesus the Nazarene recognise him as the Messiah, but those who deny his Messianic identity use this same title as an expression of scorn.

To reflect on
Jesus is both God's tender shoot and the One whom many people reject (Isa 53:2,3). What is he to you?

6

SATURDAY 7 JANUARY

Jesus Grew

Luke 2:41–52

'Then he went down to Nazareth with them and was obedient to them. But his mother treasured all these things in her heart. And Jesus grew in wisdom and stature, and in favour with God and men' (vv. 51,52, NIV).

In between Matthew's account of the holy family returning from Egypt to live in Nazareth and Mark's record of Jesus coming to John for baptism at the Jordan there is a long stretch of about thirty years. The Scriptures contain only one story of Jesus' childhood, one small glimpse of a young man growing physically, emotionally, mentally, spiritually.

Luke records the family – Joseph, Mary, a twelve-year-old Jesus, and maybe other younger brothers and sisters as well – making the annual pilgrimage to Jerusalem for the Feast of the Passover. At the end of the celebrations the family travels back towards Nazareth in the safe company of others.

As a twelve-year-old, Jesus is both child and adult. He could just as acceptably travel up front with the women and children, or at the rear with the men. Each of his parents assumes he is with the other, but in fact he is still in Jerusalem, intrigued, interested, involved in discussions at the temple. As a twelve-year-old, his presence there is not questioned. The amaze-ment from his audience is in response not to his youthfulness but to his depth of understanding.

At the end of the first day's travel, when Mary and Joseph discover he is not with either of them, they hurry together back to Jerusalem. Like the shepherd leaving the ninety-nine sheep in the wilderness while he goes searching for the one who is lost, they go searching for their lost son.

But Jesus is not lost. He knows exactly where he is. If anyone is lost, it is his parents, especially his mother who is flushed and flustered and filled with anxiety. She goes looking for her son, a child, but finds instead a young man who counters her 'Your father and I have been anxiously searching for you' with his own firm but respectful 'Didn't you know I had to be in my Father's house?'

They did not understand, records Luke. The child-man returns home with them to Nazareth and is an obedient son of the household. Mary continues to treasure and ponder these deep things in her heart.

SUNDAY 8 JANUARY
The Helper of Israel

Isaiah 41

'I am the LORD, your God, who takes hold of your right hand and says to you, Do not fear; I will help you' (v. 13, NIV).

The richly textured chapters of the book of Isaiah to be used as the Sunday readings for this edition contain both great oratory and profound theology. Comfort for ancient Israel becomes strength for us today.

Isaiah 41 is titled in some versions, 'The Helper of Israel'. It is written as a message of comfort and hope to God's people in captivity. From being in the past a strong and courageous nation under leaders such as Moses and Joshua, they are now a fearful people – fearful that God has abandoned them, fearful that their enemies will overpower them.

This is why God tells them again and again, both here and in the next few chapters: 'Do not fear. Do not be afraid.' He assures them of his presence with them. He promises to protect them against every threat. He tells them that their enemies will just evaporate (vv. 11,12). Why? Simply because 'I am the Lord, your God'. Although their outward circumstances are chaotic and overwhelming, God's help in the midst of their turmoil is certain.

I invite you to read this great chapter from Isaiah in the manner of the Benedictine monks of the sixth century. As one of their number, the only person with a Bible, read the Scripture passage for the day slowly and several times through, the other monks would listen intently, alert to a word or phrase or an image that particularly captured their attention. Then they would return to their cells to meditate on the particular word or image that God had given them.

As they mulled it over, the word would become a prayer, maybe thanksgiving, maybe repentance or questioning. It might be accompanied by tears of joy or sorrow. It might be a prayer too deep for words. Then they would rest, simply being still in God's presence. Read, ponder, pray, be still – these are the steps for this method called *Lectio Divina* (Divine Reading).

To reflect on
What word or phrase does your heart settle on as you read this chapter today? Let it become your meditation, your prayer and your place of rest.

THE FINAL JOURNEY – LUKE 22–24

Introduction

With this series we bring to a close the study of Luke's Gospel begun in September 2003. Dr Luke's 'orderly account' (1:3) has proved to be a colourful record of the birth of Jesus, his preparation and ministry in Galilee, Judea and Perea, and his last days of struggle, suffering and triumph.

Throughout, Luke portrays Jesus as the perfect example of a life lived according to God's plan – from the child living in obedience to his parents, to the adult whose nourishment was to do the task assigned to him, to the condemned man who, in the face of suffering, wanted only to do the will of God.

Yet, the writer of the letter to the Hebrews says, Jesus was human, tempted and tested 'just as we are' (Heb 4:15). So he understands our struggles and knows our need of mercy and grace.

Read these final chapters of Luke's Gospel with an open heart. Enter into the colourful scenes of the Last Supper, the Garden of Gethsemane and the Road to Emmaus. Stand by the cross as Jesus dies, and by the open tomb after his resurrection. Let Luke's story remind you of the One whose coming signals good news of great joy for all people.

> Tell of the cross where they nailed him,
>   Mocking his anguish and pain;
> Tell of the grave where they laid him;
>   Tell how he liveth again.
> Love in that story so tender,
>   Clearer than ever I see;
> Glory for ever to Jesus,
>   He paid the ransom for me.
>   Fanny Crosby, *SASB* 99

MONDAY 9 JANUARY
Enter Judas

Luke 22:1–6

'Then Satan entered Judas, called Iscariot, one of the Twelve'
(v. 3, NIV).

The last verses of Luke's previous chapter paint a picture of eagerness with the people coming each morning to hear Jesus' teaching in the temple. But his words are full of warning. 'Be careful . . . Be always on the watch . . . pray' (21:34,36). He speaks disturbingly about the signs of the end of the age. 'Nation will rise against nation . . . kingdom against kingdom.' Even as Jesus speaks of the battle on a cosmic scale, the shadows lengthen over his own life.

As the crowds gather in Jerusalem for the Passover celebrations, a dark drama plays out in the wings. Certain players step into place like figures on a chessboard lining up for a game.

The Feast of Passover, followed by the Feast of Unleavened Bread, commemorated the sparing of Israel's first-born and the nation's release from captivity in Egypt. The entire celebration recalled how Israel was 'passed over' by the angel of death and redeemed (Exod 12). It is the story of Israel's costly salvation and God's amazing grace.

During this time, the chief priests and teachers of the law are trying to find a way to remove Jesus. Luke uses the imperfect tense to describe their regular and repeated attempts to seize him. So Passover and plotting come together. What the feast celebrates – forgiveness and salvation – Jesus will actually perform. While the people recall their deliverance, the leadership plots destruction.

Enter Judas. And Satan. Whether in an attempt to force Jesus' hand or for other sinister reasons of his own, Judas goes to the leadership and offers to hand Jesus over to them. This is betrayal at the highest level. The leaders are so delighted that they pay Judas for his troubles. Betrayal money for him is relief money for them. They have their man. Now all they need is their moment.

No one can tell when Judas made his first
Surrender to himself.
But at some point along the way with Christ,
The light of loyalty had weakened, waned.
Thus, when he came to his immortal hour,
The fragile flame went out.

Catherine Baird[1]

TUESDAY 10 JANUARY
A Man Carrying a Water Jar

Luke 22:7–13

'As you enter the city, a man carrying a jar of water will meet you. Follow him to the house that he enters' (v. 10, NIV).

As Judas goes to the religious leaders and offers to betray Jesus to them, dark forces are obviously in control. With the start of the week-long Festival of Unleavened Bread, however, Jesus is clearly in control. He sends Peter and John ahead to prepare the Passover meal. He gives them no instructions about the meal itself – where to buy the lamb for the sacrifice, the bitter herbs and the unleavened bread – but very explicit details about the location for the meal.

He tells them to look for a man carrying a water jar. This is like telling them to find a man carrying a handbag. In that society a man did not fetch water. Water-carrying was women's work. This man, says Jesus, will lead them to a house where they must ask the owner to show them the guest room. They will find a large upper room already furnished, probably with reclining couches and a table set for the Passover meal.

The disciples go and find these things just as Jesus has told them. What he says can be trusted. Peter and John prepare the Passover,

thus proving that they too can be trusted.

The incident raises an important question. Did Jesus, as the Son of God, have foreknowledge of the man carrying the water jar, the exact house, the room prepared? Or were these arrangements in place simply because he, as the Son of Man, had previously made private contact with the various players?

Did that man carrying a water jar do so regularly? Was he a liberated, new-age man of the first century who thumbed his nose at social convention and carried the water anyway? Or, on that one and only particular day, was his wife sick so that he got the water-carrying task, and a tantalising place for ever in the pages of Scripture?

To reflect on
Am I a player in a cosmic drama, writing my own script, or living by God's predetermined script? What do I know for sure about God that reassures me about the things of which I am as yet uncertain?

WEDNESDAY 11 JANUARY
Do This in Remembrance

Luke 22:14–20

'He took bread, gave thanks and broke it, and gave it to them, saying, "This is my body given for you; do this in remembrance of me"' (v. 19, NIV).

The occasion was filled with symbolism. Jesus, whom John the Baptist called 'the Lamb of God', shared a meal with his disciples at which the Passover lamb was central. As they ate together they looked back and remembered the night when the angel of death had killed all the first-born of Egypt, but 'passed over' Israel's first-born who were protected by the blood sprinkled on their doorposts. That night had been a night of deliverance and salvation. 'Eat and remember.'

As Jesus broke the bread they recalled a sunny day out on a grassy hillside where they watched him accept a little boy's lunch, bless and break it and then hand it out for distribution. A crowd numbering thousands ate and were satisfied. One lunch, one blessing and a mighty multitude fed. That day had been a day of miracle and provision. 'Eat and share.'

As Jesus took the cup filled with wine they remembered another day when he told them, 'I am the Vine.' 'Take this cup now,' he said. 'Divide it among you. Share it out. Taste its sweetness and its bitterness. Drink deeply.' Within a few hours Jesus himself would be pleading with God to take the cup from him.

This meal, known as the Last Supper, needs to be read with holy respect. Some Christians receive the bread regularly and drink the wine, believing that these elements actually become Christ's body and blood. Other believers accept them as symbols of Christ's sacrifice, a reminder of the forgiveness he has won for us. Other faithful followers believe he is present at every meal, whenever Christians share fellowship together.

However we view these sacred symbols, the call is to 'Remember'. Do not forget the past – what Jesus has done in your life. Do not reject the present – he is with you now to nourish you on this journey. Do not neglect the future – God has plans to bless you and make you a blessing. Let your life be a living sacrifice (*Rom 12:1*) in the hands of the One who became a living sacrifice for you (*1 Cor 5:7*).

THURSDAY 12 JANUARY
Bent on Betrayal

Luke 22:21–23

'The hand of him who is going to betray me is with mine
on the table' (v. 21, NIV).

Unbelievably, betrayal breaks into the intimacy of the Upper Room. Even as Jesus pledges to give his body and blood for his disciples, he speaks of betrayal by one who is with him at the table.

Betrayal is now no longer 'out there' but 'in here'. Jesus will not be delivered to his enemies by one of the chief priests, nor by one of the people who have come to the temple to hear him teach, but by a friend. Love makes betrayal all the more devastating. Jesus announces, 'The hand of the one who is betraying me is at this moment on this table' (*The Message*).

How could one who has been a disciple, one who has shared the intimacy of many meals together, one who has observed and lived and breathed the things of the kingdom, now turn and betray the One he has followed? Basic to a bread covenant is that those who eat together pledge to protect and not to harm each other.

'The Son of Man will go as it has been decreed,' says Jesus, but Luke makes it clear that Judas' actions cannot be excused by appeal to God's foreknowledge. Judas is not playing out a role inescapably assigned to him. Even though Luke reports Satan as entering Judas (*v. 3*), Judas cannot say, 'The devil made me do it.' He must take responsibility for himself. His outer actions are simply the outworking of his inner choices.

Mark describes the disciples as grieved by Jesus' words concerning betrayal (*Mark 14:19*). Matthew has Judas saying, 'Surely not I, Rabbi?' (*Matt 26:25*). John reports that the disciples stare at one another in disbelief (*John 13:22*). Luke shows them asking one another which one of them it could be.

As we hear this story we need to acknowledge that we too are capable of treachery. In Judas' sandals would we do any differently? May the recognition of our capacity to sin, our bent towards betrayal, our proneness to wander help us intentionally to choose faithfulness, and to press ever closer into the arms of mercy and grace.

FRIDAY 13 JANUARY
Bending Low to Serve

Luke 22:24–30

'I am among you as one who serves' (v. 27, NIV).

To the very end, it seems, Jesus' disciples showed little understanding of his mission. To the very end he kept correcting and challenging them about the true values of the kingdom.

Just as inappropriate as talk of betrayal is a dispute that breaks out among the group. They watched as Jesus handed them the bread and wine and spoke of the deep significance of these symbols. They heard the unbelievable talk of betrayal. Now a squabble erupts about pecking order in the kingdom of God. If Jesus is tempted to throw up his hands in disgust, he shows no sign of it. Rather, he patiently reminds them yet again that they belong to an upside-down kingdom whose values are quite different from those of the world.

He gives two quick snapshots of service. The first is of 'the kings of the Gentiles' who like to call themselves 'benefactors'. That is, they lord it over the people. They like to be looked up to, to be considered great and powerful and worthy of honour. But this is not the type of leadership Jesus calls for. Leadership in Jesus' name means service, not power.

The second snapshot of service is his own example. Rather than lifting himself up, he has bent down to serve, meeting needs, bringing relief to others, embracing outcasts, healing the sick, setting people free from prisons of their own and others' making. This is the example they are to follow, bending low, doing the menial, the thankless, the unnoticed task. With bread and wine, towel and basin, he has shown them the way.

Yet Jesus is not uninterested in their status question. He knows these disciples have faithfully stood by him in his trials. Their constancy is noted and will be rewarded. At some future day when he rules all humanity they too will have a central and unique part to play.

How can I better serve thee, Lord,
Thou who hast done so much for me?
Faltering and weak my labour has been;
O that my life may tell for thee!
Bramwell Coles, SASB 488

14

SATURDAY 14 JANUARY
Betrayal and Denial

Luke 22:31–38

'I tell you, Peter, before the cock crows today, you will deny three times that you know me' (v. 34, NIV).

Betrayal and denial. One sounds as treacherous as the other. Both send a shiver down the spine. Neither is the kind of mark one would want on a character reference – 'Prone to betrayal' or 'A tendency towards denial'. Both are chilling possibilities for disciples – then and now.

Jesus, knowing what was about to happen to him, makes one last appeal to Judas. John's Gospel records Jesus dipping the piece of bread in the dish then handing it to Judas. Jesus does not point an accusing finger, nor make a big scene to humiliate Judas, but quietly tells him to do quickly what he is about to do (see *John 13:27*).

Similar foreknowledge and similar appeal come together as Jesus speaks with tenderness to Peter. 'Simon, Simon,' he says. Jesus knows that the circumstances of the next few days will all but finish off these fragile followers. Peter himself will be sifted like wheat, but a covering of prayer from Jesus means that his faith will not fail. When Peter comes through the testing, he must strengthen his companions. 'Sifted, standing, strengthen' is the mantra Peter needs to repeat over and over

to himself during the next few days.

Peter protests the prediction but Jesus makes the moment even more painful by speaking the specifics of Peter's denial – 'cock . . . today . . . deny'.

Knowing my failings, knowing my fears,
Seeing my sorrow, drying my tears,
Jesus recall me, me re-ordain;
You know I love you, use me again.

Jesus then turns to the whole group. Until now they have been dependent on the generous hospitality of others, but that is all about to change. He warns them of inevitable opposition and perilous times that will require them to carry their own resources for provision and protection. Following in the footsteps of One who is about to be arrested as a criminal is a dangerous thing to do!

For the far future I cannot see,
Promise your presence, travel with me;
Sunshine or shadows? I cannot tell;
You know I love you, all will be well.
John Gowans, SASB 294

SUNDAY 15 JANUARY
The Servant of the Lord

Isaiah 42:1–17

'I, the LORD, have called you in righteousness; I will take hold
of your hand. I will keep you and will make you to be a covenant
for the people and a light for the Gentiles' (v. 6, NIV).

This chapter of Isaiah contains a profile of the servant of the Lord. The words may apply to Cyrus the Great, King of Persia from 559 to 530 BC. In the year 539 BC he conquered Babylon and issued a decree allowing the Jews in captivity to return to Jerusalem. He authorised the rebuilding of the temple, which eventually led to the restoration of Jerusalem. Although Cyrus was a Gentile ruler he was chosen to carry out God's righteous purposes and, like David, the greatest of all Israel's kings, was called a shepherd of God's people (44:28).

Not only Cyrus but the nation of Israel itself was also called 'the servant of the Lord'. Israel was declared to be a kingdom of priests, a holy nation (see Exod 19:6), called to display the splendour of God to the world (Isa 49:3). But, like the disciples who accompanied Jesus, the people of Israel were often blind to what God was doing in their midst. With sadness more than in anger God declares, 'You have seen many things, but have paid no attention; your ears are open, but you hear nothing' (42:20).

This servant song is also sung with reference to Jesus. He fits exactly the description of one in whom God delights (v. 1), who does not break a bruised reed or snuff out a smouldering wick (v. 3). Think of how Jesus dealt with the twelve-year-old girl who had died (Mark 5:41), or the woman caught in the act of adultery (John 8:11). Matthew took these very words from Isaiah's prophecy to describe the quiet ministry of Jesus (see Matt 12:18–21). His ways were ways of gentleness and all his paths were peace.

This profile of a servant applies also to you and me as modern-day believers, walking in the footsteps of Jesus. As seekers after righteousness, light-bringers, justice-bearers, we too are called to open blind eyes, set captives free and release those who live in darkness. As you lift your heart in worship today may you catch a glimpse of some of the great 'new things' (Isa 42:9) God is doing.

MONDAY 16 JANUARY

In Gethsemane

Luke 22:39–46

'Father, if you are willing, take this cup from me; yet not my will, but yours be done' (v. 42, NIV).

Supper is over. Words of warning have been spoken. Betrayal is happening even now. Denial will soon take place. Jesus, purposeful to the end, goes 'as usual', Luke notes, to the Mount of Olives, located just to the east of Jerusalem. Dazed and confused, the disciples stumble after him in the dark.

When they reach the olive grove called Gethsemane (meaning 'oil press'), Jesus distances himself from the disciples. As the human Jesus, he needs to know they are not too far away. As the Son of God, he needs to speak with the Father on his own. This is Jesus in his loneliness.

He pours out his heart to God. He knows for himself, and he models for his disciples, that prayer is the only source of strength for the coming test. This is Jesus in his prayerfulness.

He asks God to take the cup from him. This is the cup of suffering, the terrible torture he is about to endure in the physical agony of death by crucifixion and the even greater agony of separation from God. As he dies for the sins of the world, he knows that God, the Father from whom he has never been separated, will turn his back. This is Jesus in his heaviness.

Luke is the only Gospel writer to record that an angel comes to strengthen him, and that 'sweat, wrung from him like drops of blood, poured off his face' (v. 44, *The Message*). Luke uses the Greek word *agonia* to describe Jesus' intense anguish. This is Jesus in his woundedness.

How long does he pray – one hour, two hours? When at last he returns to the disciples, he finds them fast asleep, worn out by emotional pain and grief. His anguish is now for them. He knows that the testing they are about to face is as great as the test facing him. 'Get up and pray,' he says. This is Jesus in his tenderness.

Lonely Jesus,
Praying Jesus,
Heavy Jesus,
Wounded Jesus,
Tender Jesus,
Thank you for carrying
my sin on your shoulders,
my need on your heart.

TUESDAY 17 JANUARY

Darkness Reigns

Luke 22:47–53

'Every day I was with you in the temple courts, and you did not
lay a hand on me. But this is your hour – when darkness reigns'
(v. 53, NIV).

At the beginning of Jesus' ministry, Luke records that the devil tested Jesus in the wilderness then left him 'until an opportune time' (4:13). That opportune time has now come. After three years of lurking in the shadows of Jesus' ministry, Satan has his moment.

'This is your hour – when darkness reigns,' Jesus tells the chief priests, the officers of the temple guard and the elders who suddenly burst into the quietness of Gethsemane. The darkness of the evening is matched by the depth of their enmity.

The religious leaders come with swords and clubs as if to arrest someone armed and dangerous. The Greek word *lestes* refers to a robber or highway bandit, such as the villain who attacked the traveller in the story of the Good Samaritan. Jesus complains that they treat him as a common criminal, whereas he has been with them every day in the temple. They had plenty of opportunity but they did not arrest him there.

Judas comes with a kiss. The customary gesture of greeting becomes, in this moment, the means of betrayal. How different Judas' embrace from that of the sinful woman with her alabaster jar who waters Jesus' feet with her tears, wipes them with her hair, then covers them with kisses and perfume (7:38).

In the darkness lit only by torches, a sword flashes and a man's ear is severed. But Jesus has never taught the way of violence. His response is immediate: 'No more of this!' To the very end he continues his redemptive mission, teaching his disciples and healing a man whom they have injured. A slash of violence is met by a touch of healing.

Jesus is seized and taken. On the surface, he looks like the victim and his enemies the victors. But even as he faces trial and death, Jesus remains majestically in charge. Darkness reigns in this moment, but deliverance, victory, redemption and life will have the final word.

A kiss
that should have spoken brotherhood
breathed dark betrayal.
A death
that could have signalled the end
is but the glorious beginning.

WEDNESDAY 18 JANUARY
That Look

Luke 22:54–65

'The Lord turned and looked straight at Peter' (v. 61, NIV).

Jesus is seized and taken into the house of the high priest. In the courtyard Peter faces his own test. A servant girl peers at him ('stared', NRSV) and states emphatically that he is one of Jesus' followers. Someone else sees him and says the same thing.

An hour later someone hears his Galilean accent and declares, 'Certainly this fellow was with him.' Unable to hide, unable to run, Peter does what every trapped creature does – he lashes out in fury and denial. 'I don't know him … I don't know what you're talking about.'

In the distance a rooster crows. Jesus turns and looks straight at Peter. What was that look? Was it a look of sorrow for Jesus himself, that in his moment of greatest need, his closest friend has failed to stand with him? Or was it a look of rebuke? 'Peter, I told you so. I warned you this would happen. Don't you remember what I said about being sifted?'

Whether in sorrow or in rebuke, this look recalls another day when a rich young ruler came to Jesus. He was earnest and exemplary. He had a spotless record in commandment-keeping. But Jesus saw in him one great lack. His riches were keeping him poor. He needed to give everything away in order to focus his whole attention on the concerns of the kingdom.

Shocked at the suggestion, unable to let go the things that filled his life, the young man turned and went away sad (*Mark 10:22*). The Gospel writer records that Jesus watched him go, following him with a look of love. Is not this the same look that would have followed Peter as he turned away, weeping bitter tears?

What is Jesus' look when he sees the trinkets that fill my hands and occupy my heart? Is it a look of rebuke or of love? Am I guilty of denying Jesus by giving my greatest allegiance to someone or something else, rather than to him?

At the end of a scene full of seeing and looking, Jesus is blindfolded, blasphemed and beaten.

THURSDAY 19 JANUARY
A Question of Identity

Luke 22:66–71

'"If you are the Christ," they said, "tell us"' (v. 67, NIV).

At daybreak the council, made up of chief priests and teachers of the law, meets with Jesus. There are all kind of irregularities in this so-called trial, but Luke reports only the central question – the matter of Jesus' identity. 'If you are the Christ, tell us.'

At the beginning of Jesus' ministry, this same question of identity lay at the heart of Satan's temptations in the wilderness. 'If you are the Son of God . . . If you are the Son of God' (4:3,9).

For three years of healing and helping, teaching and touching, saving and serving, blessing and binding, loving and loosing, Jesus has let his actions speak for themselves. But to the very end, it seems, his identity remains an enigma for many.

So the question for this group of Jewish leaders is all-important. 'If you are the Christ,' they say, 'tell us.' If he accepts the title, it will be enough to bring a political charge against him for being a revolutionary and for setting himself up as an alternative king to Caesar.

Jesus answers evasively, neither affirming nor denying the title. They have put the question to him but he knows their hearts are hard. They will not accept his answer, no matter what he says. He declares that the Son of Man will be seated at the right hand of the mighty God. This title, Son of Man, recalls the figure of Daniel who receives authority from the Ancient of Days and rides the clouds with God (see *Dan 7:13–14*).

His answer is more than they have anticipated. 'Are you then the Son of God?' they ask. He answers in the affirmative, 'I am,' using words that echo back to Exodus 3:14. This is all they need. He has declared himself to be the Christ, the Messiah, the Son of Man, the Son of God, and now the 'I am'. He has condemned himself out of his own mouth.

In their eagerness to fix a charge against Jesus, the religious leaders do not stop to consider that he may in fact be speaking the truth.

FRIDAY 20 JANUARY
Pilate – The Expedient Way

Luke 23:1–7

'Pilate announced to the chief priests and the crowd, "I find no basis for a charge against this man"' (v. 4, NIV).

Acting as one body, the whole Sanhedrin now deliver Jesus to Pilate for trial. Jesus' earlier appearance before the Sanhedrin concerned religious matters and specifically the question of his Messiahship. But Pilate would have dismissed such an issue as unimportant. He had little time for the Jews and their religious disputes.

So the Sanhedrin bring three political charges against Jesus – that he is guilty of perverting the nation, opposing the payment of taxes to Caesar and claiming to be a king. Such charges would be of great concern to Pilate who had the responsibility of keeping the peace and making sure that taxes were paid to Rome.

However, Pilate ignores the first two and pursues the third charge by simply asking, 'Are you the king of the Jews?' Jesus responds with an expression in Greek that means literally, 'You have said so.' It is a vague way of saying 'Yes'. Without any further ado, Pilate concludes there is no basis for a charge. Jesus has done nothing worthy of death. In Pilate's mind he is nothing more than a harmless enthusiast.

This should have been the end of the matter. Pilate dismisses the case with a wave of his hand, but the Sanhedrin will not be put off. They comment on how Jesus' teaching has stirred up the people from Galilee to Judea. Their suggestion is that he is dangerous and that it would be politically careless of Pilate to let him go.

On hearing mention of Galilee, Pilate suddenly sees a way forward. He will send Jesus to Herod, the Jewish political leader who has authority over the region of Galilee. That way, any decision Pilate makes will have Herod's backing. Courtesy, political expediency and the deft skill of buck-passing all come together in this tidy arrangement.

Is Pilate's crime in relation to Jesus one of active rejection or passive neglect? Pilate may seem like a remote figure, but his indifference, his concern to watch his own back, his anxiety to do the expedient thing, are all temptations that you and I still face today in relation to Jesus.

SATURDAY 21 JANUARY
Herod – The Entertaining Way

Luke 23:8–12

'When Herod saw Jesus, he was greatly pleased, because for a long time he had been wanting to see him. From what he had heard about him, he hoped to see him perform some miracle' (v. 8, NIV).

Pilate is cool and detached in his dealings with Jesus. Herod, to whom Pilate sends Jesus, is an altogether different character.

Herod is not concerned about expediency – he wants entertainment. He has heard of Jesus and for a long time has been wanting to see him. He is hoping for some spectacular sideshow display, a miracle or two to fascinate and thrill him.

Herod wants a God who will leap at his every command, perform at the click of a finger, a puppet–like God whom he can use to show off to his friends and impress his enemies. A God who can be held at arm's length like a remote control, to be turned off and on at will, would be most useful in Herod's particular line of business.

Herod's delight at meeting Jesus, however, quickly sours when Jesus does not perform at his command. Jesus says nothing at all, even though Herod plies him with questions. The chief priests and teachers of the law add their own voices that quickly turn to invective and accusation, but they too get no response. They are like children who come across a sick animal and, awed and horrified, prod and poke it to death.

Jesus' silence is an affront to Herod, which he answers by allowing his soldiers to make sport of Jesus. They dress him in an elegant robe, probably an old military cloak with a colour suggesting royalty, and taunt him. Herod then sends Jesus back to Pilate. Luke notes that Herod and Pilate, who had previously been enemies, become friends that very day.

Pilate and Herod had never been 'birds of a feather'. Pilate was a Roman citizen and an envoy of the emperor with responsibility for Judea and Samaria. Herod came from a hereditary, part–Jewish monarchy and was ruler over Galilee and Perea. The two men were uneasy around each other but Jesus' trial brings them together. With Pilate concerned for expediency and Herod keen on entertainment, they become united by their common problem of what to do with Jesus.

SUNDAY 22 JANUARY

Salvation – Past, Present and Future

Isaiah 43:1–21

'I am the LORD, your God, the Holy One of Israel, your Saviour'
(v. 3, NIV).

This chapter of Isaiah has both a backwards and a forwards look. Parts of it are written in the past tense: 'I have redeemed you' (v. 1), 'I created [you] for my glory' (v. 7). Parts of it are written in the present tense: 'I am with you' (v. 5), 'You are my witnesses' (v. 10). Parts of it are written in the future tense: 'When you pass through the waters, I will be with you' (v. 2), 'I will bring your children from the east and gather you from the west' (v. 5).

The prophet declares God saying, 'I am God, I've always been God and I always will be God' (v. 13, The Message). Because God is eternal, 'from everlasting to everlasting' (Ps 90:2), from vanishing point in the past to vanishing point in the future, the story of our salvation is always written in past, present and future tenses: 'God saved me; God saves me now; God will save me.' These simple words take but a moment to say but they need the whole span of a lifetime to be lived out.

Give thanks today for the past tense of your salvation, or, as Isaiah puts it, 'Review the past' (Isa 43:26). Who were the people who prayed for you, loved you in the name of Jesus and helped you walk and grow as a young Christian?

Give thanks for the present tense of your salvation – what God is doing in your life today. He may be doing 'far more than you could ever imagine or guess or request in your wildest dreams!' (Eph 3:20, The Message). If you have no awareness of God at work, then why not ask him to do the 'new thing' (Isa 43:19) he longs to do?

Give thanks for the future tense of your salvation. No matter where you go, no matter how dark and difficult the experiences you may go through in the future, God promises to be with you. He guarantees this by his own holy name: 'I am the LORD, your God, the Holy One . . . your Saviour.'

MONDAY 23 JANUARY
Pilate's Problem

Luke 23:13–25

'With loud shouts they insistently demanded that he be crucified, and their shouts prevailed' (v. 23, NIV).

Pilate's problem just will not go away. Herod, irked by Jesus' silence but finding no basis for a charge against him, sends him back to Pilate.

Pilate may not realise it but this is his defining moment. He stands between Jesus and the people but his greatest concern is for himself. A riot in his province will not go down well in Rome. His wrong handling of this situation could affect his political position with disastrous personal results.

Pilate listens, not to the voice of reason, not to the voice of courage, not to the voice of wisdom, but to the voice of the crowd. He calls together the chief priests, the religious leaders and the people and states his findings. 'You brought me this man . . . I have examined him . . . and have found no basis for your charges against him . . . he has done nothing to deserve death . . . I will punish him and then release him.'

This is Pilate's solution, the answer that satisfies every demand. But he has not anticipated the response of the crowd. With voices rising ever higher they demand Jesus' death and the release of Barabbas, a dangerous political insurgent who had been imprisoned for his part in a rebellion against the Roman government. Barabbas is in fact guilty of what Jesus is accused of – stirring up the people.

For a second time and then a third, Pilate makes his appeal on behalf of Jesus. He offers to have him flogged, a punishment severe enough to kill a man, but the crowd is still not satisfied. They want nothing less than his crucifixion. 'They kept at it, a shouting mob, demanding that he be crucified. And finally they shouted him down. Pilate caved in and gave them what they wanted' (vv. 23,24, *The Message*). Eugene Peterson's paraphrase expresses both the insistent clamour of the crowd and the inner collapse within Pilate.

Who is in charge on this day? The crowd is strident. Pilate is shaken. Jesus is silent. Yet the sovereign purposes of God are being worked out exactly according to plan.

TUESDAY 24 JANUARY
Carrying the Cross

Luke 23:26–31

'As they led him away, they seized Simon from Cyrene, who was on his way in from the country, and put the cross on him and made him carry it behind Jesus' (v. 26, NIV).

Jesus is led away to be crucified. At first he carries the cross beam to which he will soon be nailed. But he has been weakened by the severe flogging and the emotional strain of the past few days, and it quickly becomes clear that he will need help.

To carry a cross was a curse to both Roman and Jew, so a foreigner is conscripted. Someone's eye falls on Simon of Cyrene. It is obvious that he is neither Roman nor Jew. Simon is seized, forced into a task he did not seek, carrying a load he did not want, on behalf of a victim he did not know. Did something happen for Simon of Cyrene that day as he followed Jesus? What kind of look passed between them? Did they speak a few muffled words to each other?

Carry the cross, strong Simon,
You carry it for God's Son.
Thank you for being there, Simon,
You did what I would have done.

Behind Jesus surges a crowd of people, among them a group of wailing women. They may have been professional mourners whose task was to accompany anyone about to die. But Jesus addresses them as 'Daughters of Jerusalem' and speaks to them as though they are sincere mourners who understand what is happening. He urges them not to weep for him. Painful as his death will be, he knows he will be taken care of. Crucifixion is imminent, but resurrection lies just beyond.

The greater issue is what his death will mean for those who reject him. Hard days will lie ahead for the nation in which 'barren women' will be blessed. This is a reversal of the normal Jewish view that blessing comes from a fruitful womb. Jesus quotes verses from Hosea to express the terror of judgment that is soon to come upon the nation.

If this kind of fate befalls someone like Jesus (a green tree), just imagine what kind of fate is ahead for the 'dry wood' responsible for his death! This is Luke's last reported lament of Jesus over his people.

25

WEDNESDAY 25 JANUARY

Numbered with the Transgressors

Luke 23:32–34

'When they came to the place called the Skull, there they crucified him, along with the criminals – one on his right, the other on his left' (v. 33, NIV).

Throughout his ministry Jesus kept dubious company – tax collectors, prostitutes, the sick, outcasts, the marginalised. He seemed to find great delight in being with those on the edge of society, those who were not ashamed to admit their need. To the very end he kept company with those whom others wrote off as riff-raff.

Two common criminals were crucified with him – one on his right, the other on his left. The mother of James and John had asked for those honoured positions to be kept for her sons, but Jesus made it clear to Mrs Zebedee that those seats were already booked (*Matt 20:23*). Besides, the right and the left were not the place of honour but the place of suffering.

Death by crucifixion was particularly gruesome. It was usually preceded by a severe flogging that caused bleeding to speed the onset of death. After being flogged the victim carried the cross beam to the place of execution. Heavy wrought-iron nails were driven through the wrists and heel bones. The beam was then raised and fastened to the upright pole. If the victim did not die quickly, his legs were broken so he could no longer push himself up for air. Death by suffocation then happened quickly.

To die by crucifixion was considered a disgrace. Only slaves, the lowest of criminals and offenders who were not Roman citizens were killed in this way. Any possessions a crucified person had with him were taken by those who killed him. So as Jesus died, just below him his executioners threw dice for his only earthly possessions – his clothing.

Seven hundred years earlier, the prophet Isaiah said the Suffering Servant would die alongside transgressors and would make intercession for those who sinned against him (*Isa 53:12*). This is exactly what happened. As Jesus died between two criminals he spoke words of forgiveness to his executioners.

My Lord, what love is this,
that pays so dearly,
that I, the guilty one,
may go free!
And so they watched Him die,
Despised, rejected;
But oh, the blood He shed
Flowed for me!

Graham Kendrick[2]

26

THURSDAY 26 JANUARY
From Derision to Confession

Luke 23:35–43

'He said, "Jesus, remember me when you come into
your kingdom"' (v. 42, NIV).

A whole range of attitudes was there at the cross that day – from derision to confession, from 'Who cares?' to 'I care'.

The soldiers who crucified Jesus were just doing their job – indifferent, casual. They cast lots for his clothing – calculating, lucky. Jesus, suffering at their hands, prayed to the Father – forgiving, forgiving. The people stood by – watching, wondering. The rulers sneered at him – unfeeling, malicious.

The soldiers mocked him – hardhearted, brutal. They threw the 'If' word at him just as Satan had used it as a weapon against him at the beginning of his ministry: 'If he is the Christ of God . . . If you are the king of the Jews'. Their concern was not to recognise the truth of who he was, but simply to make themselves appear stronger by making him look weaker.

One of the criminals crucified alongside Jesus hurled insults at him – blasphemous, derisive. The second criminal rebuked the first – correcting, protecting. Then, turning to Jesus, he asked him to 'remember me when you come into your kingdom' – needing, pleading.

Jesus spoke words of acceptance – comforting, reassuring.

Every response to Jesus on the continuum of faith was represented there that day. Which attitude towards Jesus have you chosen to live by? Which attitude has chosen you? Do you stand with those who mock and try to ignore the Son of God? Or do you stand with the criminal who recognised, not only his own need, but the power of God to meet that need?

Simone Weil wrote, 'What I call the haven is the Cross. If it cannot be given me to deserve one day to share the Cross of Christ, at least may I share that of the good thief. Of all the beings other than Christ of whom the Gospel tells us, the good thief is by far the one I most envy. To have been at the side of Christ and in the same state during the crucifixion seems to me a far more enviable privilege than to be at the right hand of his glory.'[5]

FRIDAY 27 JANUARY

Earth's Darkest, Heaven's Brightest Moment

Luke 23:44–46

'The sun stopped shining. And the curtain of the temple was torn in two' (v. 45, NIV).

It was history's deepest, darkest day. As the Son of God hung dying on the cross, all creation mourned. The sun that normally would have been high in the noonday sky wrapped itself in dark mourning clothes. God turned his back as Jesus died with the world's sin upon his shoulders.

But darkness and death won no victory that day. As eerie shadows covered the land, the curtain of the temple was torn in two. This curtain was a veil that separated the innermost part from the rest of the temple. Inside this most holy place rested the ark of the covenant, the symbol of God's presence. Only the high priest was permitted to enter this inner sanctuary, and then only once a year, in order to atone for the sins of the people.

As Jesus died, the curtain was torn in two, thus opening the way into the most holy place. The barrier between God and humankind was broken! Limited entrance suddenly became limitless entrance! In Paul's letter to the believers at Ephesus, he explained how Jesus destroyed the barrier, 'the dividing wall of hostility' (*Eph 2:14*), that separated God from humankind. 'In him and through faith in him we may [now] approach God with freedom and confidence' (*Eph 3:12*). With the tearing of that curtain, earth's deepest, darkest moment became heaven's highest, brightest moment.

These verses invite us to pause. We can go through no darkness, no death, no despair, that he, the Son of God, has not already endured for us. But more than merely enduring the darkness, he has stepped right into it, invading and conquering it. Now there is nothing, nothing, nothing in all creation that will ever be able to separate us from the love of God that has been shown to us so powerfully in Christ Jesus our Lord (see *Rom 8:39*).

The day of resurrection!
Earth tell it out abroad;
the Passover of gladness,
the Passover of God.
From death to life eternal,
from earth unto the sky,
our Christ has brought us over
with hymns of victory.
                    John of Damascus

SATURDAY 28 JANUARY
Faith and Respect

Luke 23:47–56

'The centurion, seeing what had happened, praised God and said,
"Surely this was a righteous man"' (v. 47, NIV).

Luke's skilful account of events at the cross shows a significant change taking place after the crucifixion. The soldiers, indifferent about just another crucifixion, receive no further mention. The religious leaders seem to have disappeared. So too have the attitudes of mockery and derision that accompanied Jesus on his long and tortuous journey.

A Roman centurion, in charge of the team of soldiers who carried out the crucifixion, stands alongside the cross. He has been part of the whole event, probably on duty from the early hours of the morning. He has heard the crowd's cry, the criminals' conversation, and the words of forgiveness spoken by the man on the centre cross. From all he has seen and heard, the centurion can come to no other conclusion but that the man they have just crucified is righteous ('innocent', NRSV). The accusations against him have been false, while the affirmations have been true.

The crowds have also seen what the centurion witnessed. These nameless people, so recently baying for Jesus' blood, now beat their breasts in grief and self-condemnation. Perhaps something in the darkness has opened their eyes to the truth. Watching also with solemn devotion are acquaintances of Jesus, and women who have followed him from Galilee.

For a moment the spotlight falls on Joseph of Arimathea, a wealthy and honoured member of the Jewish council, and a secret disciple of Jesus. At considerable risk to himself, Joseph goes to Pilate and asks for the body of Jesus. With respect and compassion he takes the body down from the cross, wraps it in fine linen, then places it in a tomb hewn out of the rock. The burial is completed before sundown.

A group of women watch to see where the body is laid. Then they go home to prepare burial spices with which to anoint the body as soon as the Sabbath is over.

Notice all the expressions of faith, grief and devotion in this scene. After the derision and brutality that surrounded Jesus' trial and crucifixion, he is now given a burial fit for a righteous man.

SUNDAY 29 JANUARY
Maker, Defender, Redeemer and Friend

Isaiah 44:1–8, 21–28

'This is what the LORD says – your Redeemer, who formed you in the womb: I am the LORD, who has made all things, who alone stretched out the heavens, who spread out the earth by myself' (v. 24, NIV).

The opening words of this chapter are addressed to Jacob and Israel (also called Jeshurun). The covenant people are invited to listen because God has something of utmost importance to tell them. Once again the prophet declares what God has done for them in the past, what he is doing in the present and what he has in mind to do in the future. At the heart of all this activity lies the very nature of God himself. Who is he?

He is King (*v. 6*). As ruler and sovereign head of his chosen people he leads them in the ways of righteousness. He is Redeemer, the one who brought them out of slavery in Egypt and longs to bring them out of slavery to sin and into a restored relationship with himself. He is the first and the last, as one of the last verses of the Bible declares: 'I am the Alpha and the Omega, the First and the Last, the Beginning and the End' (*Rev 22:13*).

He is Creator (*Isa 44:24*), not only of individual people but also of the heavens and the earth. From micro to macro, from infinitesimal to infinite, he is God. He is Owner (*v. 5*) who has written proof of his ownership over all he has made. Every person, every seashell, every star tossed into space carries marks of its creator.

He is not a buddy God on equal footing with what he has made. There is no way we can approach such a God casually or carelessly. He invites our reverence and awe, yet longs for us to come into an intimate relationship with himself. He delights in our delight in belonging to him.

He is a Rock (*v. 8*), a strong and unshakable foundation on which to stand and build a life, a safe refuge in which to hide when storms threaten.

To reflect on
Take one of these images of God – King, Redeemer, First and Last, Creator, Owner, Rock – and let it become your meditation for today. What does it mean to you to belong to such a God?

MONDAY 30 JANUARY
Day of New Beginnings

Luke 24:1–12

'On the first day of the week, very early in the morning, the women took the spices they had prepared and went to the tomb' (v. 1, NIV).

This new chapter of Luke's Gospel signals a huge scene change. The backdrop of death and darkness has been rolled up for good and moved offstage. The chapter opens with the crisp feel of a fresh new morning, the sky streaked with red.

This first day of the week is a day of new beginnings. First to experience it are the women who come to the tomb. With devotion they had stood at a distance from the cross until Jesus died. They had watched where his body was laid. Obedient to the fourth commandment they had rested on the Sabbath. Faithfully they had prepared their spices.

Do they come on this new day feeling dead themselves, physically exhausted, emotionally drained? Is it some kind of automatic response that simply keeps them moving, one foot after the other? No conversation is recorded, no extra details given. We have to fill in the gaps ourselves. How would you feel on such an occasion? With what heart would you come? Imagine yourself walking to the tomb with the women on this cool, fresh morning.

At the tomb they find nothing as they had expected to find it. They thought there would be a heavy stone covering the entrance but it is rolled away. They thought they would find a body but there is none. They imagined they would be there on their own but suddenly they are joined by two angelic figures who speak words they had never expected to hear.

Walk with the women as they hurry back to tell the others. Listen in on their conversation: 'Can it really be true?' Feel the thrill of joy that leaps within when the great and glorious good news is declared: 'He is not here; he has risen!'

This is a day of new beginnings
Day of joy, no more despair
Come to the cross, see what has happened
No signs of death now linger here
Christ has risen, dispelled the darkness
Changed to day the gloom of night
Now clothed in resurrection glory
He is our everlasting light.

31

TUESDAY 31 JANUARY
On the Road to Emmaus

Luke 24:13–27

'We had hoped that he was the one who was going to redeem Israel'
(v. 21, NIV).

This account of the two companions on the road to Emmaus is a rich and beautiful story. It contains all the elements of a good tale – sadness, surprise, suspense, resolution.

The words, 'We had hoped', lie at the heart of the travellers' lament. In Jesus they had recognised the prophet of God – messenger and Messiah. They had observed his ministry of healing and deliverance. They had experienced the power of his teaching to turn life up the right way. They had thought he was the One who would rescue their nation and deliver them from their enemies.

But their lament is 'We had hoped'. Past tense. Their hopes came crashing down when the religious leaders arrested him, sentenced him to death and crucified him. To add confusion to despair there was a report that his body had disappeared. Some women had come back from the tomb with an amazing story of angels who insisted that he was alive.

As the two pour out their grief and anguish, Jesus patiently listens and awaits his moment to respond.

Then, beginning with Moses and all the Prophets, he explains the events of the past few days in the context of the much larger story.

Luke has offered you and me a gift in telling us this story. He gives us permission to feel the sadness, offer the lament and recognise the answer when we too find ourselves trudging heavy-hearted along our road to Emmaus.

Author Frederick Buechner says, 'Emmaus is the place we go in order to escape – wherever it is we throw up our hands and say, "Let the whole thing go hang. It makes no difference anyway." Emmaus may be buying a new suit or a new car . . . or reading a second-rate novel or even writing one. Emmaus is whatever we do or wherever we go to make ourselves forget that the world holds nothing sacred: that even the wisest and bravest and loveliest decay and die.'[4]

To reflect on
If you are on your road to Emmaus today, lift your eyes to the One who travels with you.

WEDNESDAY 1 FEBRUARY
Over Bread

Luke 24:28–35

'He took bread, gave thanks, broke it and began to give it to them.
Then their eyes were opened and they recognised him'
(vv. 30,31, NIV).

Late in the day, as the three travellers approach the village of Emmaus, Jesus looks set to journey on but the others persuade him to stay with them. A meal is prepared and they recline together at the table.

Here, Jesus the guest becomes Jesus the host. He takes the bread, gives thanks, breaks it and gives it to them. In the calm and quiet of their home, away from the anguish of Jerusalem, their eyes are suddenly opened. They recognise their travelling companion as Jesus himself. They have been speaking with the very One they have been speaking of! This stranger is not a stranger but a friend.

Over bread he becomes known to them. They realise he has indeed been raised from the dead. This moment takes them back to other days when they have seen him bless and break bread before their eyes.

Over bread in the wilderness he became known for his power to work miracles, to feed a mighty multitude. Over bread in the Upper Room he offered them communion with himself, his daily living presence to satisfy every need. Over bread on the beach (*John 21:13*) he would become known as One who waits to nourish, rises to bless (*Isa 30:18*) and longs to have fellowship (*Rev 3:20*) with those who follow him.

In the moment of recognition, when they suddenly see him for who he is, Jesus disappears. They recall how their hearts burned within them as he spoke to them from the Scriptures. Now it all makes sense. This news is too exciting to hold until morning so they hurry back to Jerusalem. There they find the eleven and the news that Jesus has been seen by several people. 'It is true! The Lord has risen and has appeared to Simon.' They tell how he revealed himself to them over bread. Despair becomes delight as the truth about Jesus' resurrection begins to sink in.

Over bread
Make him welcome
Know his blessing
Bid him stay

Over bread
Tell your story
Share your heartache
Seek his way.

THURSDAY 2 FEBRUARY
Standing in the Midst

Luke 24:36–43

'While they were still talking about this, Jesus himself stood among them and said to them, "Peace be with you"' (v. 36, NIV).

The air is buzzing as the eleven disciples and the two from Emmaus share their stories of seeing the risen Jesus. Suddenly he is there standing in their midst. He speaks the familiar greeting, 'Peace be with you.' Instead of responding with words of welcome, however, the disciples are startled and frightened. Luke adds that they thought they were seeing a ghost.

Jesus asks why they are troubled and doubting. He invites them to look and touch his hands and feet, where the evidence of his crucifixion can still be seen. He reminds them that a ghost (literally 'spirit') does not have flesh and bones, as he does. In other words, Jesus presents his hands and his feet as physical proof of the resurrection.

The disciples, however, still struggle to believe it all. They are filled with joy and amazement, yet can scarcely believe that he really is risen from the dead. So Jesus gives them further proof by asking for something to eat. Someone hands him some broiled fish and they all watch as he eats it.

The disciple John was present that day. Years later he wrote, 'That which was from the beginning, which we have heard, which we have seen with our eyes, which we have looked at and our hands have touched – this we proclaim concerning the Word of life' (1 John 1:1).

In this day we no longer have eyewitnesses to the resurrection. But we have many proofs that Jesus is alive. In places like soup kitchens, counselling centres, church offices, airport chapels, hospices and eventide homes, wherever an offering of love and compassion is made in the name of Jesus, the promise is that he is there, standing in the midst.

I believe in Jesus
I believe he is the Son of God
I believe he died and rose again
I believe he paid for us all
And I believe that he's here now
Standing in our midst
Here with the power to heal now
and the grace to forgive.
                                    Marc Nelson[5]

FRIDAY 3 FEBRUARY

Opening the Mind to Understanding

Luke 24:44–49

'Then he opened their minds so they could understand the Scriptures'
(v. 45, NIV).

Jesus shows his disciples his hands and feet, and his ability to eat. These things prove that he is not a ghost but a real being, formerly dead, now resurrected. He then addresses their unasked questions: How can he be here like this? What have the cross and resurrection meant?

Jesus reminds them that what was predicted has taken place. 'This is what I told you while I was still with you.' A crucified and raised Messiah is not God's 'Plan B'. This has been the purpose of God from the very beginning. The disciples have experienced what the saints of old – and even angels – longed to see (*1 Pet 1:10–12*).

He speaks of the testimony of Scripture – the law of Moses, the Prophets and the Psalms – the three parts of the Hebrew Scripture. He opens their minds to understand what was said about him, just as he had opened the Scriptures to the two travellers on the road to Emmaus and opened their eyes to recognise him as he broke the bread.

He says the message can be summed up in three verbs, three giant leaps that stride across the whole testimony of Scripture –

'suffer', 'rise' and 'be preached'. The Old Testament declared that the Christ, the Messiah, would suffer (*Isa 52:13–53:12*) and be raised (*Ps 16:8–10*). The disciples must now preach to the nations what they have witnessed. The response will be repentance; the result will be forgiveness.

Before they go out to the task, however, they need to be equipped. Jesus will send them the gift promised by the Father, and they will be 'clothed with power from on high'. Although not identified, this is clearly a reference to the Holy Spirit. The verse looks back to the prophet Joel who said the Spirit would be poured out on all people (*Joel 2:28*). It also looks forward to the book of Acts where the promise is fulfilled (*Acts 2:1–4*).

To reflect on
For so long lacking in understanding, the disciples at last seem to 'get it'. Perhaps God has an 'Aha!' moment for you today!

SATURDAY 4 FEBRUARY
Blessing, Worship and Joy

Luke 24:50–53

'They worshipped him, and returned to Jerusalem with great joy; and they were continually in the temple blessing God' (vv. 52,53, NRSV).

Blessing, worship and joy. With these key words Luke brings his Gospel to a close. The story ends where it began – in the temple. Jesus offers the blessing that Zechariah could not speak (1:22). He blesses the disciples as he departs for heaven to continue his work by God's side.

Halfway through the Gospel, Luke tells us that Jesus leaves Galilee and heads towards Jerusalem 'as the time approached for him to be taken up to heaven' (9:51). That moment of departure is now accomplished. The people who waited in the temple early in the Gospel – Zechariah, serving before God (1:8), the assembly of the people (1:10), Simeon, who praised God in the temple (2:25) and Anna, who never left the temple (2:37) – are now matched by the disciples who 'stayed continually at the temple, praising God'.

When the risen Jesus first appeared to the eleven, the disciples were terrified and thought they were seeing a ghost. Now, after the physical proofs, the instruction from Scripture, the commission, Jesus' parting blessing and his ascension, the disciples worship him. All fear and uncertainty have gone. Sight for the eyes and understanding for the mind have brought joy to the heart.

While Mark's Gospel is full of 'at once' and 'immediately' rush and bustle, the movement in Luke's Gospel is expressed by turning and returning (1:56, 2:20, 2:43). The final return in this Gospel is the disciples' return to Jerusalem in obedience to Jesus' final instruction. There they will remain for some time, as Luke records in the early chapters of Acts. The joy that was announced at the births of John and Jesus (1:14, 2:10) and anticipated in the ministry of Jesus (8:13, 10:17) is now finally fulfilled.

From here, Luke continues his story in the book of Acts, describing the coming of the Holy Spirit. He tells how the message of the gospel goes out to the far reaches of the world. The great themes of blessing, worship and joy continue.

So Luke's Gospel concludes. But the story is far from finished. You and I are the disciples now.

SUNDAY 5 FEBRUARY

The Idol Test

Isaiah 44:8–20

'All who make idols are nothing, and the things they treasure
are worthless. Those who would speak up for them are blind;
they are ignorant, to their own shame' (v. 9, NIV).

In a chaotic, unstable world, God declares himself to be the Rock, unchanging, unshaken and strong. Apart from this Rock, he says, there is nothing sturdy for beaten and battered people to cling to, no other firm foundation on which to build a life. People try to find other ways, of course, gods of their own making.

With undisguised irony, Isaiah paints a portrait of idol–makers and their futile attempts to make something strong and enduring. But, like the idols they make, these idol–makers are 'nothing . . . worthless . . . blind . . . ignorant, to their own shame' (v. 9). There is nothing of value or beauty in what they do.

The prophet describes the complex process of making an idol, beginning with the last step of plating the wooden form with precious metal (v. 12). Then he describes how the carpenter makes the wooden form (v. 13), then the process of choosing the wood for the form (v. 14). This is hard and hungry work. Unlike the eternal God who never grows tired or weary (40:28), the idol–maker is quickly exhausted by his task.

He needs to stop and eat something so he takes the wood he has chosen to shape into an idol. Using half of it he builds a fire and cooks his meal over it. The fire warms him and the food fills his stomach. With his strength restored he forms the other half of the wood into a god, then bows down to worship it. How ridiculous! The idol–maker is blind to his own folly. With his eyes plastered over and his mind closed (v. 18), he is literally feeding on ashes (v. 20).

The folly of this idolater is so obvious. But what about the more subtle idols that entrap and ensnare present–day believers like you and me? 'Above all else,' says the writer of Proverbs, 'guard your heart, for it is the wellspring of life' (Prov 4:23). To what do you and I give our hearts, our keenest attention, our greatest energy? Who are the idols that consume the best hours of our days?

HEAR A VOICE THAT ENTREATS YOU – AMOS

Introduction

This series on Amos needs to come accompanied with a health warning. Most of the book is hard to read as devotional material. There is more punishment than peace here, more woe than wonder contained in these pages. But when we read beyond the words to the issues that God addresses through his prophet, we see 'sorrow and love flow mingled down', as Isaac Watts put it (*SASB 136*). God is not fickle and vengeful but sorrowful and broken-hearted over his people's sin and waywardness.

It is to point out their wrongdoing and its consequences that Amos writes his message. He attacks Israel's sins of idolatry and complacency. He exposes the sinful ways in which the wealthy oppress the poor. Using picturesque imagery from his own pastoral background he condemns the people's thin veneer of religion, the meaningless rituals they perform to win favour with God. He calls for justice to 'roll on like a river, righteousness like a never-failing stream' (*5:24*).

This is a compelling story. Amos is both observant of the world around him and in tune with the demands of a holy God. As we study his book may we too be attentive to the entreating, pleading voice of God that calls to us in our day.

MONDAY 6 FEBRUARY

Man with a Burden

Amos 1:1

'The words of Amos, one of the shepherds of Tekoa – what he saw concerning Israel' (v. 1, NIV).

So begins the book of Amos, introducing the man and his vision. No biographical details are given other than his name, his occupation and his birthplace. Amos came from Tekoa, an area of rugged sheep country about eleven miles south of Jerusalem. As a shepherd, Amos was not a poor hired labourer but the manager or owner of a small flock. Economically independent, he was a respected man in his community. Although not trained as a professional prophet (see 7:14), Amos was obviously well informed about Israel's social conditions and religious practices, the law of Moses, and current events in Israel and the surrounding nations.

At the time, Israel had a prosperous economy but the nation was spiritually bankrupt. Idols were worshipped throughout the land and especially at Bethel, which was supposed to be the nation's religious centre. Amos' task was to call the nation back to God, back to the covenant made with their ancestors generations earlier. In a collection of short messages, using imagery from his own pastoral background, Amos tells the nation that if they do not repent and change their ways, the results of their idolatry and rebellion will overwhelm them.

A reading of the book of Amos reveals the burden of this man. Even his name has a burden attached, for it comes from a Hebrew word meaning 'to load a burden upon an animal'. His God-given task was a burden, his words of correction and judgment a heavy load to communicate to the nation of Israel.

Does a bird feel the burden of singing its song to the world? Does an artist carry his passion for beauty as a burden? Do you struggle with the burden of a huge responsibility, an overwhelming task, a privileged position? 'Cast your cares on the LORD [that is, roll back onto God the burden that he has rolled onto you] and he will sustain you,' encourages the psalmist (Ps 55:22).

To reflect on
The load God gives us to carry may be both a great burden and a glorious blessing. Is today a day for burden-rolling for you?

TUESDAY 7 FEBRUARY
The God Who Roars

Amos 1:2–8

'The LORD roars from Zion and thunders from Jerusalem' (v. 2, NIV).

Shepherd Amos and shepherd David have much in common. Both learned about the ways of God out in the pastures as they watched their animals, studied the night sky and learned the rhythms of the seasons.

Shepherd Amos and shepherd David understood the shepherding heart of God who leads and protects his flock. But at the start of Amos' message God is described not as a gentle shepherd but as a roaring lion, ready to devour those who are evil. 'The pastures of the shepherds dry up, and the top of Carmel withers,' says Amos (v. 2).

This is like saying, 'From A to Z, from the driest portion of the land to the greenest, the Lord's judgment will be felt like a severe drought that devastates the whole land.' There will be no area, however protected or secure, that will not suffer as a result of the judgment announced by this roar from Zion.

Amos pronounces God's judgment on cities and nations around Israel's borders. He has a specific word to say to Damascus, to Gaza, to Tyre, to Edom, to Ammon and to Moab. 'For three sins . . . even for four' – that is, the sin named is only one of many sins.

Fury upon fury spills forth from God. 'I will send fire . . . I will break down . . . I will destroy . . . I will not turn back my wrath . . . I will turn my hand against . . . I will set fire.' These are hard words to read. They must have been excruciating words for shepherd Amos to say.

How does this image of 'the God who roars' fit in with your theology? It is a long way from 'Gentle Jesus, meek and mild'. Augustine wrote, 'The Lord is gentle, the Lord is slow to anger, the Lord is gracious. But the Lord is also just. The Lord is also faithful. God gives you space for correction, but you love the delay of judgment more than the amendment of your ways.'

Amos' fearful description gives us pause today to reflect on anything in our lives that would have God roaring.

WEDNESDAY 8 FEBRUARY
Knowing and Sinning

Amos 2:1–8

'This is what the LORD says: "For three sins of Israel, even for four,
I will not turn back my wrath"' (v. 6, NIV).

There is a kind of perverse satisfaction in hearing my brother or sister being told off for some wrongdoing. I feel a hint of smugness as I listen. But when the accusing finger points at me and rebukes me for my sins, that is a different matter altogether.

Amos won the attention of his audience by first declaring God's judgment on the evil nations surrounding Israel. The people of Israel may have cheered as they heard his tirade. But when Amos turned and spoke God's rebuke to his own nation Judah, and then to the northern kingdom of Israel, they were suddenly silenced. Amos made it clear that the punishment for Judah and Israel would be even greater than it was for the surrounding nations. After all, the other nations were ignorant of God and his ways, but Judah and Israel knew what it meant to be the covenant people of God.

In spite of all they knew, however, they had chosen deliberately and defiantly to turn their backs on God and to violate his commandments. Every sin of Israel's was in direct contradiction to the stated laws of God. They sold the poor into slavery, even though the law of Moses forbade such a thing (*Deut 15:7–11*). They exploited the poor in defiance of God's clear command (*Exod 23:6*). They engaged in perverse sexual sins which were clearly forbidden (*Lev 20:11,12*). They illegally took security for debts (*Exod 22:26,27*). They worshipped false gods even though the first commandment clearly spoke against doing so (*Exod 20:3–5*).

Their sin was great and made even greater because they were fully aware that their actions were breaking both God's commandments and his heart. The poor, the disadvantaged and the needy were society's most vulnerable members and were to be cared for. Israel knew and understood this, yet chose deliberately to do the very opposite.

To reflect on
What is the link for you between knowing and sinning? Knowing carries responsibility with it. When is it true to say, 'I did not know, so I cannot be blamed or punished for what I did'?

THURSDAY 9 FEBRUARY

Provision and Punishment

Amos 2:9–16

'I brought you up out of Egypt, and I led you for forty years in the desert to give you the land of the Amorites' (v. 10, NIV).

Amos condemns Israel for exploiting and oppressing the poor. The nation's greatest sin, however, may well be the sin of forgetting. They have forgotten who God is and what he has done for them throughout the generations.

God speaks through Amos to remind them. 'I destroyed . . . I brought you up . . . I led you . . . I raised up.' We hear echoes of Hosea reminding his people of the gracious, tender-hearted God who loved Israel like a son, taught him to walk, led him with cords of human kindness (Hos 11:1–4).

From Egypt to exodus to explosion in the land of Canaan, every need they had was met at the hand of a merciful God. Against every strong enemy he had given them the victory. He had sent them a long line of prophets to speak the word of God. He had given them Nazirites – people set apart to live as an example of faithfulness and holiness.

'But you . . .' (v. 12). With utter disdain the people had silenced the prophets and corrupted every holy vow. They had tried to stamp out all signs of God at work in their midst.

'So this is what God is going to do,' declares Amos. He uses an image from his own pastoral background to describe how God is going to punish them and reduce them to nothing. God will crush them just as a loaded cart crushes anything that falls under its wheels.

No one will be able to save himself. The swift man will not be able to run. The strong man will not be able to fight back. The warrior will not be able to attack. A surefooted, keen-eyed archer will lose his balance. A fleet-footed soldier will not be fast enough to get away. Even a man on horseback will not have enough speed to avoid the coming punishment. The most heavily armed, most well-protected, most courageous soldier will be as vulnerable as someone wearing nothing at all. Neither inner resources nor outer covering will mean anything on that day when God comes to crush those who have opposed him.

FRIDAY 10 FEBRUARY

Hear the Voice that Entreats You

Amos 3:1–7

'You only have I chosen of all the families of the earth; therefore I will punish you for all your sins' (v. 2, NIV).

Can you hear the voice of entreaty, the tone of tenderness in this verse from Amos? The God of the broken heart speaks to his people of their 'specialness' to him. 'Out of all the families on earth, I picked *you*' (*The Message*). We hear an echo of Peter's words, 'You are a chosen people, a royal priesthood, a holy nation, a people belonging to God' (*1 Pet 2:9*).

If the first part of Amos' declaration makes them feel secure and loved, the second part must surely make them quake. 'I have chosen you ... therefore I will punish you.' On the surface, the logic seems skewed. How can specialness and punishment be linked? Simply because sandwiched between the two parts of this declaration lie years of rebellion and rejection of the ways of God. In spite of being the privileged, loved, covenant people of God, they have taken other paths, chosen other gods, given their hearts to other delights. As a consequence of turning away from God their punishment is inevitable.

Speaking on God's behalf, Amos asks seven rhetorical questions, each one using an image from everyday life. He is saying that nothing happens just by chance. If two people go for a walk it is because they have an agreement between them. If a lion roars it is because it has made a killing. If a bird gets caught in a trap it is because a snare had been set. If disaster falls on them it is in consequence of their sins. Far from being at the whim of a fickle, vengeful God, they are simply in the hands of a fate they have created for themselves.

As the prophet Isaiah wrote,

'Come now, let us reason together,' says the LORD. 'Though your sins are like scarlet, they shall be as white as snow; though they are red as crimson, they shall be like wool. If you are willing and obedient, you will eat the best from the land; but if you resist and rebel, you will be devoured by the sword' (Isa 1:18–20).

SATURDAY 11 FEBRUARY
The Prophet's Compulsion

Amos 3:8–15

'The lion has roared – who will not fear? The Sovereign LORD
has spoken – who can but prophesy?' (v. 8, NIV).

Amos speaks from an irresistible, God-given compulsion. At a given moment in time, God moved him from tending sheep to declaring a message against Israel. The message is a heavy burden for a man with a burden for a name. But just as a lion roars and creates fear, so God has spoken and Amos must speak.

The general charge against the Israelites is that they do not know how to do right. Nothing is straight, upright or honest. Evidence of their deviation from God's standards is seen in the actions of the rich upper classes who oppress and rob the poor. No one is safe from their violence.

Amos calls for unnamed messengers to travel to the cities of Ashdod and to Egypt to call their people to gather on the mountains that surround the city of Samaria. From that grandstand vantage point the pagan nations will be able to see the shameful things happening in the midst of God's chosen people.

Amos uses a vivid picture from his pastoral background to portray Israel's ultimate fate. After the enemy, God, attacks them like a lion, there will be nothing left of them but fragments – 'only two leg bones or a piece of an ear' (*v. 12*). The custom behind this verse is that if an animal was attacked by a predator, the shepherd must bring the remnants to the owner of the sheep as proof that it had been eaten by a wild animal and not stolen by the shepherd (see *Exod 22:10–13*).

These chilling words of punishment are directed towards the luxury-loving upper classes but everyone in Israel will be affected. On the day of God's wrath there will be neither religious nor material security left. Both the altars where the people worship and their superbly furnished mansions will be destroyed.

Such words of punishment need to be read and taken seriously, both by Amos' audience and in our day. But even as we read we hold our breath, for we know that punishment is not the full and final picture. We await the end of the story.

SUNDAY 12 FEBRUARY
A God Who Hides

Isaiah 45:1–15

'Truly you are a God who hides himself, O God and Saviour of Israel'
(v. 15, NIV).

The prophet Isaiah grappled with the mystery of God's presence and absence. He spoke confidently of the many ways in which God, by miracle and mercy, reveals himself to humankind. But, at the same time, God is a God who hides himself. This is not something for believers to despair about. Just as in the game of hide-and-seek, when a child hiding behind the sofa giggles and thus gives the game away, so God delights to be found.

God hides in unlikely people (v. 1). Cyrus, featured in this chapter, is a prime example. Writing more than a century before Cyrus was born, Isaiah, the prophet of God, names this Gentile King of Persia as the 'anointed' one of God. Cyrus will be used to set free the Jewish exiles in Babylon and make it possible for them to return to Jerusalem and rebuild their ruined city.

God hides in unexpected places. As the Creator of heaven and earth (v. 18), God has left his fingerprints over all he has made. Many people find God more readily on mountains, in forests or by lakes than they do in church. For many who find the Scriptures difficult to

understand, the world of creation is 'God's other book'.

God hides in unforeseen problems (v. 7). Think back to a situation in your life when you 'reached the end of your hoarded resources', as the song says, only to find that God came through for you in a way you would never have expected. There will be many times on our journey when all we can do is hold on to 'Emmanuel' – God with us, whether his presence is felt or not.

If I had not gone through the waters
I might not have learned how to swim.
If I had not passed through the furnace
I might never have come to trust him.

When the waters almost o'erwhelmed me
When the darkness around me was grim
When there was no one but God to hold on to
It was then that I learned to trust him.

MONDAY 13 FEBRUARY
Cows of Bashan

Amos 4:1–5

'Hear this word, you cows of Bashan on Mount Samaria, you women who oppress the poor and crush the needy and say to your husbands, "Bring us some drinks!"' (v. 1, NIV).

It is no more polite in our society to call someone a 'cow' than it was in Amos' day. This stinging indictment was addressed to Israel's wealthy women. In calling them 'you cows of Bashan', Amos was referring to an area in Transjordan well known for its lush pastures and well-fed cattle (see *Deut 32:14*). These pampered, self-indulgent women were maintaining their opulent lifestyle by exploiting the poor, crushing the needy and expecting to be waited on hand and foot by those around them. They had no concern, compassion or care for the weak.

When Amos declares that 'the Sovereign LORD has sworn by his holiness', the women – and men – of Israel should have been reaching for their equivalent of crash helmets and bullet–proof vests. When God says something, it will happen. When God swears an oath, it will certainly happen. When God swears by his own holy character, there is no way it will not happen.

Amos describes what will happen to the rich, indulgent people of Israel. They will be unceremoniously dragged out of the city like prisoners of war being led away by ropes fastened through hooks in their noses or lips. Those who have treated other people like animals will be likewise treated. Those who have lived in luxury will experience the bitter taste of defeat and humiliation. Fat cows will become dead carcasses.

With undisguised irony Amos describes how the people have maintained a superficial form of religion with no substance or heart to it. They have offered the whole range of religious sacrifices in the belief that, by doing so, they were keeping on good terms with God. But Amos tells them their regular pilgrimages and repeated sacrifices are nothing but a charade, a fancy parade to show off their wealth. They practise their piety in order to be seen by others (*Matt 6:1*), not in order to come close to or give glory to God.

To reflect on
Perhaps we too need to read these verses with our crash helmets on! What might God be saying to you and me today?

46

TUESDAY 14 FEBRUARY
You Have Not Returned to Me

Amos 4:6–13

'"I overthrew some of you as I overthrew Sodom and Gomorrah. You were like a burning stick snatched from the fire, yet you have not returned to me," declares the LORD' (v. 11, NIV).

When God made his covenant with the people of Israel, he made it clear that the way of obedience was the way to blessing; the way of disobedience was the way to disaster (see *Lev 26*). Life with God would be as stark and simple as that.

Repeatedly God tried to discipline them by sending them tribulations. Amos lists five occasions when God gave the people of Israel opportunity to cast themselves upon his resources. He made them endure hunger, he held back lifegiving rain, he struck their gardens with blight and mildew, he let locusts loose on their crops, he sent plagues and warfare.

All of this was to discipline them, like reining in a wild horse, but on every occasion they responded with disdain. Even when God gave them a Sodom and Gomorrah-type experience, the most chilling example in Israel's history of God's punishment for sin, the people stubbornly refused to turn to him. God provided the way to grace but the people rejected it. Out of all this disaster only a few survived, like smouldering sticks pulled out of a fire.

The writer to the Hebrews concedes that: 'No discipline seems pleasant at the time, but painful. Later on, however, it produces a harvest of righteousness and peace for those who have been trained by it' (*Heb 12:11*). It was a lesson, however, that they refused to learn.

In ancient Israel if a lamb was a 'congenital stray' – that is, if it refused to stay with the flock – the shepherd would break its leg. This was not an act of cruelty but of kindness, for the shepherd would then carry the lamb in his arms until the leg healed. By that time the lamb would not want to be anywhere but close to the shepherd.

This is what God had tried to do with Israel. He had all but broken the nation but still the people went their wayward way. They refused to learn from God's discipline or to acknowledge his sovereignty. Now, says Amos, they will have no choice but to face God's judgment.

WEDNESDAY 15 FEBRUARY

Seek the Lord and Live

Amos 5:1–17

'Seek good, not evil, that you may live. Then the LORD God Almighty will be with you, just as you say he is' (v. 14, NIV).

Both longing and lament sound throughout this passage. The God who allows punishment to come upon his people is also the God of the broken heart who grieves over their sin.

The name of God is proclaimed at the beginning – 'the Sovereign LORD' (v. 3), in the middle – 'the LORD' (v. 8) and at the end – 'the Lord, the LORD God Almighty' (v. 16). The theme of the passage is Israel's death, brought on by its failure to honour God by true worship and just dealings in its law courts.

The passage begins and ends with wailing for the dead. These words would be shocking to Amos' first audience. After all, Israel was at that time wealthy, prosperous and a strong military power. But with his prophet's eye Amos can see things the people cannot see. He knows they are enjoying their final days of the good life.

His lament is for the people who have brought corruption to Bethel and Gilgal, locations that at one time in Israel's history were 'thin' places of encounter with God. Now they have become shrines celebrating idolatry and shame. The people have perverted justice and righteousness, tainted the things of God and turned good into evil, truth into lies.

They have trampled on the poor and oppressed the righteous. They have spent their energies in futile ways, building flash stone mansions that they will never live in and planting lush vineyards whose wine they will never taste.

Doing wrong, loving the wrong things, putting their energies into the wrong places, the people have only one hope of rescue – God himself. 'Seek me and live . . . Seek the LORD and live . . . Seek good, not evil, that you may live,' pleads God through Amos.

'There is life for a look at the crucified one,' wrote songwriter Anna Matilda Hull (*SASB 271*). Amos declares the same message. For the people of his day, seeking God would mean letting justice, goodness and righteousness become the rule, the norm, the standard. What would it mean for you?

Intentionally 'seek God and live' as you go through this day.

THURSDAY 16 FEBRUARY
Let Justice Roll On

Amos 5:18–27

'Let justice roll on like a like a river, righteousness like a never-failing stream!' (v. 24, NIV).

Amos declares woe upon those in Israel who long for the day of the Lord. They seem to think it will be a glorious day of celebration when God will win victory over all his enemies and bring the nation's troubles to an end.

Not at all, says the prophet. Far from being a day of light and joy, it will be a day of darkness and humiliation. Israel's theology is correct – God will defeat his enemies, but they fail to realise that their sins have made them too into enemies of God. They are as deserving of his judgment as any pagan nation.

Amos uses a graphic image to illustrate how bad that day will be. A man fleeing from one danger (a lion) runs smack into another (a bear). That same man reaches the safety of his house and goes inside, relieved to be home, but is bitten by a snake. 'You think things are bad now?' asks Amos. 'You ain't seen nothing yet!'

His voice rises to thunder pitch as he declares God's judgment on Israel. 'I hate, I despise . . . I cannot stand . . . I will not accept . . . I will not listen.' It is not the religious rituals themselves that are the problem, but the mechanical, meaningless way in which they are offered. They do not come from a heart of love or with a commitment to act in righteous ways.

Amos exhorts the people to pay close attention to what it means to worship. Worshipping God means walking in his ways. Justice should flow continually like a full river all year round, not like an undependable wadi that has water in it only when it rains. Justice is not an optional extra but a key value, a non-negotiable in the life of a believer.

This, as contemporary songwriter Matt Redman says, is the heart of worship. More than merely bringing a song, it is a matter of bringing the heart from which the song sings.

To reflect on
Is justice rolling on steadily in your life? Is righteousness flowing like a never-failing stream?

FRIDAY 17 FEBRUARY
Too Long at Ease in Zion

Amos 6:1–7

'Woe to you who are complacent in Zion, and to you who feel secure on Mount Samaria, you notable men of the foremost nation, to whom the people of Israel come!' (v. 1, NIV).

In Amos' day when someone died there would be a large banquet with both mourning and feasting. Amos discovers, however, that the wealthy people at these funeral banquets in Samaria are not grieving at all for the person who has died. Careless and carefree, they are simply there to enjoy themselves.

Amos thus offers his own lament over the coming death of Israel. He can see a day coming when these opulent funeral feasts will cease and the nation will be taken off into captivity. First he laments the people's false sense of security. The inhabitants of Zion, the capital of Israel, have no worries about military threats or the state of the economy. They are strong, confident and self-righteous. Compared to their neighbours, they feel bigger and better than all the rest.

They live every day in carefree ease and security. They have everything money can buy. They sprawl on expensive couches inlaid with ivory. They eat top-quality tender beef from prime fattened calves and choice lambs. They enjoy the finest music, imagining that they are great musicians in the style of King David. Unlike David, however, who sang his songs to bring glory to God, these people sing their songs to glorify only themselves. They drink to excess using huge wine bowls, and massage their skin with expensive lotions and perfumes.

So preoccupied are they with enjoying themselves, they do not even notice their nation falling apart. The poor are being oppressed, the moral and economic fibre of the nation is crumbling, and Israel's military power is under threat. Amos warns that these wealthy upper-class people of Israel – the 'notables of the first of the nations' (v. 1, NRSV) – will be the first to go into exile (v. 7). Revelry and sprawling at feasts is about to come to an end. The party is over!

To reflect on
'Too long at ease in Zion I've been content to dwell,' wrote songwriter W. Walker (SASB 482). What similarities can you see between Amos' day and our own times? Make one of these issues your focus for prayer today.

SATURDAY 18 FEBRUARY
Words of Condemnation

Amos 6:8–14

'The Sovereign LORD has sworn by himself – the LORD God Almighty declares: "I abhor the pride of Jacob and detest his fortresses; I will deliver up the city and everything in it"' (v. 8, NIV).

Amos portrays God swearing by his own eternal and almighty nature, the strongest guarantee possible, that he hates and condemns Israel's pride. This is the root of all Israel's sin. In its pride, the nation believes itself to be self-sufficient, able to rely on its own resources and security rather than relying on God. They sing, 'A mighty fortress is our God,' forgetting that it is not a stronghold of bricks and mortar, but God alone who can provide them with refuge and protection.

Amos gives an example of what will happen. There may be a house with just a few people left in it but they too will die. A relative, maybe from a different village, will come to give them a decent burial. The person will search the house for any survivors, calling out, 'Is anyone with you?' What he really means is, 'Is anyone still alive in here?', but the answer will be 'No'. At such a grievous time, when it would be natural to call on God for help, people will be afraid even to mention God's name in case of further punishment.

'The LORD has given the com-

mand,' says Amos. God's direction and the prophet's words are always mingled together. Even as the prophet speaks, God's judgment begins.

As a way of pointing out Israel's foolishness, Amos asks two foolish questions: Do horses run over rocks? Does one plough the sea with oxen? The answer to both questions, obviously, is: Of course not! The rocky terrain would ruin the horses' legs and the oxen would drown in the sea. But this kind of foolishness is exactly what Israel has practised in the law courts, turning justice into poison. The righteous, God-given order of Israel's society has been tainted and distorted by corruption and sin.

In a final divine reversal of Israel's fortunes, God, the Lord of hosts, the Lord over all nations, announces that an unnamed enemy will be raised against them and will take their whole land. Because of the nation's stiff-necked rebellion and persistent failure to honour God, Israel's fate is sealed.

51

SUNDAY 19 FEBRUARY
The God Who Carries

Isaiah 46:1–13

'Even to your old age and grey hairs I am he, I am he who will sustain you. I have made you and I will carry you; I will sustain you and I will rescue you' (v. 4, NIV).

'Come to me, all you who are weary and burdened, and I will give you rest' (*Matt 11:28*). Next to Psalm 23, this verse must be one of the earliest pieces of Scripture that many of us memorised. As *The Book of Common Prayer* puts it, these are 'comfortable words'. Being weary and burdened ('heavy laden', AV) is not necessarily the result of sin or failure, but simply an inevitable part of life, an integral aspect of being human.

Isaiah the prophet speaks of the tremendous burden of carrying false gods – those things in which hope is wrongly placed in times of hardship. Bel was the chief deity of the Babylonians; Nebo was the god of science and learning. These 'gods', far from being powerful, needed animals and people to carry them around and could not even save themselves from being carried off into captivity.

In a masterful contrast, Isaiah declares the faithfulness and unfailing strength of God who has carried Israel 'since you were conceived ... even to your old age and grey hairs' (*vv. 3,4*). There is a profound tenderness in this image. Think of the concentration and care with which a young woman carries her first baby in the womb. Think of the pride with which a baby is carried and shown off to family and friends. Think of the joy of carrying a child in the arms or on the shoulders. Think of the care with which a frail elderly person is carried.

'From womb to tomb' Israel has been and will be carried. This promise is sealed by the everlasting nature of God himself: 'I am God, and there is no other; I am God, and there is none like me' (*v. 9*). When it comes to carrying his children, no one can do it the way God does!

To reflect on
Think back over the various stages of your life – infancy, childhood, adolescence, adulthood. Do you recall a memory of God's grace carrying you at each stage? As you look ahead affirm your trust in the grace of God to continue carrying you.

MONDAY 20 FEBRUARY
Standing in the Gap

Amos 7:1–9

'I cried out, "Sovereign LORD, forgive! How can Jacob survive? He is so small!"' (v. 2, NIV).

A television news item showed the devastating effect of a plague of locusts spreading across several African nations. The ground and air were white with flying, swarming insects.

With the prophet's eye, Amos sees a similar plague coming upon the land of Israel. It will happen at a strategic agricultural time, when the king's share of the crop has been harvested and just as the young, tender spring crops are sprouting. Knowing that such a plague at such a time will cause untold hardship for poor peasant farmers, Amos cries out for mercy. Not on the basis of their repentance but on the basis of the nation's smallness, he asks God to forgive. He is pleading for a pure act of grace. With an almost audible sigh of relief, Amos reports, 'So the LORD relented.'

For a second time Amos sees a threat coming upon the land – fire, a clear symbol of judgment. Once more, in the style of Abraham interceding for the inhabitants of Sodom and Gomorrah (see *Gen 18*), Amos cries out to God, pleading Jacob's (that is, Israel's) smallness and inadequacy. Once more God relents.

Amos, the praying prophet, illustrates the power of standing in the gap between God and people. He is a perfect example of the righteous man, mentioned in James' letter, whose prayer is 'powerful and effective' (*Jas 5:16*). He prays with the confidence Jesus recommends, asking, seeking, knocking (see *Matt 7:7*).

Then Amos sees a third vision. This time the Lord is standing by a wall, holding a plumbline, a device used to ensure the straightness of a wall. God's covenant with Israel, his clear commandments, his setting apart of the nation to be holy, his blessings and favour upon the people, made Israel in the past a straight wall, an example of righteousness in a pagan world. Idolatry and faithlessness, however, have thrown the wall out of line. The nation is no longer standing true and strong. Israel has been 'weighed on the scales and found wanting' (*Dan 5:27*).

To reflect on
On whose behalf could you 'stand in the gap' in prayer today?

TUESDAY 21 FEBRUARY
A Calling to Fulfil

Amos 7:10–17

'I was neither a prophet nor a prophet's son, but I was a shepherd, and I also took care of sycamore-fig trees. But the LORD took me from tending the flock' (vv. 14,15, NIV).

In the midst of the doom and gloom Amos speaks; there are yet signs of mercy. As he reports his vision of the plumbline, he records God calling Israel 'my people' (v. 8). For all their sin and shame, they are still, in the eyes of God, his beloved covenant people.

Amos' very presence is itself a sign of mercy. If it were not for the prophet, where would the people be? If he did not speak God's words, how would they know what is on God's heart? If it were not for his prayers on their behalf, what would happen to them?

Amaziah, the high priest at Bethel, makes a report concerning the prophet to Jeroboam, King of Israel. The priest's words are inflammatory and designed to make a scapegoat out of Amos but unwittingly he speaks the truth. Jeroboam (that is, his house or dynasty) does die by the sword, with the assassination of his son Zechariah (see *2 Kgs 15:8–10*). The warning about Israel going into exile away from their native land (*Amos 7:11*), unbelievable as such a prediction may sound, is exactly what Amos has told them will happen (*v. 17*).

'Away with you!' the priest tells Amos. 'Go stand on another street corner. Find another pulpit. You're disturbing the peace around here. Go spread your doom and gloom somewhere else!' With the confident composure of a man who is sure of himself and his vocation, Amos tells the priest how God called him to his task.

He had no special privilege or preparation. He was just an ordinary man with an ordinary background doing an ordinary job when God called him to leave shepherding and become a shepherd of Israel. In spite of the priest's constraints, Amos declares he cannot be constrained.

A God–given vocation can be a heavy load to carry at times. May Amos' example help you and me to be faithful right where we are.

To serve the present age,
My calling to fulfil,
O may it all my powers engage,
To do my Master's will!
        Charles Wesley, SASB 472

WEDNESDAY 22 FEBRUARY
A Basket of Ripe Fruit

Amos 8:1–7

'"What do you see, Amos?" he asked. "A basket of ripe fruit,"
I answered. Then the LORD said to me, "The time is ripe for my
people Israel; I will spare them no longer"' (v. 2, NIV).

This passage contains the most extreme statement in the book of Amos: 'I will spare them no longer.' No more chances, no more blessing, no more forgiveness. In a vision Amos sees a basket of ripe summer fruit and God tells him the time is ripe for judgment. It is not just the king and temple that will be destroyed (7:9), but the nation of Israel itself, God's own special covenant people.

'In that day' (v. 3) joyous singing at the temple will turn into wailing. In the place of life and worship there will be dead bodies lying everywhere. They will be left unburied – the ultimate disgrace – as food for vultures and wild animals. The scene will be so tragic and so unbelievable that a deathly silence will fill the temple. Amos names no enemy and gives no explanation of how this tragedy will happen, but gives one reason why.

Earlier he accused the 'cows of Bashan' (4:1) of oppressing the poor. Now he focuses on the merchants who trample over the needy. Those who need help and cannot make it on their own receive no compassion or assistance, but are taken advantage of.

The merchants' motivation is money. They have a thin veneer of religiosity, attending the New Moon festivals and observing the Sabbath as a holy day, but they are always impatient for these non-working, non-profit-making days to be over so they can get back to selling, scheming and short-changing.

When buying grain they measure it out in oversized containers; when selling it they use undersized containers. They have two sets of weights for their scales – one for weighing heavy and the other for weighing light. A little chaff or dirt scooped up off the floor also helps to bring a measure up to weight.

Through such dishonesty the wealthy merchants end up 'buying the poor with silver' (v. 6). As their debts mount up, the poor have no choice but to sell themselves or their children into slavery. These brutal practices are, of course, all unlawful and will be punished. 'I will never forget,' thunders God.

THURSDAY 23 FEBRUARY
A Different Kind of Famine

Amos 8:8–14

'"The days are coming," declares the Sovereign LORD, "when I will send a famine through the land – not a famine of food or a thirst for water, but a famine of hearing the words of the LORD"' (v. 11, NIV).

A world where famine stalks is not hard to imagine. We catch ghastly glimpses of it all too regularly on our television screens – bloated stomachs of listless children, dazed mothers with empty breasts trying to feed newborn babies. The images are horrifying and all too real.

Amos speaks of a different kind of famine coming upon the land – a famine of hearing the words of the Lord. The people made no response when prophets like Amos declared the word of the Lord. Because of their apathy, God said he would take away even the opportunity to hear it. Amos describes people groping blindly after God, desperate to find him, but he will not be found. They will stagger like a man searching for water, or like a confused and desperate traveller, but every trace of God will be gone.

Imagine praying but hearing only silence, the raw silence of absence and emptiness. Imagine going through a grievous loss and looking to God for comfort but feeling no everlasting arms around you. Imagine seeking guidance from God but hearing no 'This is the way I want you to go'. Imagine doing something so shameful that only forgiveness from God could set you free, but not being able to find such forgiveness.

Imagine a world in which the standards of righteousness, truth and justice are no longer used. Imagine the fruits of the Spirit – love, joy, peace, patience, kindness, goodness, faithfulness, gentleness and self-control – being shrivelled up and wasted. Imagine a world without compassion, without tenderness, without service. Imagine turning towards God only to find he has turned away from you.

Our local newspaper features the story of a seven-month-old baby girl being beaten to death by her father. A local fourteen-year-old is killed in a car crash after going for a joyride with her boyfriend in a stolen car. This past Christmas the shops carried a popular new range of Bob the Builder and Barbie Advent calendars.

I read Amos' words, look around my world and can come to no other conclusion but that the famine has already begun!

FRIDAY 24 FEBRUARY
Standing in the Place of Mystery

Amos 9:1–10

'Though they dig down to the depths of the grave, from there my hand will take them. Though they climb up to the heavens, from there I will bring them down' (v. 2, NIV).

I have to confess that the book of Amos is a challenge to my theology. I love the promises of Scripture that God is always with me (*Heb 13:5*). I hold fast to the reassurance that no matter what I go through, God will be there (*Isa 43:1,2*). I am comforted by the fact that there is no distance too great for God's love to reach me (*Ps 139:7–10*). I marvel that God saw me, knew me, loved me and had my whole life planned even before I was born (*Ps 139:13–16*). I delight in a God who calls me his beloved, in a Jesus who prays for me, in belonging to a family of faith into which I am cemented like a brick in a building (*Eph 2:19–22*).

I have built a theology – my whole life, in fact – on these and other wonderful assurances from Scripture. I love believing in a God who is bent on blessing me. But the book of Amos portrays quite another side of God that I seldom consider – a God bent on punishment.

Today's reading seems to bring these two conflicting aspects of God to a head. God, standing by the altar, declares it to be a place of destruction, whereas in Israel's history the altar was always a place of refuge. God declares there will be no escape, neither in depth nor in height – a stark contrast to Psalm 139. There will be no hiding place, not even on Mount Carmel, the place of Elijah's great battle and God's amazing victory.

Most chillingly of all, God says, 'I will fix my eyes upon them for evil and not for good' (*Amos 9:4*). This is El-Roi, the God who sees, who fixed his eyes in blessing on Hagar, Sarah's maidservant (*Gen 16:13*).

So how do we hold together the tension of God as Love and God as Punisher? We stand yet again in the place of mystery, one hand holding firmly what we know to be true of God, the other hand open, letting rest there all that we do not yet fully understand.

SATURDAY 25 FEBRUARY
Reversal and Restoration

Amos 9:11–15

'I will bring back my exiled people Israel; they will rebuild the ruined cities and live in them. They will plant vineyards and drink their wine; they will make gardens and eat their fruit' (v. 14, NIV).

At last a glimmer of hope shines through. At last a reversal is declared, a promise of restoration announced. 'I'll make everything right again for my people Israel' (*v. 14, The Message*). Amos says the restoration will be lavish. The seasons will run together with no interval between sowing and reaping. There will be a continuous supply of fresh produce. New wine will drip from the mountains and flow from all the hills.

Israel will be planted, established, settled once more, and will grow like a great oak or solid kauri that will never again be destroyed. Amos' picture sounds like a return to Eden. Certainly it is a great reversal of the devastation described earlier (see *4:6–11*) when starving people staggered from town to town, desperate for water, and when blight, mildew and locusts devastated their crops. Not only the land, but the people themselves will again be productive and secure. 'I will bring back . . . they will rebuild . . . I will plant.'

Just when all this will happen, and how, and who will be the blessed recipients of God's favour, Amos does not make clear. But this is more like the God we know – the God of abundant grace, the God of lavish love, the God who does in us and for us 'far more than you could ever imagine or guess or request in your wildest dreams' (*Eph 3:20, The Message*).

Our relief at reading the end of Amos' story must not make us deaf to the voice that entreats us throughout his book. Through Amos, God warned the people of Israel that an outward show of religion, accompanied by no heart obedience, was unacceptable. Their idolatrous indulgent lifestyle and their oppression of the poor were wrong and would be punished. With graphic imagery, Amos made the message clear that God's desire was always to discipline them, not destroy them.

In these days may we also be responsive to the voice of discipline, the voice of love that calls us home.

Hear a voice that entreats you,
O return ye unto God!
Fanny Crosby, SASB 272

SUNDAY 26 FEBRUARY
The Way We Should Go

Isaiah 48:1–19

'This is what the LORD says – your Redeemer, the Holy One of Israel:
"I am the LORD your God, who teaches you what is best for you,
who directs you in the way you should go"' (v. 17, NIV).

In the Orthodox tradition, the Sunday before the beginning of Lent is called Forgiveness Sunday. The community of believers gathers for a service where each member kneels before each other member and asks forgiveness for anything they may have said or done during the past year that caused hurt or offence.

Today is the Sunday before the beginning of Lent. As you read today's portion from the book of Isaiah, hear the voice of God pleading for his children to come back into relationship with him. Hear also his promise to guide and teach and direct us in the way we should go. God declares that following this way will lead to peace and righteousness (*v. 18*), fruitfulness and blessing (*v. 19*).

These verses echo the confident assurance of psalmist David that God will 'instruct you and teach you in the way you should go . . . counsel you and watch over you' (*Ps 32:8*). For a couple of years when I myself was instructing, teaching and counselling others I took this verse from the Psalms as God's daily promise to me.

'The way we should go' is not some ethereal, mystical experience but is grounded in the reality of everyday life. We catch a glimpse of how the first believers in the Early Church walked in this 'way'. The way took them in four directions – upwards, downwards, inwards, outwards – but, far from being scattered, they were centred on the Lord Jesus, gathered together around him (see *Acts 2:42–47*).

They lifted their hearts to God in worship, praise and thanksgiving. They spent time in prayer and gave daily attention to fellowship, communion and teaching. They reached out in compassionate service to others, ministering to any in need. Both in public – 'in the temple courts' – and in private – 'in their homes' – their fellowship was characterised by unity and joy, and God blessed them daily with new converts.

To reflect on
Reflect on how God has led you 'in the way you should go'. Give thanks that the way of worship, fellowship, prayer, service, teaching and forgiveness is still open to you today.

FORGIVEN AND FORGIVING

Introduction

Forgiveness has been described as the thorniest bush with the most splendid roses. It was the subject of much of Jesus' teaching.

'Keep us forgiven with you and forgiving others' (*Matt 6:12, The Message*). 'You can't get forgiveness from God ... without also forgiving others' (*Matt 6:15, The Message*). 'Forgive one another as quickly and thoroughly as God in Christ forgave you' (*Eph 4:32, The Message*).

Jesus made it clear that forgiveness is both a gift from God and a grace to pass on to others. These are the two hands of forgiveness. With one hand we receive it; with the other hand we offer it.

Forgiveness is clearly not an optional extra but an integral part of kingdom living. Henri Nouwen says, 'The lifelong struggle to forgive lies at the heart of the Christian life.' So we need to get it right. This series will, I pray, help us all in that process.

MONDAY 27 FEBRUARY

Forgiveness Begins with God

Ephesians 1:3–14

'In him we have redemption through his blood, the forgiveness of sins, in accordance with the riches of God's grace that he lavished on us with all wisdom and understanding' (v. 7, NIV).

Creation began with God. 'In the beginning God created the heavens and the earth' (*Gen 1:1*). Holiness begins with God. 'Be holy, because I am holy' (*Lev 11:44*). Love begins with God. 'We love because he first loved us' (*1 John 4:19*). So does forgiveness. In fact, everything that is true, noble, right, pure, lovely, admirable, excellent or praiseworthy (*Phil 4:8*) has its beginning in God.

God is the initiator in every aspect of our salvation. If God were not holy, we would have no model of holiness to follow. If God did not love us, we would have no love to pass on to others. If God were not a forgiving God, we would have no hope of being forgiven, no example of forgiveness to live by, no grace to offer forgiveness to others.

If you want to know how much God identifies with you, look at the baby in a Bethlehem manger. This child is Immanuel, God with us, wrapped in love and human flesh. Paul tells how Jesus made himself nothing, humbling himself, taking on the very nature of a servant, coming right down to where we stand (*Phil 2:7,8*).

If you want to know how much God loves and forgives you, look at the cross. Jesus' open arms embraced all the world long before you or I had any sense of sin, any awareness of our need for God. From the cross Jesus spoke words of forgiveness to soldiers and sinners alike: 'Father, forgive them, for they do not know what they are doing' (*Luke 23:34*).

This God in whom all beginnings begin had you and me, love and forgiveness, redemption and restoration in mind long before we even existed.

You did not wait for me to draw near to You
but you cloth'd Yourself in frail humanity.
You did not wait for me to cry out to You,
But You let me hear Your voice calling me.

And I'm forever grateful to You,
I'm forever grateful for the cross,
I'm forever grateful to You
that you came to seek and save the lost.
Mark Altrogge[6]

61

TUESDAY 28 FEBRUARY

God of Forgiveness

Psalm 103

'As far as the east is from the west, so far has he removed
our transgressions from us' (v. 12, NIV).

A golden seam of forgiveness weaves its way right through the Old Testament and into the New Testament. From the Garden of Eden through the laws of Leviticus, the pronouncements of the prophets and the wise sayings of Proverbs, the clear testimony of Scripture is that God is a God of forgiveness and mercy.

This is how God described himself when he gave Moses the Ten Commandments: 'Compassionate and gracious ... slow to anger, abounding in love and faithfulness ... forgiving wickedness' (*Exod 34: 6,7*). God is not a cosmic spoilsport lurking in the shadows, planning vengeance and retribution, setting traps for us, waiting to trip us up, watching to see how hard we fall, rubbing his hands in glee at our helpless state. Rather, he is bent on blessing us, he longs to be gracious to us, he rises to show us compassion, he gives strength to all who look to him.

Psalm 103 is a glorious statement of faith and trust in this compassionate, forgiving God. Using strong active verbs, David the psalmist describes how God forgives, heals, redeems, crowns, satisfies, renews, works righteousness, abounds in love, removes transgressions, has compassion, remembers. We receive all these 'benefits' (*v. 2*) without deserving any of them. We deserve to be punished for our sins, not forgiven. But God is merciful, gracious and slow to anger. He has removed our sins as far as east is from west. That is a distance that can never be spanned, for east and west can never meet.

There is only one proper response to make – praise. The psalmist calls on 'all my inmost being', or 'all that is within me' (NRSV) to praise, bless and not forget all the benefits of this forgiving, healing, redeeming God.

Read the psalm slowly aloud. Stop when you come to a word that invites you to pause. Reflect on what it means for you. Let the breadth and depth of this exquisite psalm fill you with gratitude and wonder today.

To reflect on

Grace is getting what we don't deserve. Mercy is not getting what we do deserve.

WEDNESDAY 1 MARCH

Forgiveness Flows from the Father

Luke 23:32–43

'Jesus said, "Father, forgive them, for they do not know what they are doing"' (v. 34, NIV).

Today is Ash Wednesday, marking the beginning of the season of Lent. On this day of beginnings we celebrate a completion.

As Jesus hung on the cross, humiliated and in deep pain, people milled around watching, waiting, mocking, berating. The religious leaders sneered, soldiers taunted, one of the criminals hurled insults. In the midst of this dark morass of hatred and invective, Jesus cried out words of forgiveness. Notice to whom he addresses his prayer. He does not say, 'I forgive you', but 'Father, forgive them'.

Jesus, who had had unbroken fellowship with the Father since before the creation of the world, is, in these moments of suffering and torment, abandoned by God. The Father turns his back as Jesus dies with the sins of the world upon his shoulders. But, even though he is cut off from the Father's presence and blessing, Jesus knows to direct his prayer to the only One who can extend forgiveness.

As he asks for forgiveness to flow, Jesus is obviously referring to the soldiers who are in the very act of carrying out his crucifixion.

'Father, forgive them, for they do not know what they are doing.' He is no doubt looking at the religious leaders and others who had such an insidious part to play in his death. 'Father, forgive them . . .' He is aware of the criminals on the crosses alongside his own. 'Father, forgive them . . .'

Is it possible that Jesus saw more than the crowds who were present that day? His words of forgiveness, his cry, 'It is finished' (John 19:30), and the torn curtain in the temple suggest that something more than an ordinary death took place. The power of sin was broken. With Jesus' death a redemptive work was completed. Forgiveness can now flow from the Father to all who 'do not know what they are doing'.

'Sorrow and love flow mingled down,' wrote Isaac Watts (SASB 136). Indeed they do, and forgiveness flows down as well, down through the centuries and generations, right down to where you and I stand in our need before God today.

THURSDAY 2 MARCH
Forgiveness Is God's Habit

Psalm 130

'If you, GOD, kept records on wrongdoings, who would stand a chance? As it turns out, forgiveness is your habit, and that's why you're worshiped' (vv. 3,4, *The Message*).

Habits are strange things. They sneak up on you, move in and quickly take up residence. You may not think you have any habits until your usual routine is disrupted and then you suddenly realise how deeply ingrained your habits have become.

Habits are helpful in giving structure and order to life. But habits can also be destructive. A habit of overspending, eating to excess or driving too fast can have consequences ranging from troublesome to tragic. Habits that are good and helpful need to be affirmed, while habits that are harmful to ourselves or others need to be axed.

God has habits too. 'Forgiveness is your habit,' says Eugene Peterson's paraphrase of Psalm 130:4. God's usual way of being and responding is with forgiveness. What great news this is for those who get caught up in destructive ways of doing things. What wonderful news to know that habitual wrongdoing and failure are met by God's habitual forgiveness.

Paul describes a new Christian as 'a new creation' (*2 Cor 5:17*) with new habits. Some ways of doing things change immediately but others take longer. The big ship called Character with its cargo of habits may have been heading in one direction for a long time. Repentance means turning the heavy ship around, changing course, being guided by a new star or compass.

The apostle John said that when we become Christians through faith in Christ we do not keep on sinning – that is, we do not keep up with the habit of sin. Our tastebuds change. The things that used to delight and entice us no longer hold any appeal. The things of God that were previously unknown to us become sweet and nourishing.

Even so, sin can still trip us up. No matter how old we are in the faith, we need to remember that, 'If we confess our sins, he [that is, God] is faithful and just and will forgive us our sins and purify us from all unrighteousness' (*1 John 1:9*). When we fall and sin, God, whose habit is forgiveness, is there ready to catch us.

FRIDAY 3 MARCH
Forgiveness Restores

Leviticus 25:8–13

'Consecrate the fiftieth year and proclaim liberty throughout the land to all its inhabitants. It shall be a jubilee for you; each one of you is to return to his family property and each to his own clan' (v. 10, NIV).

In the Garden of Eden, sin broke the pure fellowship that Adam and Eve had with God and opened their eyes to their naked state. To cover their shame and their sin God made garments of animal skins. No chastisement is recorded, no words of forgiveness spoken, but from this moment a picture begins to form of a God who not only hates sin, but knows what to do about it. His action restores the relationship.

As the children of Israel wandered round and round in the desert, learning what it meant to be the covenant people of God, a weary cycle of rebellion, sin and repentance developed. Sin was never without its consequences, but repentance was always met by God's forgiveness and restoration. Long generations of prophets spoke the same message as Moses. 'Turn from God and you will face the consequences. Turn to God and he will forgive and restore you.'

Forgiveness was written into the very fabric of Israelite society. The book of Leviticus, for all its tedious lists of laws, is really a book of forgiveness. 'If a member of the community sins unintentionally ... he must bring as his offering ... the priest will make atonement for him' (*Lev 4:27,28,31*). A sin offering brought and slaughtered became the means of forgiveness and restoration. But another day brought another sin, requiring another sacrifice.

Forgiveness was even planted in the soil. Every seventh year the land was to be rested. The people were instructed not to plant their fields or prune their vineyards. In that year God would provide all they needed. After seven cycles of seven years, the fiftieth year was to be a holy year when all land that had been sold was returned to its original owner. All debts were cancelled, all slaves freed. This year of Jubilee was to be celebrated as a year of restoration, forgiveness and freedom. If there was any need, God would supply it. If there was any shortfall, God would make it up.

To reflect on
What is God forgiving, restoring, setting free in your life in these days?

SATURDAY 4 MARCH
Forgiveness Is the Key

Psalm 32

'Blessed is he whose transgressions are forgiven, whose sins are covered' (v. 1, NIV).

The psalmist David knew the joy of forgiveness. He had sinned against God, against a woman and her husband, and against himself (see 2 Sam 11–12). His outer, visible sins were the big ones of adultery and murder. His inner, invisible failure was that he had fallen short of all he was destined to be as 'a man after God's own heart'.

Thankfully, David found forgiveness. Psalm 51 records his anguish and pleading. Psalm 32 records the sense of freedom he found when he finally confessed his sin. Before confession, he was burning up on the inside. 'My bones turned to powder ... all the juices of my life dried up' (vv. 3,4, *The Message*). After confessing his sin, he was a man restored, redeemed, forgiven, set free.

I knew a woman once who suffered a grievous hurt but could not bring herself to forgive the person who had hurt her. She cut herself off from the world and locked herself up in her house. She became a prisoner, with bitterness and anger her prison guards. As she lived, so she died.

Another person, a man who had been a member of a church for many years, became, in his later years, an unhappy, grumpy old man. Then a sudden illness hospitalised him. Close to death, he realised how his attitudes had offended people.

When he recovered sufficiently he sent a message to all the members of the church, asking them to come and see him. As each person came, he apologised and asked for forgiveness. With relationships restored and friendships renewed he gradually returned to full health and to a positive, active role in the church.

Corrie ten Boom, a Dutch woman who spent months in a German concentration camp during the Second World War, wrote that unforgiveness is a prison. 'Forgiveness is the key that unlocks the door of resentment and the handcuffs of hate. It is a power that breaks the chains of bitterness and the shackles of selfishness.'

To reflect on
Do you need to use the key of forgiveness to let yourself out of prison today?

SUNDAY 5 MARCH

An Antidote for Discouragement

Isaiah 49:1–7

'But I said, "I have laboured to no purpose; I have spent my strength in vain and for nothing"' (v. 4, NIV).

Before he was born, God chose his servant, the Messiah, to bring the light of the gospel, the message of salvation, to the world. His calling and commissioning are described in tender, personal terms. 'God put me to work from the day I was born. The moment I entered the world he named me. He gave me speech that would cut and penetrate. He kept his hand on me to protect me. He made me his straight arrow and hid me in his quiver' (vv. 1,2, *The Message*).

Then suddenly, unexpectedly, there is a jolt. 'I have laboured to no purpose.' Can this be Jesus, the Messiah, speaking? In spite of the opposition Jesus encountered from his enemies and the obtuseness of his disciples, he kept going, as the writer to the Hebrews puts it, 'for the joy set before him' (*Heb 12:2*).

I came across this verse in Isaiah many years ago when a mission station in Africa, where hundreds of young people had been educated, was forced to close because of terrorist activity. I remember these words when I hear of a child, brought up in a loving Christian family, going off the rails in adolescence. I recall this verse when a friend tells me of her son who, in spite of his longing to have legal custody of his children, has lost even his right of access.

I weep this verse when I hear of Christian leaders resigning, or when I notice that a once vibrant Christian has drifted away from fellowship. I think of this verse when I see a garden that was once tilled and fertile now neglected and overgrown with weeds.

There are many scenarios on our Christian journey that make us conclude that we have laboured in vain. In such moments we need to be reminded of the 'big picture' – the words of God's calling that precede this verse (vv. 1–3) and his great commission that follows it (vv. 5–7). God's purpose in allowing us to go through discouragement is never to destroy us but always to make us press more firmly into him.

MONDAY 6 MARCH

Loving Your Enemies

Matthew 5:38–42

'I tell you, Do not resist an evil person' (v. 39, NIV).

Imagine you are walking home on your own one dark night. Suddenly two men step out of the shadows. They beat you up and leave you lying semi-conscious on the cold ground. When you come to, you feel your swollen cheek and your aching ribs. You realise your attackers have taken your wallet, your new jacket and your shoes. Is your first thought, 'I love those people who beat me up. I forgive them. I wish they had taken my shirt and my socks as well. I wish I had turned the other cheek so that they could have punched and bloodied that one too'?

Hardly! Yet that seems to be the force of these verses from Matthew's Gospel. Jesus seems to be saying that forgiveness means letting ourselves be hit on both cheeks rather than one, and not only allowing our cloak to be taken from us, but even giving away our tunic (our undergarment) as well. Such teaching will surely result in nothing but resentment and passivity.

Will a ten–year–old boy who has saved all year to buy a bike rejoice when someone steals it? Will a group of poor workers in Guam or Guatemala extend forgiveness when those who have power over them make their living conditions even more difficult? Can Jesus really expect a battered wife to be a doormat for her husband's feet and a punching bag for his fists?

Such teaching would not be in line with all we know of Jesus. He loved sinful people, but he loved them too much to leave them in their sin. He loved people who lived at the extremity, on the edge, on the margins of society, but his love did not ostracise them further. Rather his love drew them in, made them welcome, assured them of acceptance, helped them to change.

So we need to read these verses with fresh eyes. Could Jesus in fact be inviting us to see that forgiveness, far from being passive and self-abusive, actively resists evil, maintains our dignity and challenges the person who hurts us to change what they are doing?

TUESDAY 7 MARCH
Turning the Other Cheek

Matthew 5:38–42

'If someone strikes you on the right cheek, turn to him the other also'
(v. 39, NIV).

Imagine you are a slave in ancient Israel. Your master is angry and is about to strike you. He cannot hit you with his left hand for the left hand was used only for tasks considered unclean. So he must use his right hand.

He strikes you on your right cheek with the back of his right hand. In Jesus' culture, hitting someone with the back of the hand was a gesture of humiliation, used by those in a position of power against someone considered to be beneath them. Masters would backhand slaves. Romans would backhand Jews. Husbands would backhand wives. Parents would backhand children. The message of the backhand was: 'Remember that your place is beneath me!'

Now read the passage again. Jesus says, 'If someone strikes you on the right cheek, turn to him the other also.' If your master has back-handed you on your right cheek, he will have to use a fist or the open palm of his right hand to hit you on your left cheek.

In Jesus' culture, this gesture was used only between equals. Perhaps it is like the 'high five' that people give each other today in our society, striking their open right hands together in a gesture of friendship.

By turning your left cheek to your master, you, as a slave, have reminded him of your dignity as a human being. You have also invited your master to examine the lie by which he lives, namely that one human being is better than another. What is more, you have done all this without the use of violence, without striking your master back. Turning the other cheek is therefore not a sign of weakness and passivity, but a gesture of strength. It is a reminder of the dignity and worth of every creature, no matter what their status in life.

An Indian evangelist was sharing the gospel with a group of people when a man threatened to slap him. 'I presented my cheek to him,' he said. 'Suddenly the man's hand stopped in mid-air and he never hit me!' (*Bible Society Newsletter*).

WEDNESDAY 8 MARCH

Let Him Have Your Underwear

Luke 6:27–31

'If someone takes your cloak, do not stop him from taking your tunic'
(v. 29, NIV).

Imagine you are a poor farmer. You have a little plot of land where you grow vegetables, some for your family to eat and some to sell at market. You pay rent on your land every month. On the week that the rent is due, your family has less to eat because you need to sell as much as possible in order to get enough money to pay your rent.

One day the man who owns the land comes to tell you that he is doubling your rent. Your heart sinks. You know this means further hardship for you and your family. In fact, it makes your situation impossible. It means you will not be able to grow enough, sell enough or earn enough to feed and clothe your family. The landowner is literally stealing the shirt off your back.

Speaking to this situation, Jesus says, 'If someone demands your cloak, then give him your tunic as well.' In Jesus' day, a tunic could be worn by itself in public without embarrassment but, since nothing was worn underneath the tunic, giving it away would be the same as, in our culture, giving away one's underwear.

Thus you would be naked. In Jesus' culture it was not so scandalous to be naked yourself, as it was to look at another person in that state. Therefore, the landowner to whom you give your cloak and your tunic will experience the humiliation of reducing you to nakedness and poverty. Without violence you have regained your dignity (even though you are now naked), and you have made the one who oppresses you face his responsibility for your dire situation.

A man coming out of a bus station came face to face with an armed robber waiting outside. The man thought quickly. Taking off his jacket, he said, 'My, it's cold out here. Why don't you take my jacket?' The gunman was taken aback. Quickly the man continued, 'I was just going to get something to eat. Why don't you join me?'

To reflect on
No one can steal from you what you freely give.

THURSDAY 9 MARCH
Going the Extra Mile

Matthew 5:38–42

'If someone forces you to go one mile, go with him two miles'
(v. 41, NIV).

Imagine you are a peace-loving villager living on the outskirts of Jericho or Jerusalem in ancient Israel. One day you are on your way into the city when a Roman soldier stops you and demands that you carry his pack. At first you feel annoyed. The soldier's pack is heavy and uncomfortable but you have no choice. The law stipulated that a civilian could be forced to carry a Roman soldier's pack for one mile.

As you stagger along beneath the weight, you recall Jesus' teaching, 'If someone forces you to go one mile, go with him two miles.' You decide to put that teaching to the test and see what happens. When you come to the road marker that indicates you have covered one mile, you tell the Roman soldier that you will carry his pack for a second mile.

A few steps later, everything suddenly changes. The law that required a civilian to carry a Roman soldier's pack for one mile also stipulated that if a soldier demanded more than one mile he could be punished. So as you walk along, voluntarily carrying the heavy pack for a second mile, the soldier is at first confused, then alarmed. Before too long he begs you to stop and hand over his pack. He no longer wants you to carry it because he is afraid of being punished.

Without striking the soldier or getting caught up in a cycle of violence, you have exercised your power to choose your own response, refused to act as a victim and kept your dignity.

This week's readings about loving one's enemies, turning the other cheek, handing over one's tunic and going the extra mile illustrate the proactive side of forgiveness. By responding positively and not passively to those who demand something of us, we may well defuse a situation of potential violence, get under their defences and cause them to change.

To reflect on
When some difficult demand is laid upon you today, think about how you can 'go the extra mile' and voluntarily give more than would be expected of you.

FRIDAY 10 MARCH
Growing a Flap of Forgiveness

Romans 12:14–21

'Do not repay anyone evil for evil' (v. 17, NIV).

Now and again you meet someone who makes Scripture come to life, not so much by what they say, but by how they live. A woman who I'll call Rita is a perfect example.

Rita grew up in a family that looked good on the outside, but on the inside was a festering mess. She suffered abuse and betrayal from those who should have loved and protected her. At a defining moment in her adult years, however, Rita realised she had a choice. She could either continue the patterns of denial and pretence she had grown up with, or she could face, challenge and change them.

Thanks be to God, she chose the latter way. It took a long time, many years in fact. Forgiveness for those who had wounded her deeply did not happen overnight. But gradually, one painful step, one desperate prayer after another, she found healing and, with it, the confidence to step out of shame and hurt into freedom and life.

Rita's woundedness will always be a memory. It is part of who she is. But she has diluted, defused and disempowered it by refusing to let it go any further or hurt her any longer.

Recently out walking, Rita came across a young gum tree growing up towards a large immovable rock. The tree had no way round, so it had grown a flap of trunk up and over the rock. Just as an oyster makes a pearl out of an irritation, the tree had used the obstacle of the rock to hold on to and support itself.

Writer Gale Webb says, 'The only way to conquer evil is to let it be smothered within a willing, living, human being. When it is absorbed there, like blood in a sponge or a spear thrown into one's heart, it loses its power and goes no further.'[7]

'Do not be overcome by evil,' says Paul, 'but overcome evil with good' (v. 21). Grow a flap of forgiveness, a pearl of peace, a layer of love over the hurt that threatens to destroy you.

SATURDAY 11 MARCH
Forgiveness Is a Grace from God

Matthew 18:23–35

'The servant's master took pity on him, cancelled the debt and let him go. But . . .' (vv. 27,28, NIV).

When the king in Jesus' parable decides to settle his accounts, he finds that one of his servants owes him ten thousand talents. That is like saying 'millions of dollars'. It is an overwhelming debt. With an earning capacity of just a few cents a day, the servant will obviously never be able to repay such a huge amount.

He falls on his knees and begs the king for mercy. He actually asks for an extension of time, a delay, mistakenly believing that, if he is given enough time, he will be able to repay the money. The master's idea of forgiveness, however, is quite different. With a heart of compassion, he cancels the servant's debt and lets him go free. So the servant goes out, his debt completely cancelled, his slate wiped clean. However, he thinks he has simply been given an extension of time – which is what he asked for – so that he can repay the debt he thinks he still owes.

He catches sight of a fellow servant who owes him just a few dollars, an easily repayable amount. The second servant falls on his knees (as the first servant had done) and begs for an extension of time (exactly as the first servant had done). 'But he refused,' says Jesus (v. 30). The first servant throws his fellow debtor into prison until he can repay his debt in full.

When the king hears what the first servant has done, he is understandably shocked and angry. He reinstates the debt, then turns him over to the jailers to torture him until he can repay the whole huge, impossible, multi-million-dollar amount.

Jesus concludes, 'This is how my heavenly Father will treat each of you unless you forgive your brother from your heart.' There is a spiritual law at work here. Forgiveness is a gift of grace from God. When we accept his forgiveness and pass it on to others, we ourselves are blessed. When we do not pass on God's forgiveness, we are handed over to the Fearsome Foursome tormentors whose names are Guilt, Resentment, Striving and Anxiety.

SUNDAY 12 MARCH
A Celebration of Restoration

Isaiah 49:8–23

'Then you will know that I am the LORD; those who hope in me will not be disappointed' (v. 23, NIV).

This chapter is a celebration of restoration, written to the Jewish people exiled in Babylon. Far from their homeland, they feel forsaken and forgotten, far from God himself. They cannot think of home without weeping. They cannot sing the songs of faith they once sang so full-heartedly. All they can do is weep and remember, remember and weep (see *Ps 137*). But to these lost and longing ones the prophet Isaiah speaks words of comfort, words of compassion.

God, declares the prophet, is even now working out their restoration. One day soon, 'in the time of my favour . . . in the day of salvation' (*v. 8*), God is going to do something so remarkable, so unbelievable that they will not be able to contain their joy. The impossible will become gloriously possible.

What was once desolate and devastated will be restored. Those who were once held captive will be released. Those who have lived too long in darkness will be led out into the light. Every barren place will burst forth, lush and prolific. Impassable mountains will be levelled for easy passage. Those who have been afflicted will be comforted – given strength. All that was once blighted, barren and bereaved will be fertile again, abundant and over-flowing. A tragic exile will become a triumphant return.

Israel says, 'I've been forsaken, forgotten, abandoned.' But God says, 'How could you be? I could no more forget you than a mother could forget her child. But, even if she could, I could not! You are engraved on the palms of my hands. A mere glance at my hands reminds me of you.'

While these amazing words were written to the exiles in Babylon they are also words today for anyone in the exile of barrenness, forsaken-ness or sin. One day, 'in the time of my favour', God's people will be brought together. There will be no more exiles, refugees, marginalised, lost or displaced people. Every tear will be wiped from every eye. There will be no more death or mourning, crying or pain (*Rev 21:4*). God himself declares this to be so.

MONDAY 13 MARCH
Dealing with Unfinished Business

Matthew 5:21–26

'If you are offering your gift at the altar and there remember that your brother has something against you, leave your gift there in front of the altar. First go and be reconciled to your brother; then come and offer your gift' (vv. 23,24, NIV).

Imagine you are standing in a beautiful holy place such as a cathedral. The banners and tapestries on the walls are rich in colour and texture. You catch the fragrance of the candles. You feel the deep stillness, the quiet dignity, the sacred majesty of the place. Truly this is the house of God.

With reverent steps you bring your gift to the altar. But as you prepare to offer it, a face flashes through your mind – a face with a name and a memory of pain and hurt. It is an uncomfortable moment. You know that person is angry with you. They have told you so. Suddenly you feel distracted. You can no longer concentrate on making your offering. What do you do?

Matthew records Jesus saying that if this happens to you one day when you are in church, you must put down your offering (your songbook, your music, your money for the offering) and you must go immediately and deal with the unfinished business. Notice the direction of forgiveness in this scenario. Someone is angry with you, but you are to take the initiative in going and seeking reconciliation.

Mark gives a similar instruction. 'When you stand praying, if you hold anything against anyone, forgive him' (*Mark 11:25*). Same awesome place, same atmosphere, same altar. But this time, when a face flashes through your mind as you stand there preparing to make your offering, the anger belongs to you. You are the one holding a grudge against someone else.

Mark does not say anything about going and being reconciled, but simply, freely, sincerely in your heart, releasing that person with your forgiveness. Notice the direction this time – I am angry with someone else. I forgive them.

Forgiveness means living in right relationship with both God and others. Forgiveness means reconciliation. Whether asking for or offering forgiveness to someone else, the Scriptures make it clear that forgiveness, reconciliation and worship are inextricably woven together. Just ask Zacchaeus – he'll tell you (*Luke 19:1–10*).

To reflect on
Forgiveness is the fragrance that flowers breathe out when they are trampled on.

TUESDAY 14 MARCH
The Two Hands of Forgiveness

Colossians 3:12–14

'Forgive as the Lord forgave you' (v. 13, NIV).

The word 'forgiveness' is not really a proper word, because it is just a verb with 'ness' added to it. What other verb makes a noun in this way? Jumpness? Walkness? Singness? The correct way to make a noun out of 'forgive' would be to take the past participle 'forgiven' or the adjective 'forgiving' and make it 'forgivenness' or 'forgivingness'. A moment's reflection on these two words shows us the two sides of this action.

Forgiveness has two hands. With one we receive and with the other we give. Jesus said, 'If you forgive, you will be forgiven. But if you do not, you will not.' He was not meaning a linear mathematical formula like two plus two equals four, but rather a holistic, integrated way of living.

Just as you cannot genuinely offer mercy to someone who hurts you unless you experience God's mercy yourself, so you cannot live in forgiveness for yourself and, at the same time, live outside it when it comes to others.

Paul takes this theory and puts flesh on its bones. Writing to the Christians at Colosse, he reminds them of who they are – 'God's chosen people, holy and dearly loved'. They are a forgiven people. But Paul is realistic enough to know that in any kind of community living there will inevitably be clashes and complaints. He reminds them of how they are to deal with each other.

They are to clothe themselves with garments of compassion, kindness, humility, gentleness, patience, forgiveness and love. These are not dressing–up clothes that children put on for fun, like Mum's lipstick and high heels, or Dad's big boots and carpenter's belt.

Bearing with others means accepting them for who they are, even with their weaknesses and faults, yet acknowledging their worth. Forgiving others means passing on the forgiveness that we have received from God himself (see 1:14). These are the two hands of forgiveness. With one we receive it; with the other we pass it on.

To reflect on
Forgiveness is not a cup we drink on our own but a bowl we share with others.

WEDNESDAY 15 MARCH
Doing the Work of Forgiveness

Ephesians 4:25–32

'Be kind and compassionate to one another, forgiving each other, just as in Christ God forgave you' (v. 32, NIV).

In order to do the work of forgiveness I need to understand that forgiveness is, first of all, a decision. It is not just a warm, fuzzy feeling but a choice, a decision of the heart to deal with all that prevents love and life flowing through me.

Forgiveness is a risk. If I offer forgiveness to you, what will you do with it? Will you receive it and bless me, or will you take advantage of my vulnerability and hurt me more? I do not know. I only know that in not forgiving I face an even greater risk of harm to myself.

Forgiveness is a journey that winds its way around hills of heartache and mountains of memory, through valleys of dark shadows and across open plains of open pain.

Forgiveness is a process. Just as a wound takes time to heal, so the raw hurt of woundedness needs time to be opened, cleaned out and exposed to healing sunshine.

A man whose adult son was killed by a neighbour felt an overwhelming weight of anger towards his son's murderer. When he asked God to take away the anger, the only answer he received was, 'Wait.' A year later, when the case went to court, the young man who had committed the crime made a heartfelt apology for his action. When the father heard the words, 'I am truly sorry', he sensed God saying, 'This is what I have been asking you to wait for.' The father wrote to the young man in prison, thanking him for his apology and expressing his own words of forgiveness.

Forgiveness is a release, a giving up of one's anger, resentment and right to judge, condemn or get even with another person. Forgiveness is restoration to fellowship with God and maybe with the one who has wronged us. In Peru, when an offender wants to be reconciled with the one he has offended, he says, 'Speak to me.'

Forgiveness is finally an act of faith that leaves the issues of fairness and justice, of right and wrong, for God to work out.

THURSDAY 16 MARCH
Be Forgiven, Be Forgiving

Matthew 6:5–15

'Forgive us our debts, as we also have forgiven our debtors'
(v. 12, NIV).

At the heart of this prayer that Jesus gave as a model of how we ought to pray lurks what has been called 'the unnatural act' of forgiveness. It is summed up in the little word 'as'. 'Forgive us . . . [according to the same measure] as we forgive.'

When Archbishop Desmond Tutu asked an old woman what she wanted from the Truth and Reconciliation Commission, she replied, 'I want you to find the person or persons who tortured my husband and who murdered my son so that I can look them in the eye and say, "I forgive you".'

Forgiveness of this magnitude is indeed an unnatural act. But, as that woman knew, and as countless others also know, forgiveness is the only way to break the cycle of violence. Forgiveness loosens the stranglehold of guilt and anger. Forgiveness builds a bridge between offender and offended and puts both on the same side.

One of the probing questions of the Welsh revival, which swept thousands of people into the churches, was, 'Have you forgiven everybody, everybody, everybody?' It is a good question to ask daily of ourselves also. Forgiveness is a key to life. We step into freedom when we receive God's forgiveness; we offer that same freedom to others who have hurt us when we release them with our forgiveness. But if we imprison others in chains of unforgiveness, we will discover that those very chains hold us prisoner as well.

'Freely you have received, freely give,' said Jesus (*Matt 10:8*). Literally it means, 'As a gift you have been given, as a gift give.'

Not long before he died, David Watson wrote about how God was showing him that his love for God meant nothing unless he was truly able to love others. 'As the Lord put various names into my mind, I began to write letters . . . asking for forgiveness. It was the most painful purging and pruning I can remember in my entire Christian life. But fruitful!'

To reflect on
'It is a joy to accept forgiveness, but it is an almost greater joy to give forgiveness.'

Corrie ten Boom

FRIDAY 17 MARCH
Great Love, Great Forgiveness

Luke 7:36–50

'I tell you, her many sins have been forgiven – for she loved much.
But he who has been forgiven little loves little' (v. 47, NIV).

Where forgiveness is, there is love. Where one is absent, the other is nowhere to be seen. A group of Pharisees was given a living demonstration of this one day when a woman of the street barged in on a dinner party in the home of Simon, one of their number. In the middle of the scene Jesus reclines, enjoying a meal.

On one side, Simon – proud, quick to judge, critical, offering Jesus an open home, but no real hospitality. On the other side, a woman with a precious jar of perfume and a huge amount of love to pour out. Oblivious to the mutterings of the gathered crowd, she weeps over his feet, dries them with her hair, then covers them with kisses and perfume.

Jesus, who is able to read the innermost thoughts of a person's heart, tells Simon a story. Two men, two debts, one large, one small, both cancelled. 'Which of the two is going to be more grateful for his cancelled debt?' he asks. The answer is obvious, but it is a trick question. When Simon answers, 'The one who had the bigger debt cancelled,' Jesus swings the story round and points

it straight at him. 'Do you see this woman, Simon? Great love, great forgiveness. But you, Simon, small love, small forgiveness.'

Consider this man for a moment. He is a Pharisee, an upright religious leader, a man of standing. But there is something lacking in Simon. He offers formalities but no feeling, company but no courtesy.

As with many of Jesus' stories, not all the background colours are painted in. We have to fill in the gaps ourselves, put ourselves in the picture and write our own ending. What would you have done if you had been in Simon's sandals that day? Shrugged your shoulders and missed the point of Jesus' illustration? Or would you have recognised that Jesus was holding out an invitation of great value?

'My dear friend,' Jesus says, 'if only you knew how loved–and–forgiven you are, you too would pour it all out, just as this woman is doing.'

SATURDAY 18 MARCH

Forgiveness – Seeing Myself as God Sees Me

Psalm 23

'You prepare a table before me in the presence of my enemies.
You anoint my head with oil; my cup overflows' (v. 5, NIV).

The morning is cold and damp. I feel grey myself as I pull back the curtains. As I bring to prayer the feelings that accompany my awaking, God reminds me of the default function on my computer. It is set on Times New Roman at font size 10, but whenever I begin a new document I change it to Arial at size 12.

'Why the reminder, God?' I ask. He speaks gently. 'You need to change your inner default settings. You wake weary and anxious. You look out on a grey morning and feel grey yourself. Have you forgotten my love for you? Don't you remember, "new morning, new mercies"?' 'Sorry, God,' I mumble. 'Help me to see myself as you see me, your beloved child.'

God reminds me too of the table he sets before me every day in the presence of my enemies. Now and then these shadowy figures are actual people I know, but more often they are fragile or broken parts of myself that need to be embraced and welcomed to the table. 'Come on, Weariness, here's your seat. Anxiety, you sit here.

Blame and Shame, pull your chairs up closer.'

I need to change the default setting on my internal computer so that I see myself with God's eyes, loved lavishly, forgiven fully, having all I need for today. Henri Nouwen says:

You are my Beloved, on you my favour rests. I have moulded you in the depths of the earth and knitted you together in your mother's womb. I have carved you in the palms of my hands and hidden you in the shadow of my embrace. I look at you with infinite tenderness and care for you with a care more intimate than that of a mother for her child.[8]

This is the voice I need to hear on a grey morning. So I pray today:

Gentle God, you call me your Beloved, but sometimes I do not feel lovable. Help me to forgive myself, to see myself as you see me and learn to love myself as someone created in your image.

Morning by Morning

Isaiah 50:1–9

'The Sovereign LORD has given me an instructed tongue, to know the word that sustains the weary. He wakens me morning by morning, wakens my ear to listen like one being taught' (v. 4, NIV).

The morning is a great time to pray, a great time to listen to God, a great time to receive one's instructions for the day. Miraculously a good night's sleep seems to put to rest the fears and failures of the previous day. The morning is like a seashore washed clean by the tide, or a new exercise book at the start of a school year. While not everyone is naturally a 'morning' person, many Christians find that when time in the morning is given to God, the whole day flows better.

For the past six years as part of my morning prayer ritual I have knelt before God and read the words of Isaiah 50:4. This verse is the promise God gave me when I began as author of *Words of Life*. My part is to put myself in the place of listening; God's part is to give a word to sustain the weary.

Does God get tired of my praying this verse every morning? I think not. Do I ever reach the end of his help? I suspect not. Does he ever say, 'Okay, Barbara, you've squeezed all the juice out of this verse?' I hope not! This verse has become for me a sustaining promise that God continues to honour morning by morning, week by week, month by month, year by year.

Was Mother Teresa's sustaining promise: 'Whatever you [do] for one of the least of these brothers of mine, you [do] for me' (*Matt 25:40*)? Would Billy Graham's be: 'If you confess with your mouth, "Jesus is Lord," and believe in your heart that God raised him from the dead, you will be saved' (*Rom 10:9*)?

If you do not have a sustaining promise to live by, why not ask God to give you a verse of Scripture that you can take hold of as his word to you morning by morning?

Great is thy faithfulness!
Great is thy faithfulness!
Morning by morning new mercies I see;
All I have needed thy hand hath provided;
Great is thy faithfulness, Lord, unto me!

Thomas Chisholm, SASB 33

MONDAY 20 MARCH
When Forgiveness Seems Impossible

Mark 11:22–25

'When you stand praying, if you hold anything against anyone, forgive him, so that your Father in heaven may forgive you your sins' (v. 25, NIV).

Forgiveness is not easy. At times it is downright difficult. It cannot be forced. We may mouth the words, 'I forgive you', but a rage within tells us our words are a lie. How can those three words let someone off the hook who has hurt, betrayed, robbed, shamed and all but destroyed us?

A woman who had suffered a deep hurt wrote about her long journey towards forgiveness. She found that forgiveness and healing are travelling companions. 'Both require stamina, commitment, persistence and much grace to overcome resistance, doubt, fear and painful brokenness,' she wrote. She discovered that forgiveness was not something she could grit her teeth and force herself to do. 'Forgiveness is, instead, an act of grace, and the source of that grace is God.'

Corrie ten Boom wrote about the grace of forgiveness. After the Second World War, still suffering physical and emotional scars from the brutality of the Nazi concentration camps, she felt called to preach forgiveness throughout Europe. One day at the end of a church service in Munich, a man approached her, his hand outstretched. 'How grateful I am for your message of forgiveness,' he said.

Corrie recognised him as one of the former secret service guards who had watched and sneered as she and the other women prisoners had been forced to take delousing showers in front of him. In that moment the raw memory filled her with pain and shame. She felt not the slightest desire to offer forgiveness to this man. But as his hand remained outstretched, she breathed a silent prayer, 'Jesus, I cannot forgive him. Give me your forgiveness.' With a strength that she knew did not come from herself, she raised her arm and grasped his hand.

Forgiveness in such a situation is a gift of God, a mystery. There is no other explanation. How else could Elizabeth Elliot and Marge Saint go back to the Auca Indians and share the gospel with the very people who had killed their husbands?

If forgiveness seems overwhelmingly difficult for you today, let God in his grace do it for you.

82

TUESDAY 21 MARCH

The Mathematics of Forgiveness

Matthew 18:21–22

'Peter came to Jesus and asked, "Lord, how many times shall I forgive my brother when he sins against me? Up to seven times?"' (v. 21, NIV).

Paul's command to 'Pray continually' (1 Thess 5:17) is matched by Jesus' command to 'Forgive continually'. That is not exactly how Jesus says it, but it is what he means.

Peter finds it a tough call. He had come to Jesus asking about the mathematics of forgiveness. 'How often?' he asks. He wants Jesus to pick a number. He expects him to say something like, 'Once – that's normal. Twice or three times – that's big-hearted. Four, five, six times – that's really generous. Seven times – now that's perfect.' But Jesus explodes Peter's tidy number like a stick of gelignite blowing fish out of a pond. 'Seven! Hardly. Try seventy times seven' (The Message).

The story Jesus tells in reply to Peter's question is a story about a king, a servant and a huge debt that the servant could never hope to pay. It is a story set in the context of God's grace. The point is that our debt to God is totally and forever beyond our ability to repay. So, out of his infinite grace, God extends to us his forgiveness. The only condition he places upon us is that we pass on the gift. We are to look at others through the eyes of mercy.

Gracilla Martinez tells how she learned to forgive when her fifteen-year-old son, who had recently become a Christian, was executed under Cuba's Batista regime. The boy's last words to her were, 'Don't hate them, Mamacita, forgive them. Forgive them, or they will be the victors.' But she could not. In her heart she vowed revenge.

For ten years she carried the burden of that hatred, fuelling it with plans for retaliation. Then, one day, she said, 'I saw how destructive my hate was, how it consumed my energies, crippled my friendships and disabled any good that I wanted to do. I wanted to be freed from the prison I had erected in my life. I saw, finally, the truth of my son's words.'

To reflect on

Forgiveness is not to be an occasional act, but a permanent attitude. It is to become the very way we live.

WEDNESDAY 22 MARCH
Forgiving and Forgetting

Hebrews 12:1–6

'Let us throw off everything that hinders and the sin that so easily entangles, and let us run with perseverance the race marked out for us' (v. 1, NIV).

Forgive and forget, says the old adage. It sounds easy. But can a mother forget the man who murdered her beautiful daughter? Can a man forget the merciless taunting of his workmates that gave him no choice but to resign? Can a young man forgive and forget the school bully who beat him up regularly? To pretend that such things did not happen or did not matter is simply a form of denial. It merely drives the pain and anger underground, from where they seep out later.

Forgiveness does not equal forgetting. There may even be times when we need to forgive and remember in order to learn from the experience.

When Paul wrote to the Philippians, 'One thing I do: Forgetting what is behind and straining towards what is ahead, I press on towards the goal' (Phil 3:13,14), he was not putting out of his mind all that had gone before. The word 'forget' here means 'letting go'.

The writer to the Hebrews picks up this same image of the Christian life as a race. He urges his readers to kick off the shackles and get rid of the things like unforgiveness that trip us up and hinder us from running well.

Forgiveness is about getting free and setting free. It is about releasing others from their hold on us. It is about withdrawing our right to get even with, or get revenge over, the person who wronged us and caused us to suffer. It means refusing to let the hurtful past dictate how we live in the present.

The story is told of an indigenous American grandfather telling his grandson about a tragedy that happened and how he felt about it. He said, 'I feel as if I have two wolves fighting in my heart. One wolf is vengeful, angry and violent. The other wolf is loving and compassionate.' His grandson asked, 'Which wolf will win the fight in your heart?' The old man replied, 'The one I feed!'

To reflect on

A youngster said, 'Forgiveness is not about getting your own back; it's about getting your life back.'

84

THURSDAY 23 MARCH

A Community of Forgiveness

James 5:12–20

'Confess your sins to each other and pray for each other so that you may be healed' (v. 16, NIV).

When Jesus healed people he usually sent them back home to tell their family and friends what had happened to them. He told the demon-possessed man, 'Go home and tell...' (see *Mark 5:1–20*). He said to the paralysed man, 'Get up, take your mat and go home' (see *Mark 2:1–12*). He said similar words to the blind man at Bethsaida (*Mark 8:22–26*).

Jesus knew that a healing miracle would have its greatest impact back home where the person was best known. He knew also that healing is best maintained in the company of others. The village community would both support the healed person and hold him accountable to the change he had experienced.

The letter of James, a practical, down-to-earth book on Christian living, picks up this theme of a healing, forgiving community. James declares that as we engage in Christian living – speaking truthfully, being obedient, listening and doing, praying for one another, singing together, encouraging each other – we are in fact learning how to be open to God's grace and blessing. While God deals individually and personally with every believer, the Christian life was never meant to be lived out in isolation.

James says, 'Make this your common practice: Confess your sins to each other and pray for each other so that you can live together whole and healed' (*v. 16, The Message*). Such openness will make us feel vulnerable, of course. Pride and shame would urge us to keep our sins private and hidden. But whether with the support of a large congregation, a small house group or simply with one trusted friend, we all need help to stand and grow as a Christian.

In this we are just like a tree in the forest that stands most strongly when it is surrounded and supported by other trees. The storms of life are too tough for anyone to face on their own.

To reflect on

Are you part of a community of healing and forgiveness? How can you create such a community, right where you are, that offers support and strength to someone else?

FRIDAY 24 MARCH
Forgiveness Is a Health Issue

Habakkuk 3:17–19

'The Sovereign LORD is my strength; he makes my feet like the feet of a deer, he enables me to go on the heights' (v. 19, NIV).

'Why should I forgive that person?' I ask when a friend challenges me. 'The very thought of forgiving him makes me sick.' I speak a deeper truth than I realise. I am 'sick'. Unforgiveness is sapping my strength, robbing me of sleep and leaving me exhausted. 'Perhaps you do not understand what forgiveness is,' my friend says. 'Let's go over it again.'

Forgiveness is not pretending that something bad did not happen or that it did not matter. Forgiveness does not alter the hurt of the past, but it can certainly affect the health of the future.

Forgiveness is not dismissing or minimising the wrong done to me. It is not saying, 'Oh, never mind, that's okay. I'll get over it.' Forgiveness involves taking the offence seriously, not passing it off as insignificant. My forgiveness does not prevent the other person facing the consequences of their actions.

Forgiveness is not tolerating sinful habits or abusive practices. Forgiveness is not excusing the wrong done to me, but rather looking for a healthy way to love myself and the other person as well.

Forgiveness is not a passive resolve to wait the problem out in the hope that time will heal the wound. Forgiveness may not always mean reconciliation. It takes two people for this grace to occur and there are times when one may be unable or unwilling to respond in this way.

Forgiveness is not a sign of weakness, but rather of true inner strength. When I forgive I throw away my crutches of anger and hatred and I walk free. When I forgive, I find the antidote for the bitter poison of revenge and I release the other person from my right to get even. 'I take heart and gain strength. I run like a deer. I feel like I'm king of the mountain!' (v. 19, The Message).

To reflect on
'Forgiveness is God's cure for the deformity our resentments cause us. It is how we discover our true shape, and every time we do it, we get to be a little more alive.'

Barbara Brown Taylor[9]

SATURDAY 25 MARCH

Forgiving Oneself

Romans 8:1–4

'Therefore, there is now no condemnation for those who
are in Christ Jesus' (v. 1, NIV).

Forgiving oneself may be the hard-est part of all, letting go the regrets, the 'if onlys', the laments that linger long in our heart. 'If only I had not given in to . . . If only I had not agreed to . . . If only I had not gone along with . . .'

Author Lee Strobel writes,

Though I am tarnished by sin, God nevertheless considers me worth loving. He has been willing to restore me by wiping away my wrongdoing, not on the basis of my personal performance but because he has chosen to be gracious to me. My mistakes do not destroy the image of God that is inscribed in me, so my errors cannot eliminate the reason why I have value in his eyes.[10]

The demons of blame and shame can do their taunting dance in our mind long after other people have forgotten the matter, and long after God has extended his forgiveness to us. At times we need a ritual of forgiveness, some symbolic action to represent the fact that unforgive-ness has paid its dues and is now released. I stood on top of a high bridge with a young woman as she threw a crumpled list of regrets into the raging waters beneath. On an-other day a friend and I dug a hole in the sand to 'bury' a painful in-cident.

Visit a grave, speak words of release to someone who has died, plant a tree or a rose bush, write a letter or a poem – do whatever it takes to receive the forgiveness and to hear the words of 'no condem-nation' that God speaks. Forgiving oneself might be the final prison door to pass through on the way to freedom.

'With the arrival of Jesus, the Messiah, the fateful dilemma is resolved. Those who enter into Christ's being-here-for-us no longer have to live under a con-tinuous, low-lying black cloud . . . The Spirit of life in Christ, like a strong wind, has magnificently cleared the air, freeing you from a fated lifetime of brutal tyranny at the hands of sin and death' (vv. 1,2, The Message).

SUNDAY 26 MARCH
The Ransomed of the Lord

Isaiah 51:1–16

'The ransomed of the LORD will return. They will enter Zion with singing; everlasting joy will crown their heads. Gladness and joy will overtake them, and sorrow and sighing will flee away' (v. 11, NIV).

There is a timeless quality to the book of Isaiah. It is written primarily to God's exiled people in Babylon but, beyond that, it has a universal reach. The prophet speaks of salvation for all generations (v. 8), for all time (v. 6) and for all the people of the earth (49:6).

Isaiah reminds the people of Israel of their history – the rock from which they were cut (51:1). He recalls how God took a single couple and from them brought forth a whole nation. Having done so much for them in the past, it is impossible for God to abandon them now. He will not leave them in the ruin of despair or in the wasteland of sin but will restore them to the kind of beauty first on display in the Garden of Eden. The God who brought the world into existence and created it to be filled with splendour, harmony and blessing will not rest until the world is once more a place of joy and gladness, thanksgiving and celebration.

Isaiah calls the people to listen (vv. 1,4,7) and to lift up their eyes (v. 6). Something momentous is about to happen. Something amazing is on its way. God is bringing his ransomed home. On that day sorrow and sighing will be banished forever. Gladness and joy will be carried high on the shoulders of the people as they come. This will be a homecoming ticker–tape parade unlike any other!

We catch our breath as we realise that these words from the prophet Isaiah are written for you and me as well. 'Blessed are those who wash their robes, that they may have the right to the tree of life and may go through the gates into the city,' declared the writer of Revelation (*Rev 22:14*). You and I too, brother and sister, are the ransomed of the Lord.

From every tribe and every race,
All men as brothers shall embrace;
They shall come from the east, they
*   shall come from the west,*
And sit down in the Kingdom of God.
        John Gowans, SASB 170

WORTHY OF GOD'S CALLING
– 2 THESSALONIANS
Introduction

Paul's second letter to the Thessalonians was written just a few months after his first. Having heard some news of the believers, he writes to encourage them for their faithfulness in the face of persecution and to correct their confusion over the matter of the second coming of Jesus. While some members of the congregation are troubled at the prospect, others have opted out altogether, giving up work to wait for the Day.

As always, Paul writes a blend of good theology and practical application. He encourages the believers not to be troubled but to have faith, to keep working at their God-given task and to live worthily of God's high calling.

May his words be a well-timed message for us also!

MONDAY 27 MARCH

Grace and Peace

2 Thessalonians 1:1–2

'Grace and peace to you from God the Father and the
Lord Jesus Christ' (v. 2, NIV).

The opening verses of Paul's second letter to the Thessalonians follow the standard pattern of most of Paul's letters. He identifies the senders and recipients then expresses a blessing of goodwill.

The fact that Paul's name is put first, and his occasional use of 'I' throughout the letter, suggest that he is the actual writer. But the frequent use of 'we' suggests that it comes from all three – Paul, Silas and Timothy.

Silas (also known as Silvanus) was a prophet from Jerusalem who was delegated, along with Judas Barsabbas, to deliver the results of the Jerusalem Council to the church at Antioch (*Acts* 15:22). After Paul and Barnabas separated, Paul chose this man Silas as his co-worker and the two travelled through Galatia, Asia Minor, Macedonia and Greece on Paul's second missionary journey. Paul viewed Silas as a fellow apostle for he played a significant role in establishing churches in both Thessalonica and Corinth, as did Timothy who joined Paul and Silas as a junior member of the team early in their travels. Timothy is described as 'God's fellow-worker' (*1 Thess* 3:2), a young man whom Paul looked on as a dearly loved son (see *1 Cor 4:17*).

This second letter to the Thessalonians was probably written about six months after the first. The situation in the young church has not changed markedly, nor have Paul's reasons for writing. He wrote the first letter to strengthen the Thessalonian Christians in their faith and to remind them of how they ought to live as they prepared for the sure return of Jesus. He now writes this second letter to clear up some confusion about the second coming.

Paul is a larger-than-life figure. From his first appearance in Scripture he comes across as a passionate follower, a firm advocate, a challenging teacher, a hardy traveller, a man of fierce intensity and conviction. He will have some tough things to say to this young church but, as always, he begins on a note of grace and peace.

Look for an opportunity to express grace and peace in your dealings with someone else today.

TUESDAY 28 MARCH
Painting a Picture of Faith

2 Thessalonians 1:3–4

'Among God's churches we boast about your perseverance and faith in all the persecutions and trials you are enduring' (v. 4, NIV).

Artist Paul picks up a paintbrush. With just a few brushstrokes he paints a picture of a thriving church that, in spite of problems, is filled with love, faith and steadfastness. Against a dark backdrop of persecutions and trials he paints the clear, luminous colours of perseverance and faith.

The fact that the Thessalonian believers' faith is growing and their love for each other increasing is a clear indication that God is at work. After all, these are the very things Paul has been praying for them 'night and day' (see *1 Thess 3:10,12*). This band of hardy believers has become 'Exhibit A' for Paul as he moves around the other churches. Towards God they are evidencing faith. Towards each other they are showing the fruits of love. Towards those who oppress them they are standing firm with perseverance and steadfastness. No wonder Paul boasts about them, quotes them as an example to copy and gives thanks to God for them.

This is both great praise and good psychology. Paul is holding up a standard and encouraging them to keep living up to it. He is like a minister I know who holds a crown of goodness and integrity and faithfulness over his people and helps them grow into it.

If you were to follow Paul's example today and paint a picture of the church fellowship to which you belong, what colours would you use? What sombre tones would you need to express the problems or trials your church faces? What bright colours would express the faithfulness and steadfastness of the people? What shades would convey the blessings of recent answers to prayer? How would you capture the colour of intercession, the wonder of worship, the freedom of forgiveness?

Remember, whether painting a picture of the church at Thessalonica or the body of believers to whom you belong, this church is the radiant bride of Christ.

Jesus, thy blood and righteousness
My beauty are, my glorious dress;
'Midst flaming worlds, in these
arrayed,
With joy shall I lift up my head.
Nicolaus Ludwig von Zinzendorf,
translated by John Wesley,
SASB 116

WEDNESDAY 29 MARCH

God Is Just

2 Thessalonians 1:5–10

'All this is evidence that God's judgment is right, and as a result you will be counted worthy of the kingdom of God, for which you are suffering' (v. 5, NIV).

If you find yourself reading these verses more than once in order to understand them, take heart. In the original Greek, verses three to ten are one long loose sentence. Paul's words are like autumn leaves bouncing over rapids.

At the heart of the passage stand the words, 'God is just.' Evidence of God's justice is seen in the Thessalonians' strong stand against persecution. Not only are they trusting and persevering in the midst of their trials, but actually growing in faith and increasing in love. Such steadfastness and firmness in the face of suffering are sure signs of God's blessing and grace at work.

Paul goes on to outline the two sides of God's justice. One is negative and one is positive. The negative side has to do with retribution – that is, payback to those who trouble God's people. These troublers are broadly defined as 'those who do not know God and do not obey the gospel of our Lord Jesus'. They are not simply ignorant or uninformed. They have heard the gospel of Jesus but have made a deliberate choice not to accept his claims.

They will be punished 'with everlasting destruction', Paul declares. 'Eternal exile from the presence of the Master and his splendid power is their sentence' (v. 9, The Message). His definition of destruction is the exact opposite of his definition of salvation as being with the Lord for ever (1 Thess 4:17) and sharing in God's glory (Rom 8:17,18).

In sharp contrast to those who do not obey the gospel are those who have believed – among them the Christians at Thessalonica. These faithful believers will experience both the presence and the glory of the Lord himself.

The discussion surrounding matters of heaven and hell, the immortality of the soul, and the general judgment at the end of the world are deep and complex. But Paul gives us here a simple focal point – God is just. When all is said and done, our eternal destiny rests in that truth. Exile or exaltation, separation or salvation – which outcome of God's justice do you choose to rest in today?

THURSDAY 30 MARCH
Worthy of His Calling

2 Thessalonians 1:11–12

'We constantly pray for you, that our God may count you worthy of his calling, and that by his power he may fulfil every good purpose of yours and every act prompted by your faith' (v. 11, NIV).

'What on earth am I here for?' So begins *The Purpose Driven Life*. It is, according to author Rick Warren, 'life's most important question'. Answer that question, he says, and you will understand the 'big picture' – how all the various pieces of your life fit together.

Paul had no doubt at all about the purpose of his life or that of the Thessalonian believers. They were created for relationship with God. This holy purpose was the constant focus of Paul's prayers on their behalf. In his earlier letter Paul had urged them to 'live lives worthy of God, who calls you into his kingdom and glory' (*1 Thess 2:12*).

Although he says 'every good purpose [literally 'every resolve of goodness'] *of yours* and every act prompted by *your* faith', it is clear that God is the starting point. God has taken the initiative in their salvation and placed a calling on their lives to become like Christ (see *Rom 8:29*).

God has a blueprint, a pattern of righteousness and faith for them to follow. Paul's constant prayer is that they might be worthy and live 'worthily' of this great calling.

They are, as he reminded the believers at Ephesus, 'God's workmanship [literally, 'God's poem'], created in Christ Jesus to do good works' (*Eph 2:10*). This is their true value, their great worth, their high calling.

In his sermon, 'The Drum Major Instinct', Martin Luther King Jr asked not to be remembered for his Nobel Peace Prize, his numerous awards or where he went to school. He asked, rather, to be remembered as someone who 'tried to love and serve humanity'. Our names may never be famous, but such a high calling, such a great purpose, is within the reach of us all. So we pray today:

Make us worthy, Lord,
to serve others throughout the world
who live and die in poverty or hunger.
Give them, through our hands,
this day their daily bread,
and by our understanding love,
give peace and joy.

Mother Teresa

FRIDAY 31 MARCH
Like a Ship Adrift

2 Thessalonians 2:1–4

'Concerning the coming of our Lord Jesus Christ and our being gathered to him, we ask you, brothers, not to become easily unsettled or alarmed' (vv. 1,2, NIV).

In his first letter to the Thessalonians Paul told the believers that the Day of the Lord would come when least expected and would surprise all who were unprepared. He used metaphors of a thief in the night and the sudden labour pains of a pregnant woman to express the unexpected nature of Jesus' return.

Since receiving that first letter, some members of the congregation had become convinced that the 'Day' had already arrived. This rumour was causing great upset among the community of faith. Paul uses the word 'unsettled', which in Greek was often used to describe a ship adrift from its mooring, unstable and unsafe.

This unsettling had come about either by a prophecy (that is, a prophetic utterance spoken by one of the congregation or by a visitor); by a report (that is, a spoken message or teaching); or by a letter (that is, a forged letter claiming to come from Paul himself). Concerned as he is about the source of the confusion, Paul is even more concerned about the teaching. He tells them that it is impossible for the Day of the Lord to have arrived already because certain events and developments, which had not yet taken place, must first occur.

The two things that must first happen are 'the rebellion' and the revealing of 'the man of lawlessness'. Paul takes for granted that his readers know what he means by the rebellion (see v. 5) and says nothing further about it. Like other New Testament writers, he probably has in mind a time of wrongdoing and general opposition to God.

The leader of this rebellion is someone who will stand in defiant opposition to God and will exalt himself over everything that is holy and worshipped as God. Paul declares that this person is 'doomed to destruction'. For all his proud claims, his final overthrow is certain.

To reflect on
Just as bank tellers learn to identify counterfeit money by handling real money, so believers learn to recognise what is false by staying close to the One who is the Truth (see John 14:6).

SATURDAY 1 APRIL
The Splendour of His Coming

---

2 Thessalonians 2:5–12

'Then the lawless one will be revealed, whom the Lord Jesus will overthrow with the breath of his mouth and destroy by the splendour of his coming' (v. 8, NIV).

Paul brings two comings together in this passage. He writes first of the coming of 'the man of lawlessness'. Deception and opposition are his bodyguards. Counterfeit miracles and signs and wonders are his tools of trade. Evil, lies and wickedness are his delights.

Paul makes it clear that the secret power (literally, 'mystery') of lawlessness is already at work. The persecution being suffered by the Thessalonians, for example, is proof of this. But lawlessness is being restrained at present. Just who or what this restraining influence is, Paul does not make clear. After all, he has already taught the Thessalonians about this (v. 5), but we can only guess. The restraining influence could be the Roman Empire with its laws, or the ministry and teaching of the Church and especially of Paul, or it could be the work of the Holy Spirit. Even Augustine said on this point, 'I frankly confess I do not know what he means.'

At some future time, however, the lawless one will be revealed. He will come with all the pageantry and pomp of an emperor's arrival.

But his grand display will be short-lived. As the man 'doomed to destruction' (v. 3), he will be overthrown and destroyed by the far greater power and splendour of the Lord's own coming. In comparison to its counterfeit imitation, Jesus' coming will be sudden, unexpected and attended by overwhelming greatness and glory. The writer of Acts, quoting Joel, described wonders in the heavens and signs on earth, the sun being turned to darkness and the moon to blood, before the coming of 'the great and glorious day of the Lord' (Acts 2:19,20).

Evil will be defeated! This sure fact has emboldened countless people down through the centuries – such as Martin Luther King Jr, Gandhi, Archbishop Romero, Nelson Mandela – to take a stand for truth and to fight against injustice and oppression. May we who follow in their steps lift our eyes from the mud and muck of evil, turn our eyes upon Jesus, and live and work for the day when he will come again with glory and great splendour.

SUNDAY 2 APRIL

Coming on Quiet Feet

Isaiah 52:1–12

'How beautiful on the mountains are the feet of those who bring good news, who proclaim peace, who bring good tidings, who proclaim salvation, who say to Zion, "Your God reigns!"' (v. 7, NIV).

In Isaiah 47, Babylon was called to go down from the throne and sit in the dust in rags, nakedness and shame. In today's reading the prophet tells Jerusalem to do the very opposite. She is called to shake off the dust, put on garments of splendour and take her throne (vv. 1,2). The city of God is about to be transformed from slave to queen, not as the result of some deal between God and the captors, but as a sign of God's power.

Isaiah illustrates this amazing act of God by picturing a besieged city waiting for news from a delivering army. Will the army be able to break through the besiegers? If so, there is hope. If not, all is lost. Suddenly the watchmen on the city walls begin to shout for joy. They have seen a messenger far off on the mountains who is signalling the good news of victory.

God has indeed bared his holy arm and delivered his people. Nothing remains but for Israel to take hold of this promise in faith and to turn away from her old, sinful ways. Set free by the power of God, the people of God are now to live in that freedom.

Every time I read a book or hear a sermon that calls me to greater freedom in Christ, I catch the sound of a peacemaker's quiet tread. Every time I encourage another believer into the *shalom* wholeness, fullness and blessing that Christ has made possible, I too become a peacemaker.

Peacemaking has both an outer and inner aspect, both action and reflection. It drives us to find new, creative ways to resolve conflict and to be mediators for peace right where we are. It also encourages us to nurture an imagination for peace, to embrace the joy and sorrow, the sacredness and sin of the world and to bring it all to God whose love alone can transform darkness into light and death into life.

Peacemaker, Lord! Now I am stirred to wonder;
O take me, and my calling seal!
                    Arch Wiggins, SASB 529

MONDAY 3 APRIL

The Grace that Comes Before

2 Thessalonians 2:13–15

'From the beginning God chose you to be saved through
the sanctifying work of the Spirit and through belief in the truth'
(v. 13, NIV).

Today's verses can be read in about thirty seconds flat, but meditating on them will take a lot longer and living them out will take a lifetime.

The whole time frame of the gospel is contained here: a backward glance – 'from the beginning God chose you', to a forward glimpse – 'that you might share in the glory of our Lord Jesus Christ'. Each member of the Trinity is mentioned. God 'chose' and 'called'. The Holy Spirit sanctifies. Jesus is the One, now glorified, who will share his glory with those who put their trust in him. Paul's part is mentioned – 'our gospel' and 'the teachings we passed on to you'. The believers' part is itemised – they are to 'stand firm and hold to the teachings' they have received. Each word of this rich passage will reward reflection.

As usual, my heart settles on the God–verbs. God loved, chose, saved and called. These are the actions of the God who is always the beginning point in our salvation. Long before we even existed, God saw us, knew us and had a purpose laid out for our lives. 'Before the creation of the world . . . he chose us . . . to be holy' (*Eph 1:4*). 'While we were still sinners' (*Rom 5:8*), unlovely and unlovable, fallible and fickle, he saw our helplessness and loved us. He did not wait until we had cleaned up our act, taken a course in self-improvement or become nicer persons. God took the initiative in saving us by sending Jesus to die in our place.

This is what theologians call the 'prevenient' grace of God – God's grace and gifts that 'come before' us. That grace may have touched our life through a Bible–in–Schools teacher, a youth group leader, a praying grandparent, a religious programme on television, a Gideon Bible in a motel room, or in countless other ways.

To reflect on

Consider today how you came to faith in Christ. Reflect on some of the ways this prevenient grace of God has 'come before' you. Give thanks for every initiative God has taken – and continues to take – in your salvation story.

TUESDAY 4 APRIL

Eternal Encouragement and Good Hope

2 Thessalonians 2:16–17

'May our Lord Jesus Christ himself and God our Father, who loved us and by his grace gave us eternal encouragement and good hope, encourage your hearts and strengthen you' (vv. 16,17, NIV).

Eternal encouragement and good hope. What amazing, life-giving qualities these are! What world-changing impact individuals have had who knew God's 'unending help and confidence' (*The Message*).

The Revd Lohnan Zuzul, the Anglican minister at a church in Kadarko, in Nigeria's Plateau State, daily faces the threat of attack from those opposed to Christianity. In 2003 his village was ransacked, his home burned down, and many people killed. Armed mobs brought grass into his church to burn it down. 'But,' he says, 'God was at work, and the church would not catch fire.' Pray that this man and the Christians in Kadarko will stand firm with eternal encouragement and good hope.

Deborah Xu Yongling is a Chinese house church leader. Ten years ago she escaped from the communist authorities and has been on their wanted list ever since. Her unsettled lifestyle has resulted in chronic health issues, but Deborah's zeal for the things of God is untiring. Pray that this woman and the persecuted Christians in China will stand firm with eternal encouragement and good hope.

Pastor Alfredo has seen his church in central Colombia grow from twenty-five people to 275. He preaches against violence, calling his congregation to live lives that are dignified and full of good works. He and his congregation are caught between attacks from left-wing guerrillas and right-wing paramilitaries. 'We often think about fleeing the area,' he says, 'but then we think, "If we go, who will do this work? Who will make a difference?"' Pray that this man and the Christians in Colombia will stand firm with eternal encouragement and good hope.

Zeeshan is a teenage Christian student at a secondary school in Pakistan who was kidnapped and beaten for his faith. He was told, 'Christians are not good. They are used to cleaning the dirt and they smell all the time. You should not be a Christian.' In spite of the threats and beatings, Zeeshan says, 'I always remember Jesus Christ in my heart.' Pray that this young man and the Christians in Pakistan will stand firm with eternal encouragement and good hope.

WEDNESDAY 5 APRIL

Faithless and Faithful

2 Thessalonians 3:1–5

'Not everyone has faith. But the Lord is faithful' (vv. 2,3, NIV).

With the word 'Finally', Paul heads towards the conclusion of his letter. He still has much to say, some of it quite harsh and direct, but he continues to write with grace and peace.

Prayer has frequent mention in his two letters to the Thessalonians. 'Brothers, pray for us,' he asked them earlier (1 Thess 5:25). 'Pray continually,' he exhorted (5:17). 'We constantly pray for you,' he told them (2 Thess 1:11). Now he makes two prayer requests of the believers. One is that the word of the Lord might 'spread rapidly' – that is, that it might 'run swiftly'. Paul often used athletic language to speak about his ministry, but here the emphasis is on the running of the word. The image recalls the psalmist: 'He sends his command to the earth; his word runs swiftly' (Ps 147:15).

Part of this request is that the word might be honoured – that is, acknowledged, accepted and acted upon, 'just as it was with you'. Paul takes every opportunity to commend the Thessalonian believers for their faithful living out of the gospel.

His second prayer request is that he and his team might be delivered from opposition. This man Paul is a towering figure of the Church, yet his continual use of 'we' and 'us' makes it clear that he does not see himself as a lone hero. Opposition against one believer is a matter for the whole body of Christ to address.

Paul contrasts the wickedness of the unfaithful with the faithfulness of God. Proof of God's faithfulness will be seen in the continued strengthening and protection of believers, their ongoing obedience, and all the ways in which they will be helped to live out their faith with 'God's love and Christ's perseverance'. Paul's words are rich and full of confident hope.

To reflect on
Follow Paul's pattern today and pray the contrasts as a faith exercise:
'I am not always faithful, but you, Lord, are faithful.'
'I am not strong, but you are mighty.'
'I am often shallow, Lord, but you are deeper than the ocean.'
'I cannot, but you can!'

THURSDAY 6 APRIL

Command and Example

2 Thessalonians 3:6–10

'In the name of the Lord Jesus Christ, we command you, brothers, to keep away from every brother who is idle and does not live according to the teaching you received from us' (v. 6, NIV).

When the community of believers was first established at Thessalonica, Paul apparently instructed them to devote themselves to their own concerns rather than those of others, to work for their own living, and not to be dependent on others (see *1 Thess 4:11–12*). He also encouraged the congregation to warn those who were idle (*5:14*).

Now he rises to his full apostolic authority as he writes. 'In the name of the Lord Jesus Christ, we command you . . .' From his perspective, there should be no need to 'command' the Thessalonians about keeping away from any believer who is idle (Greek *atakos*), for he has already taught them this. The rule was summed up in the expression, 'If a man will not work, he shall not eat' (*2 Thess 3:10*).

In Paul's opinion, living in idleness is clearly a negative behaviour, one that stands in contrast to living worthily of God and responsibly towards others. But living in an idle, lazy way is not merely a passive, couch–potato kind of existence. The active side of the state of idleness is described in verse 11 where Paul accuses certain ones of being busy-bodies. They are not inactive, but active in the wrong way, meddling in the affairs of others.

Paul puts the antidote to this behaviour in the form of a command, reminding the Thessalonian believers of what he has already taught them. They must eat their own bread – that is, work responsibly to support themselves and stop being an unnecessary burden on the rest of the community.

This is the example that he and his team gave the believers when they were among them. 'We were not idle . . . nor did we eat anyone's food without paying . . . [but] we worked night and day . . . so that we would not be a burden.' Paul's unashamed example is their model, their pattern to follow.

To reflect on

With God there is no unemployment. Every person, even the poorest or the least qualified, has a God-given task to do, a part to play in the body of Christ. How are you playing your part?

FRIDAY 7 APRIL
Let Us Not Be Weary

2 Thessalonians 3:11–15

'Brothers and sisters, do not be weary in doing what is right'
(v. 13, NRSV).

In Paul's mind, the most effective antidote to idleness is busyness – but of the right kind. Settle down, work quietly, live responsibly. This is what he means. No one can accuse Paul of being so heavenly minded that he has no earthly common sense. In a phrase that sums up his encouragement to all, he tells the believers at Thessalonica not to be weary in doing what is right. 'Don't give up, don't slack off,' he is saying.

With the kind of punishing schedule Paul seems to live by, he must have an intimate knowledge of this kind of weariness. It is more than the weariness of too many hot days or too many wet weeks, more than the load of too many demands and not enough respite, more than the heaviness of too much criticism and not enough encouragement.

Paul puts his finger on the problem, to which we have given a contemporary title – compassion fatigue. The disciples knew what that was. Remember how they went across the lake to have some time on their own with Jesus. Somehow the crowd guessed where they were heading, and when the disciples arrived they found thousands of people waiting for them. 'Oh no, Lord,' they must have groaned inwardly. 'Send them away, we need a break.' Jesus, however, not only welcomed the crowd but also spoke to them about the kingdom, healed their sick, then fed them all with just a couple of fish and a few loaves of bread (see *Luke 9:10–17*).

You and I are probably also familiar with compassion fatigue. It happens when people's needs seem endless. When others take and take and never say thank you. When needy ones drain life out of us and never pour any life back in. When people make no change for the better, in spite of all our efforts.

What does this kind of weariness need? Forgiveness or refreshment – such as an afternoon nap, a foot massage, a silent retreat? How can we be wise stewards of our bodies and resources, and at the same time give active attention to God's call?

SATURDAY 8 APRIL

A Double Blessing

2 Thessalonians 3:16–18

'Now may the Lord of peace himself give you peace at all times
and in every way . . . The grace of our Lord Jesus Christ
be with you all' (vv. 16,18, NIV).

Paul's conclusion to this letter is unique. Every other letter written by Paul and preserved for us as Scripture ends with a single blessing, but this letter concludes with a double blessing. It is like a rare and valuable postage stamp, a collector's item of great value. It is like a double-scoop ice cream, a child's delight on a summer's day. It is like Elisha asking for a double portion of Elijah's spirit (*2 Kgs 2:9*), the sign of a great gift.

'May the Master of Peace himself give you . . . The incredible grace of our Master, Jesus Christ, be with all of you!' (*The Message*). This double blessing is addressed to all – even the troublers, even the busybodies among the congregation.

In blessing them all with peace, Paul has in mind more than the mere absence of conflict. He is praying for them the *shalom* gift of wellbeing and wholeness, characterised by reconciled relations with God, with each other in the congregation, and even with those outside the community of faith.

In blessing them with grace, Paul is referring the believers at Thessalonica to the redeeming activity of God, as revealed in the ministry, death and resurrection of Jesus. Paul would not have known the acronym of grace as **G**od's **R**iches **A**t **C**hrist's **E**xpense, but this is what he means when he uses the word.

So Paul ends where he began – with peace and grace, grace and peace. He began his letter encouraging the Thessalonians for their faith and faithfulness. He has taught them about the evil man of lawlessness. He has had some firm things to say about not being busybodies but working quietly, intentionally, earning their living, paying their own way. He has urged them not to get weary of doing what is right. Now he concludes his letter with the spotlight, focus and emphasis firmly on Jesus.

Like John the Baptist, Paul is a signpost pointing to someone greater than himself. He knows that Jesus is the One on whose grace, power and faithfulness the lives of the Thessalonians depend. So it is for us all.

EASTER EPOCH

Introduction

This series was prepared by Major John Townsend who, at the time of writing, had recently returned to New Zealand from missionary service in Pakistan. John was born in Uralla, New South Wales, Australia, the son of an Aboriginal mother and a German father. He had a very impoverished background but was converted when a creative and innovative Salvation Army officer took an interest in the young people of the town.

As an officer John studied hard, gaining three degrees and commencing work on his doctorate. Most of his officership was spent in corps and training work. John's unique way of seeing things made him an ideal guest contributor for this edition of Words of Life. In the course of writing, however, John became ill and was promoted to Glory on 24 November 2004.

With the permission of Major Val Townsend, John's wife and soulmate for many years, the series has been completed, holding to John's unique turn of phrase and honouring his spiritual insights into the Easter story.

John Townsend was a fine officer, a great husband, father and grandfather, and a dearly loved colleague to many Salvationists in Australia, New Zealand and Pakistan.

Through this series of Easter meditations his voice continues to speak. John writes:

The 'Act of Easter' begins in the heart of God in heaven. However, the 'Purposes of Easter' are earthed and validated in the villages, towns and cities just where you live.

Christian communities the world over will celebrate Easter with a multiplicity of sights, sounds, tastes and theological expressions according to their particular cultural and historical background. So, as we walk Calvary's path this season, it will be to our benefit to thoughtfully reflect on a few defining moments of the Easter epoch.

None of us lives to himself alone and none of us dies to himself alone. If we live, we live to the Lord; and if we die, we die to the Lord. So, whether we live or die, we belong to the Lord (Rom 14:7,8).

SUNDAY 9 APRIL

Entry into Jerusalem

Luke 19:28–42

'As he approached Jerusalem and saw the city, he wept over it'
(v. 41, NIV).

By riding into the city of Jerusalem on a lowly donkey Jesus presented himself to the nation as Messiah and King (see *Zech 9:9*). In doing this he triggered an avalanche of divine and human emotions that engulfed everyone in its path.

The crowd's 'Hosanna' cries were jubilant and festive. Excited people waved palm branches and acclaimed Jesus by crying passages from the Festival Psalms: 'Blessed is the king who comes in the name of the Lord!' (see *Ps 118:26*). 'Peace in heaven and glory in the highest!' Perhaps their fervour was further enlivened by the report of the raising of Lazarus from death (*John 12:17,18*).

For the Pharisees, however, it was very different. They had been ruined by a religious system that promoted power, fear, jealousy and greed, so this joyous occasion served only to heighten their bitterness and resentment. 'Teacher, get your disciples under control!' they complained (*Luke 19:39, The Message*).

This was the moment when the leadership rejected Jesus as their Messiah. They were saying, 'These people are calling you "King of Israel" when we know there is only one king and he is Caesar.' The corrupt spiritual leaders knew this demonstration had all the makings of a revolt. If everyone were to acclaim Jesus as King, then the Romans would come and take away both their temple and their nation (see *John 11:48*).

The grief of Jesus was publicly displayed (*Luke 19:41–44*). He knew that the crowd's popular acclamation would quickly change and, within a few days, they would disown him. He wept as he foresaw the dreadful consequences of that rejection.

Divine and human emotions mingled together on Palm Sunday. That day saw both strength and weakness, power and vulnerability, celebration and grief displayed in the impending cosmic/earthly dealings of God with humankind at Calvary.

To reflect on

Easter is not an event that happens in a nebulous vacuum somewhere out there on the rim of the universe. Easter is about God and humanity, heaven and earth vigorously engaging each other here on earth. Amazingly, you and I are caught up in this great togetherness.

MONDAY 10 APRIL

Cleansing the Temple

Luke 19:45–48

'Then he entered the temple area and began driving out those who were selling' (v. 45, NIV).

The temple was the religious heart of Israel. Magnificently built of dazzling white marble, much of its exterior was coated with silver and gold. The temple was a majestic, imposing, gleaming structure on the skyline of the city of Jerusalem. Every nook and cranny of the temple reminded the Jews of their sacred history and supremely validated their existence as the covenant people of God.

What did Jesus find when he went into the temple? Instead of an environment of reverence and a prayerful composure of souls encountering their God, he found that the temple management had sold out to a greedy marketplace mentality. He found squawking birds, bleating animals and sky-high prices. He found a concoction of unholy traffic that had invaded and defiled the temple precincts.

This cacophony was all taking place in the temple's outer courtyard, known as the Court of the Gentiles. In the book of Isaiah, God's people were told to do what was right and to observe the Sabbath. For those who did what pleases God – keeping the Sabbath,

loving and worshipping him – God said he would bless them and bring them to Zion and give them joy in his house of prayer, a place of prayer for all nations (see *Isa 56:4–7*). But when Jesus came into this outer courtyard, far from finding it a place of worship and prayer, he found it filled with the sounds and smells of a sale yard.

Enough is enough! With fearless zeal Jesus drove the unsavoury mob from their market stands. He declared that his Father's house was no place to ply their ill-gotten trade, leeching on the significance of Holy Week and the victimisation of poor pilgrims. After this incident the chief priests (who are also credited with having a financial interest in these matters) had still more cause to despise Jesus.

To reflect on

'All in the name of God and religion' can be construed as a valid licence to commit all kinds of evil deeds against humanity. So let us pray today, 'Lord, please help me to keep a close watch over my personal motives.'

TUESDAY 11 APRIL

It Was Passover Time

Luke 22:1–6

'Now the Feast of Unleavened Bread, called the Passover,
was approaching' (v. 1, NIV).

Passover was the first of three great Jewish feasts of the year to commemorate the deliverance of the Jews from Egypt (see *Exod 12:12–15*). The Jews held a one-day Passover celebration, followed by a seven-day Feast of Unleavened Bread. Jews from all parts of Israel and from other lands thronged to Jerusalem. Jesus and his plucky companions came too.

Luke exposes the undercurrents beneath the surface of the Passover events. Two fateful plans are afoot, in sharp counterpoint with each other – a plan of destruction and a plan of salvation.

Jesus' enemies are scheming to eliminate Jesus. They would prefer a time when there are fewer of his followers about but the deed cannot be postponed so they decide to use the occasion of the Passover for their purposes. The next step in their evil scheme is to find someone to engineer the arrest of Jesus. Judas Iscariot fits the role perfectly because he is 'one of the Twelve'. Finally, Luke alone among the evangelists mentions the activity of Satan. This dreadful plot could be born in human hearts only by the influence of the evil one.

Thus, with Passover the occasion, the leaders of Jewry the plotters, Judas Iscariot the betrayer, and Satan the instigator, the baited trap is set waiting to be sprung.

Luke entwines his story in such a way as to show that Jesus, far from being a helpless victim in this evil scheme, is himself pursuing another plan which keeps pace step by step with Satan's evil doings.

For the Jews the Passover commemorated their physical deliverance from Egypt into Canaan. Soon Jesus will give that event a whole new meaning, signifying a deliverance of the most profound kind, from sin and death into eternal life. Moses' exodus will be fulfilled in Jesus' exodus. Powerfully, wonderfully, Jesus' counterplan is set also. His mission of tragedy and glory has begun. The fulfilment of God's divine plan is at hand. God is in control.

Settle your heart and mind on the living God, no matter what your present situation may be. God can be trusted.

WEDNESDAY 12 APRIL

The Last Supper

Luke 22:7–16

'When the hour came, Jesus and his apostles reclined at the table'
(v. 14, NIV).

The Upper Room is probably where Jesus appeared to his disciples on the day of his resurrection (*Mark 16:14*) and the room to which the disciples returned after Jesus' ascension (*Acts 1:13; 2:1*). Alternatively, the room may have been in the house of Mary, the mother of John Mark (see *Acts 12:12*).

Using wine and unleavened bread, a basin and towel as visual aids, Jesus symbolically and theologically prepared his disciples for what lay ahead. For him there would be betrayal, arrest, death and resurrection. For them there would be confusion, scattering and many things they could not yet understand.

He used part of the meal – the sharing of the bread and wine – to teach that they were to receive his own Spirit within them. It was by virtue of his blood shed for them that this new covenant would be established (see *Jer 31:31–34*). He used the basin and towel to teach the way of humble service. There could be no deeper symbol of their total dependence on him, no greater evidence of their commitment.

Jesus gave clear and vital indicators about the role of the Holy Spirit in the disciples' future ministry. Then in their hearing in that Upper Room he prayed his great intercessory prayer (*John 17*).

The last meal was about common unity, fellowship and commitment to the task of taking salvation to the whole world. Tragically, the disciples' puny desires for self-importance and aggrandisement kept getting in the way. Worst of all, there was a traitor with his feet under the table. Why God should entrust such a huge mission to such frail humanity remains a profound mystery.

The striking of the Shepherd and the scattering of the sheep indicates chaos and disaster. Though the events of this time appear tragic, nothing falls outside God's sovereign control. Jesus predicted that after his resurrection there would be a glorious reunion of Shepherd and sheep in Galilee.

Long ago, the prophet Isaiah said, 'By his wounds we are healed. We all, like sheep, have gone astray' (Isa 53:5,6). The ministry of God's grace is ours today. Hallelujah!

THURSDAY 13 APRIL

To the Mount of Olives – Gethsemane

Luke 22:39–46

'Jesus went out as usual to the Mount of Olives, and his
disciples followed him' (v. 39, NIV).

The Garden of Gethsemane was on the lower slopes of the Mount of Olives. It was a place filled with gnarled and twisted trees, an appropriate setting for Jesus' anguished prayer battle. His prayers were prayers of entreaty – that he might be spared from drinking 'this cup', and of trustful surrender – that the Father's will be done.

The bitter dregs of Jesus' 'prayer cup' were manifold. There was family pain, knowing that Mary, his mother, would be forced to witness the cruel spectacle of her son's crucifixion and death. There was concern for the spiritual and physical wellbeing of his disciples. There would no doubt be deep grief over Judas' betrayal. There would be sorrow for the whole nation's rejection.

The cup may suggest the fierce struggle of temptation for Jesus to go another way instead of the Father's way. He was not a joyful martyr bent on self-destruction. We recall the starkness of Paul's words who declared, 'God made him who had no sin to be sin for us, so that in him we might become the righteousness of God' (*2 Cor 5:21*). So

Jesus bore God's wrathful judgment, the awful consequences of humanity's sin. There in Gethsemane the crushing intensity of black evil and the beauty of God's righteousness clashed.

Jesus was fully aware of the cost of being faithful to his Father's will. So it is little wonder that in this supreme hour of crisis, when the wrath of the One he called 'Abba' (Daddy) was turned loose on him, he longed for divine and human intimacy and companionship.

In company and yet alone, Jesus knelt in that garden and came face to face with the thundering silence of heaven. There was no reassuring voice from heaven proclaiming, 'This is my Son, whom I love.' No dove descended, no angels came to minister. There were only slumbering disciples oblivious of the critical moment.

Never is God more fully and forcefully present than in the hour of human loneliness. God is not an abandoning God. Take a few moments right now to acknowledge his abiding presence with you.

FRIDAY 14 APRIL

Jesus' Arrest

Luke 22:47–53

'While he was still speaking a crowd came up, and the man
who was called Judas, one of the Twelve, was leading them.
He approached Jesus to kiss him' (v. 47, NIV).

The fact that Judas the betrayer was 'one of the Twelve' surely served to sharpen the point of a cruel betrayal. Judas approached the praying Jesus with a representative group of chief priests, teachers of the law and elders. This was no motley bunch of hit-men, but rather pillars of Judaism, supported by soldiers with their swords at the ready.

With torches and lanterns and glistening steel blades they burst out of the darkness of the night. For Jesus there was never going to be a mere physical altercation. His struggle involved body, soul and mind, a struggle with eternal consequences. Jesus was not about returning violence with violence but rather initiating a powerful yet fragile and vulnerable community known as the kingdom of God.

Thus the hour arrived, the prayer battle as good as won, and Jesus steeled himself for what lay ahead – the cruel act of execution. Jesus understood his destiny, that this was the painful way of the Father's will for him.

For days Jesus' enemies had had ample opportunity to arrest him while he taught in the temple courts. Why then did they come at night? And why did they choose to arrest him outside the city? The obvious answer is that they feared the people's reaction to Jesus' arrest, and so, under cover of darkness, they moved swiftly.

Then there was that kiss. It was customary for disciples to greet a respected teacher in this way. Thus Judas' gesture would not be suspected for what it really was – a heinous act of betrayal. Having become involved in the wicked affair, Judas could not afford to make a fiasco of his part. But who was the trapped one now? The attending disciples did not linger long enough to find out but scattered in every direction.

The future expansion of the gospel depended on the ministry of the disciples but, alas, heels vanishing into the shadowy night did not look very promising at all. Thank God for the second and more chances he gives us. We are all beneficiaries of God's grace, mercy, forgiveness and restoration.

SATURDAY 15 APRIL

Jesus' Trial

Luke 22:63–71

'At daybreak the council of the elders of the people, both the chief priests and teachers of the law, met together, and Jesus was led before them' (v. 66, NIV).

The Jewish elders' decision that Jesus must die was long-standing. The Pharisees, with whom he had come into conflict in Galilee, had arrived at this decision early in his ministry. The chief priests and Jerusalem elders had conflicts with him during his visits to the city and had made several attempts to get rid of him (John 7:1; 8:59). These religious parties, so much at variance with each other at other times, found common ground in plotting Jesus' death.

The crowd's exuberant response to the triumphal entry, the cleansing of the temple and the resurrection of Lazarus served only to ignite further hatred towards Jesus.

Each group of enemies had their own reasons for hating him but one reason was common to them all. Jesus exposed and condemned their corruption. They would neither admit it nor repent of it. By planning to bring the full force of Jewish and Roman powers against Jesus they sought a corporate solution to their personal dilemma.

Jesus' so-called 'trial' was grossly corrupt. It was nothing more than a litany of lies, false accusations and gross inaccuracies, supported by a rigged jury. The Jewish trial essentially nullified itself because it sat illegally at night. The Roman trial by both Pilate and Herod found Jesus innocent. On all accounts Jesus should have been discharged and offered protection but mob-psychology won the day, resulting in a trumped-up charge of high treason being laid against him.

Handwashing was not normally a Roman custom but, having lived for several years among the Jews, Pilate picked up one of their own customs and contemptuously used it against them. He washed his hands of the whole matter, not out of justice but out of political and moral cowardice and fear of the mob.

How could one expect a fair trial by people whose hearts and minds were poisoned by hatred, warped by sin, and set on self-preservation? But there is no escape for us either. Human solidarity and depravity means that Caiaphas' guilt of putting Jesus to death is our guilt too. How great is our need for pardon!

SUNDAY 16 APRIL
Beautifully Shameful

---

1 Corinthians 1:18–25

'The message of the cross is foolishness to those who are perishing, but to us who are being saved it is the power of God' (v. 18, NIV).

At the heart of the Easter odyssey is a cross. I invite you today to focus on the beautiful simplicity and the sacred mystery of the scandalised 'old rugged cross'. In your imagination see the cross before you. Take time to touch and smell the sweet-bitter, rough-smooth wooden texture. Consider with awe the fact that long before Jesus' cross stood on Golgotha's hill, it was a splintered shaft embedded in the heart of God.

The cross is far less than many would hope simply because it is a symbol of shame and disgrace, of weakness and vulnerability. Anyone looking for mighty displays of force, miraculous feats or startling prophecies will be sadly disappointed. Dietrich Bonhoeffer captures Calvary's deepest moment in his description of people 'standing by God in his hour of need'.

On the other hand, the cross is far more than anyone ever dreamed because it is a sign of eternal hope, God's mighty power revealed in glory – a glory often clothed in suffering and weakness.

In Jesus' day the Roman authorities wanted executions to be excruciatingly painful and as public as possible in order to deter crime and violence. There was no debate about lethal injections or humane methods or appropriate prison sentences for crimes committed. Death by crucifixion was a harsh lesson of rejection, public humiliation, suffering, anguish and revulsion.

Is it any wonder that the beautifully shameful cross of Christ is still woefully misunderstood by so many today, an enigma and stigma theologically and culturally? For the courageous and searching person who draws near to Jesus' cross, however, a reward beyond measure awaits. God wants to speak to us and he does so powerfully through the cross. In prayer today hum or sing one of your favourite songs about the cross of Jesus, and quietly reflect on the significance of the words for your soul's nourishment.

On a hill far away stood an old rugged cross,
The emblem of suffering and shame,
And I love that old cross where the dearest and best
For a world of lost sinners was slain.
George Bennard, SASB 124

MONDAY 17 APRIL

The Crucifixion

Luke 23:26–38

'When they came to the place called the Skull, there they crucified him, along with the criminals – one on his right, the other on his left' (v. 33, NIV).

Crucifixion was an abomination to the Jews and an abhorrence to the Romans. No Roman citizen could be crucified without a direct edict from Caesar, and Jews regarded a crucified man as being 'cursed of God' – a belief that increased the 'stumbling-block' of a crucified Messiah (see *Deut 21:23*).

Jesus could not have been crucified without his own consent (*see John 10:17,18*). Why, then, did he submit himself as a lamb to the slaughter? Simply put – there was no other way. Jesus' conflict with evil was irreconcilable. It was the final act of the divine revelation he came to give – that only by his stripes are we healed from the disease of sin (*Isa 53:5*).

Calvary's cross can be viewed in two ways. First, it is an act of mankind in all its base depravity; and second, it is an act of God in all his sovereignty and unlimited grace. And God won.

The Jews mocked Jesus as Messiah, and the Roman soldiers ridiculed him as King. Ironically both were correct. The men who crucified Jesus were not abnormal villains. They were as we are – sinful, proud and selfish humans.

The crucifixion is a climax of human blindness and iniquity spilling over in brutal outrage against God's Son. It shows a world that has gone topsy-turvy. Jesus is King but he died an outlaw's death. Jesus is Messiah but he was rejected by the people he came to deliver. Jesus is the mighty Son of God who did not use his powers for himself but died a seemingly powerless death. All the traditional symbols have been reversed. Weakness is a sign of strength. Death is the means of life. God-forsakenness leads to reconciliation with God.

It serves little purpose to sketch the horrors of Jesus' crucifixion, nor is there a nice way of saying that evil engulfed him on the cross. How can we explain God forsaking his Son and the terrible abyss of abandonment? We can only bow in humble adoration and whisper:

It was for me that Jesus died
On the cross of Calvary.
                    Sarah Graham, SASB 128

TUESDAY 18 APRIL

The Burial

Luke 23:50–56

'Then he took it [Jesus' body] down, wrapped it in linen cloth and placed it in a tomb cut in the rock, one in which no-one had yet been laid' (v. 53, NIV).

It was the Roman custom to leave the body of a crucified victim on the cross until death brought a merciful release. Some poor creatures remained alive for three days or more. The Jews would not tolerate this practice, not because of mercy, but because exposed bodies would pollute the Festival Sabbath. So the bodies had to be disposed of without delay.

To the surprise of many, Jesus was already dead. This meant that he was spared having his legs smashed, a common way of hastening death because a person being crucified could no longer push up with his legs in order to breathe. By the compassionate action of Joseph of Arimathea, Jesus was saved from a felon's burial in an unmarked, uncelebrated and un-recorded grave. Joseph provided the tomb and linen wrappings and Nicodemus brought the costly spices (John 19:38,39). The burial was done hurriedly because the Sabbath was fast approaching.

The tomb was naturally secure as it was hewn out of solid rock. But the chief priests were afraid that Jesus' disciples or robbers might come and remove the body so they sealed the tomb by rolling a heavy stone across the face of it. They then posted a guard on duty to watch over it.

Why was it left to Joseph of Arimathea and Nicodemus of Jerusalem to bury Jesus? These two men had common ties. Both were members of the Council of the Sanhedrin but, more importantly, both had been secretly drawn to follow Jesus.

It is sufficient to say that these two rich men showed the regard they had for Christ's person and teaching. They showed by their actions that their devotion was not lessened by the reproach of the cross. The crisis of the moment may have triggered their natural disin-clination to courage, but there is plenty of ground at the foot of the cross, even for genuine secret seekers after truth.

Fringe faith, which at first is like a bruised reed, may afterwards resemble a strong cedar. Faith has to start some-where, and when it does blossom – what extravagant love is displayed!

113

WEDNESDAY 19 APRIL

The Resurrection

Luke 24:1–12

'He is not here; he has risen!' (v. 6, NIV).

The crucifixion of Jesus shattered the disciples so much that they lapsed into mourning and despair. They regarded the event as bringing to an end all that Jesus had lived and worked for, and all that they had believed in. 'Our own hope was that he would be the redeemer of Israel; but he is dead, and that is three days ago!' (*Luke 24:21*, JFM).

Yet a mighty transformation was soon to burst upon them. Their whole outlook changed dramatically when they learned that Jesus had not only risen from the dead but was alive for ever in unassailable power and glory. Easter Sunday heralded a triumphant cry and the disciples of Jesus would never be the same again. Hallelujah!

The cry, 'He is risen!' thus became, and continues to be for believers in every generation, the supreme announcement of Christian hope to a world so painfully bereft of hope.

Where is hope in the dark sullen eyes of a scantily dressed street child banging on a passing car window and pleading to sell a handful of shrivelled-up wild flowers? Where is hope in the smouldering ruins of a bomb-flattened apartment block? Where is hope at the end of a smoking gun barrel? Where is hope in the fervency of religious beliefs and ideologies? Where is hope in the principles and prejudices of powerful nations?

Is hope that elusive, mystical quality that we look forward to, reach out towards, but can never quite grasp with our hands? Is there yet hope on earth?

The resurrection of Jesus answers all our questions about hope in a resoundingly positive way. Nails, rocks, official seals and unbelieving hearts could not completely snuff out hope. On the contrary, the living Lord is a sure sign to the world that he is our glorious hope for today, for tomorrow and for ever. Hope wins overwhelmingly against all the odds.

The grave now is empty, the stone is rolled away,
And Christ is alive in my heart.
The death that he conquered in me has no part
For Christ is alive in my heart.
Author unknown

114

THURSDAY 20 APRIL
On the Road to Emmaus

Luke 24:13–35

'When he was at the table with them, he took bread, gave thanks, broke it and began to give it to them. Then their eyes were opened and they recognised him' (vv. 30,31, NIV).

The two people on the road to Emmaus walked with their heads down, their feet heavy and their hearts overwhelmed. They walked in a kind of daze. Again and again they went over the events of the previous few days, but it was like doing a jigsaw puzzle with several pieces missing. There was just no logic, no sense to what had happened. With the dashing of their highest hopes and their greatest dreams, they felt abandoned, wretched and bereft.

That is what grief does. It blinds the eyes. It weighs heavy on the body. It wraps the heart in a dark shroud.

Then a stranger joined them. They scarcely noticed his coming but suddenly he was alongside them, walking in step, asking questions. How did he not know what had happened? But it was a relief to have someone else to tell their story to.

'We had hoped,' they said, 'that Jesus was the answer to all our needs. He was undoubtedly God's prophet, popular with the people, amazing in his miracles. He spoke words of life. But the religious leaders arrested him, killed him, silenced him. Then just this morning some women came and said that he was alive. Now we don't know what to think. We're confused and puzzled so we're going home, back to where things are quiet.'

Jesus, ever the gentle companion, listened, responded, explained. When they reached the village they invited him to come and have a meal with them. As he broke the bread their eyes were opened and at once they recognised him. Amazingly, it was Jesus himself, right there with them. Suddenly the jigsaw pieces all fitted together. With joy they hurried back to tell the others.

Grief blinds us but joy opens our eyes, lifts the weight from our body, casts off the heavy blanket from around our heart. If you are walking an Emmaus Road today, lift your eyes and look around to see who travels with you. The risen Lord is wherever his people are, exchanging joy for sorrow, giving hope to all those who feel bereft.

FRIDAY 21 APRIL

The Ascension

Luke 24:36–53

'When he had led them out to the vicinity of Bethany, he lifted up his hands and blessed them. While he was blessing them, he left them and was taken up into heaven' (vv. 50,51, NIV).

After his resurrection Jesus appeared to his disciples on numerous occasions. He walked with the two on the road to Emmaus. He joined the group in the Upper Room. He was waiting for the weary fishermen on the shore of Lake Galilee (see *John 21*). Paul wrote to the Corinthians, 'After that, he appeared to more than five hundred of the brothers ... Then he appeared to James, then to all the apostles, and last of all he appeared to me also' (*1 Cor 15:6–8*).

Then the day came when Jesus led his band of disciples out of the city of Jerusalem, down into the Kidron Valley, and up the Mount of Olives to a location near Bethany. They had often been to Bethany where Jesus' dear friends Lazarus, Martha and Mary lived. Now they had come for a different purpose.

In our readings some days ago of Jesus in Gethsemane, I suggested that in that place of agonised prayer he came face to face with the silence of heaven. How dramatically the situation has changed! Jesus now ascends into heaven from the Mount of Olives. He goes from a place of crushing to a place of exultation (see *Phil 2:9–10*). He moves from a place of loneliness to a seat at the right hand of God (*Luke 22:69*).

And what of the disciples? From being a bunch of dispirited deserters they become a worshipping, praising, joyous and obedient group. What a turnaround!

The Easter epoch reminds us that all is well. Jesus has fought the spiritual battle, won the victory and completed his mission on earth. We can live in his victory and wait in ever-rising anticipation for his promised return. Therefore, let us rest in the prayer of Jesus to his Father: 'I have brought you glory on earth by completing the work you gave me to do. And now, Father, glorify me in your presence with the glory I had with you before the world began' (*John 17:4–5*).

To reflect on
Glory and suffering are inextricably bound together. It is almost impossible to welcome one without experiencing the other.

SATURDAY 22 APRIL
So Where to from Here?

Matthew 28:16–20

'Go and make disciples of all nations, baptising them in the name of the Father and of the Son and of the Holy Spirit, and teaching them to obey everything I have commanded you. And surely I am with you always, to the very end of the age' (vv. 19,20, NIV).

The historical Easter epoch was never intended to signal the completion of the ministry of Jesus on earth. On the contrary, it heralded the beginning of a new Christian history that would be continually written and lived by the followers of Jesus down through the ages. What happens next, then, is up to you and me.

In every respect, the Emmaus Road journey could track its path to your high-rise city apartment, or your leafy suburban street, or your dusty village compound. The question is – will you recognise Jesus when he comes? At its heart Easter is about you and Jesus walking, talking, enjoying intimate fellowship together, and sharing the good news of salvation with others.

A key component of the Easter story is about communication – God opening his heart and speaking to the world through the cataclysmic actions of his Son Jesus. Communication invites listening, and listening brings about understanding that ultimately enhances humanity by fostering positive qualities of tolerance, forgiveness, justice, equality, peace and faith.

God knows how much the peoples of our turbulent world desperately need to listen to each other. From the highest levels of political, economic, religious and community leaders, right down to our nearest neighbour, listening to one another is basic to our survival as a community. As we listen with compassion and without judgment, we begin to see each other with new eyes and to appreciate each other, in spite of our differences.

So I invite you to hand-pick an Easter lesson that God through his Holy Spirit has communicated to you during these days. Then be determined to let that new learning infiltrate and dictate your walk with God from this day forward. There is much to do before Jesus returns. Easter ignites the power of hope within each of us. On the calendar, Easter comes but once a year, but for the Christian, Easter happens every single day.

Christ is alive! His Spirit burns
Through this and every future age,
Till all creation lives and learns
His joy, his justice, love and praise.
Brian Wren, SASB 42

SUNDAY 23 APRIL

The Servant King

Isaiah 52:13–53:3

'He had no beauty or majesty to attract us to him, nothing in his appearance that we should desire him' (v. 2, NIV).

These words are a description of Christ the Paradox. He is both Suffering Servant and King of Kings. He is both meekness and majesty. He is both despised and desired. He is a man of sorrows familiar with grief, and the One whose presence fills us with joy (Ps 16:11).

Rejected by people, he was God's beloved Son (Luke 3:22). Acclaimed by the thronging crowd in Jerusalem on Palm Sunday, he was harangued by that same crowd just a few days later. Cries of 'Hosanna!' turned quickly to 'Crucify!' He rode into the city on a donkey, a beast of burden, but was led out of the city carrying the burden of his own cross.

Jesus' whole life was a paradox. Some listened and loved, others heard and hated. Those with full hands who had no sense of need received little from him. Those whose hands were empty and whose hearts were hungry for God received more than they could contain. There was nothing attractive about him yet he attracted people to himself and transformed their lives.

Those closest to him often understood him the least. Those who had no right to be close to him – blind men, women, lepers and sinners – seemed instinctively to know who he was and that he could help them. He served people, healing diseases, setting tortured souls free, washing his followers' feet. He humbled himself all the way to the cross but from that lowest place God raised him to the highest place.

Mary's gentle lamb grew to be the Lamb of God who takes away the sin of the world (John 1:29). 'Worthy is the Lamb, who was slain, to receive power and wealth and wisdom and strength and honour and glory and praise!' (Rev 5:12).

From heav'n You came, helpless babe,
enter'd our world, Your glory veil'd;
not to be served but to serve,
and give Your life that we might live.
This is our God, the Servant King,
He calls us now to follow Him,
To bring our lives as a daily offering
of worship to the Servant King.

Graham Kendrick[11]

A NEW CREATURE IN CHRIST
– 2 CORINTHIANS 5:17

Introduction

Therefore if any person is ingrafted in Christ, the Messiah, he is a new creature altogether, a new creation; the old previous moral and spiritual condition has passed away. Behold, the fresh and new has come! (2 Cor 5:17, Amplified Bible).

This verse from Paul's second letter to the Corinthians is a wonderful statement of faith. 'A new creation' sounds like a makeover of the extreme kind. But what does this new creation look like? What are the implications of this radical new identity? How is this new life to be lived out day by day in the midst of chores and choices, demands and duties, overdue library books and odd socks?

With the help of a magnifying glass and some real–life stories, we will take a long look into the depths of this exquisite verse.

MONDAY 24 APRIL
A New Creation

2 Corinthians 5:17

'If anyone is in Christ, he is a new creation; the old has gone, the new has come!' (NIV).

A 76-year-old woman called June was recently enrolled at our local corps as a senior soldier (full adult member) of The Salvation Army. June's family travelled some distance for the occasion, and her Home League (women's group) friends were also there in abundance. There was a real party atmosphere.

June, in full uniform, was beaming. She said she could not quite believe what was happening. The journey had been a long one. She did not go into the details of her earlier years, but the lines on her face tell their own tale.

I remember walking home with June one evening a year or so ago after a social event at the corps. As we staggered along, arms around each other, I asked June about her relationship with God. She said, 'Oh, God and I aren't on speaking terms.' At that stage she was still recovering from the sad loss of her husband.

But things changed for June. A neighbour knocked at her door, and kept coming, even when June was rude to her. A group of Home League women befriended her, a house group prayed regularly for her, faithful corps officers visited and cared for her. Slowly, one step after another, she moved from grief and bitterness of heart into openness and acceptance of God's love.

The promises she made on her enrolment day – 'I will maintain Christian ideals . . . I will be a faithful steward . . . I will abstain from tobacco' – would have been unthinkable for June a year or so ago. But she made them confidently, positively, sincerely. How could she do that? Simply because, in becoming a Christian, June is what the Scriptures call 'a new creation'. She will always be June, of course – that smile, that warmth, that fun streak. But as June herself says, 'I feel as though I am a completely new person now. Everything's different. I can't explain it but I love it.'

Praise God that he is still in the business of creating. These days it is not new planets, but new people.

TUESDAY 25 APRIL

A New Conduct

2 Corinthians 5:17

'When someone becomes a Christian he becomes a brand new person inside. He is not the same any more. A new life has begun!' (Living Bible).

For many people who become Christians, the contrast between the 'old' life and the 'new' is minimal. An elderly friend who grew up in a loving Christian family says she cannot remember the day of her conversion. It is as if she has always 'lived in the light'. For others, however, the contrast is stark.

A young musician, interviewed recently in the New Zealand *War Cry*, spoke of the hate he felt as a child for his father who was a very violent man. Every time there was a party at their home, he and his sister knew what to expect at the end of the night. 'It was like waiting for a storm to hit. We knew it was coming but hoped it would never arrive.'

At the age of twelve this young man started drinking alcohol and experimenting with cannabis and other drugs. He grew to love the party scene of drink, drugs and girls. 'Before long,' he said, 'I became reliant on drugs. I was addicted to cannabis and spent almost every cent I had on it. I even started to buy in bulk, dealing to whoever would buy. As I sank deeper into this dark world I allowed demons to slowly destroy me. I hit rock bottom, felt worthless and without purpose.'

Then, whether by the personal invitation of a friend, or by some inner nudge, he started attending the local Salvation Army corps and began reading his Bible. 'I was earnestly looking for a better life and a way out.' He spoke of meeting Jesus, feeling an overwhelming love, knowing that God was doing something momentous in his life. He spoke of being released from things that had long kept him bound. He spoke of finding a new purpose and passion for living.

Corrie ten Boom said: 'Jesus Christ is able to untangle all the snarls in my soul, to banish all my complexes, and to transform even my fixed habit patterns, no matter how deeply they are etched in my subconscious.' The stains of sin may run deep but God's transforming work reaches far deeper.

WEDNESDAY 26 APRIL
A New Courage

2 Corinthians 5:17

'If anyone is in Christ, there is a new creation: everything old has passed away; see, everything has become new!' (NRSV).

Growing up, Betty was not afraid of anything – spiders, brothers, not even her father's angry outbursts. Nothing could dampen her bright, bubbly personality. But at the age of twelve, Betty met something fearful – death. Betty's nineteen-year-old brother died in tragic circumstances. Suddenly Betty found herself facing something she could not understand. The easiest way was to avoid it, deny it. For the next forty years Betty could not bring herself to attend a funeral.

When Betty's niece died, she drove her parents to the funeral but stayed outside in the car under the pretext of looking after her mother who was unwell. But a friend, a Salvation Army officer, noticed her in the car and insisted on looking after the mother. 'Your place is in there,' she said to Betty.

Betty still did not go in, but the experience marked a turning point in her life. For the first time she faced her fear of death and began looking for God and some answers. 'I found God in people's eyes,' she said. 'People of faith seemed so full of hope and joy, and it showed on their faces.' Betty's search led her eventually to the Church and to a community of believers.

These days Betty is passionate about her garden. She knows all there is to know about growing tomatoes. She is also a keen golfer. But Betty's greatest passion is to journey with people facing death. She is a bereavement-support person in her parish and an advocate for the elderly residents at a local rest home.

In sharing her faith Betty has helped many others face their fear of dying. She says the journey began when her brother died, then gathered momentum with her niece's death. She says, 'I am amazed when I look back and see how my God has led me.'

At times the call of God seems impossible, the challenge an overwhelming and fearful thing. But one step, one experience, one stretching of faith after the other, God leads us graciously, gently, giving us courage for the unique task to which he has called us.

THURSDAY 27 APRIL
A New Condition

2 Corinthians 5:17

'Anyone united with the Messiah gets a fresh start, is created new.
The old life is gone; a new life burgeons!' (*The Message*).

Frank is a poet, artist, singer and musician. He practically grew up on the stage, giving his first performance at the age of thirteen. He went to church now and again as a child, but in his early twenties had an urge to attend more regularly. Although he heard the gospel clearly preached, and his wife and two of his children were converted, Frank himself was forty-five years old before he became a Christian.

One Sunday evening when his family had gone to church, Frank stayed home. Feeling 'fed up' with arguing with God, he asked Jesus to come into his life. At 17.55, he said, he fell asleep a sinner and at 18.10 woke up a saint. 'I knew Christ had died for me.'

Frank's life after that dramatic, life-changing evening took him in a completely new direction – into teaching, counselling, ministry to children and nationwide evangelistic missions. He became an accredited local preacher in the Methodist Connexion and, in his early sixties, completed an honours degree in theology.

Frank's move from sinner to saint illustrates the new condition of the person who becomes a Christian. The author of the book of Hebrews writes that, in giving himself as a redeeming sacrifice, Jesus 'has made perfect for ever those who are being made holy' (*Heb 10:14*). Note the tenses of the verbs here. 'He has made' is past tense, meaning that Jesus' action is done and completed. It is a finished action. 'Are being made holy' is a present–continuous tense. A person who becomes a Christian lives in the process of being made holy every day. The old condition has gone; a new condition has come.

John Newton wrote: 'I once was lost, but now am found, was blind but now I see.' For Frank, the change was just as dramatic: 'I fell asleep a sinner. I woke up a saint.'

I am a new creation,
no more in condemnation,
here in the grace of God I stand.
My heart is overflowing,
my love just keeps on growing,
here in the grace of God I stand.
                    Dave Bilbrough[12]

FRIDAY 28 APRIL

A New Conviction

2 Corinthians 5:17

'Anyone who is joined to Christ is a new being; the old is gone, the new has come' (GNB).

There was a time when the only convictions Kim knew about were the legal kind – and there were plenty of them. Her first partner went to prison for kidnapping, her second partner was imprisoned for murder, and Kim herself served a brief prison sentence for her part in a petrol-bomb incident. Kim lived in a world of drugs and alcohol, violence and abuse. One tattoo after another on her body recorded the sad journey.

In her mid-twenties, with four children, Kim decided to start a new life. Moving to a new city, she stayed with a family friend who, in the strategy of God, just happened to be a Christian. This friend talked to Kim about faith, God and choices. 'We don't make mistakes, Kim,' she said, 'just wrong choices.'

When the children started going to Sunday school, Kim decided she needed to learn what they were learning. Her friend took her to an *Alpha* course where, she said, 'I asked all the hard questions and tried to prove the Christians wrong!' But as time went on, Kim started to enjoy the course, and by the last week was ready to give her life to Jesus. 'I said the prayer about six times,' she said, 'just in case God didn't hear me.'

The next morning Kim woke up with a joy she had never before experienced. But on that very day, her seven-year-old son was killed on his way to school. The day that began in joy ended in devastation. Christian friends loved and supported Kim but she plunged back into drugs, trying to ease her pain. Months later, she asked God to take away the desire for drugs, and began to pick up the threads of her life again.

These days Kim is a fervent, radiant Christian. The tattoos have been removed from her arms, leaving just the scars of her old life. Now married, she and her husband are training to become Salvation Army officers. Kim is learning the Army's doctrines, 'I believe . . . I believe . . . I believe.' These are the new convictions that now shape her life.

SATURDAY 29 APRIL

A New Community

2 Corinthians 5:17

'For anyone who is in Christ, there is a new creation; the old creation has gone, and now the new one is here' (JB).

In the African bush, miles from anywhere and thousands of miles from my homeland, I found a community of God's people to whom I belonged. They were black-skinned and radiant-faced, poor yet clothed in the rich garments of salvation, uneducated but knowing intimately the One in whom they had put their trust. We met as strangers but quickly discovered we were brothers and sisters in Christ.

In the community of believers, Paul declares, differences of race, age, gender, background or status matter not at all (see *Col 3:11*). Education and wealth, prestige and privilege are no measure of one's value or right of entry. No one is excluded. All are welcome. 'No longer foreigners and aliens,' says Paul (*Eph 2:19*). Differences become far less important than the things we hold in common – the love of God, the salvation of Jesus, the presence of the Holy Spirit.

The Christian life was never meant to be a lone existence. For sure, God calls each person individually and has a unique purpose for every person's life, but he has programmed us for community.

Paul uses the image of a building to describe how each individual Christian is a part of the whole. Each believer is like one brick alongside another, or a post in a fence, or a book on a library shelf. Author Michel Quoist says Christians are like a wire fence, standing together and 'holding hands around the holes'.

The privilege of being part of such a community is matched by an awesome responsibility. When Christians are starving in Sudan, persecuted in Eritrea, or in need in Nepal, then I too have a part to play. I need to feel their pain, do what I can to relieve their desperate situation, and pray for them as my brothers and sisters in Christ.

To reflect on

'We are the Church, a ragged band of miracle workers: ragged because we are often contentious, scared, lazy, undependable, and – in a word – flawed; miracle workers because we've had to take straw and build a cathedral of hope for every generation that crossed our threshold.'

Renita Weems[13]

SUNDAY 30 APRIL
The Wounded Healer

<u>Isaiah 53:4–12</u>

'He was pierced for our transgressions, he was crushed for our iniquities; the punishment that brought us peace was upon him, and by his wounds we are healed' (v. 5, NIV).

In December in my country, New Zealand, large red sheep trucks collect spring's fattened lambs from farms and transport them to freezing works where they are slaughtered. Squeezed tightly on the trucks, the lambs make no sound. Do they know they are on their way to die? Do they know that this is what they were born for?

At his trial before Pilate, Jesus was silent, like a spring lamb on a New Zealand sheep truck. He must have known he was on his way to death. He must have known that this is what he was born for. The gift of myrrh at his birth gave a hint of that from the very beginning. The writer of Revelation declares that he was 'the Lamb . . . slain from the creation of the world' (*Rev 13:8*). The Baby of Bethlehem is the Christ of Calvary, the Lamb of God.

Henri Nouwen gives him yet another name – Wounded Healer. How can he heal? Because he himself has been wounded, stricken, stripped, smitten, crushed, pierced, afflicted, oppressed, tortured, mocked, beaten, bruised and bloodied. How can he give life?

Because he lived and died and now lives again. How can he save? Because he is the Saviour. How can he take away the sin of the world? Because he had no sin of his own to carry (*Heb 4:15*).

Film director Mel Gibson called Jesus' story *The Passion of the Christ*. By enduring the passion of suffering, he has opened up for you and me the passion of overflowing, inexplicable, uncontainable joy. His hurt has become the source of our healing.

The words of Isaiah 53 are a deep pool inviting our long gaze, our careful reflection, our grateful consideration. Read the chapter until a word takes hold of your heart. Let that word become your meditation, your prayer, your place of rest today.

Worthy is the Lamb, seated on the throne;
Crown You now with many crowns,
You reign victorious.
High and lifted up,
Jesus, Son of God;
The Darling of heaven crucified.
Worthy is the Lamb.
Darlene Zschech[14]

NOTES

1 Catherine Baird, 'One Word for Judas', taken from her book *Reflections* (The Salvation Army, 1975).

2 Graham Kendrick, 'My Lord, What Love Is This', copyright © 1989 Make Way Music, PO Box 263, Croydon, Surrey, CR9 5AP, UK.

3 Simone Weil, *Waiting for God* (Perennial, 1992).

4 Frederick Buechner, *The Magnificent Defeat* (Chatto & Windus, 1967).

5 Marc Nelson, 'I Believe in Jesus', copyright © 1987 Mercy/Vineyard Publishing. Administered by CopyCare, PO Box 77, Hailsham, BN27 3EF, UK, music@copycare.com. Used by permission.

6 Mark Altrogge, 'I'm Forever Grateful', copyright © 1986 Sovereign Grace Praise. Administered by CopyCare, PO Box 77, Hailsham, BN27 3EF, UK, music@copycare.com. Used by permission.

7 Gale Webb, *The Night and Nothing* (SPCK, 1964).

8 Henri Nouwen, *Life of the Beloved* (Hodder & Stoughton, 1992).

9 Barbara Brown Taylor, *Gospel Medicine* (Cowley Publications, 1995).

10 Lee Strobel, *God's Outrageous Claims* (Zondervan, 1997).

11 Graham Kendrick, 'From Heaven You Came (The Servant King)', copyright © 1983 Thankyou Music/Adm. by worshiptogether.com songs excl. UK & Europe, adm. by Kingsway Music, tym@kingsway.co.uk. Used by permission. Thankyou Music.

12 Dave Bilbrough, 'I Am a New Creation', copyright © 1983 Thankyou Music/Adm. by worshiptogether.com songs excl. UK & Europe, adm. by Kingsway Music, tym@kingsway.co.uk. Used by permission. Thankyou Music.

13 Renita Weems, *Listening for God* (Simon & Schuster, 1999).

14 Darlene Zschech, 'Thank You for the Cross (Worthy Is the Lamb)', copyright © 2000 Darlene Zschech/Hillsong Publishing/Kingsway Music, tym@kingsway.co.uk for the UK. Used by permission.

INDEX

(as from Advent 2000)

Words of Life Bible reading notes
are published three times a year:

Easter
(January–April)

Pentecost
(May–August)

Advent
(September–December)

In each edition you will find:

- informative commentary
- a wide variety of Bible passages
- topics for praise and prayer
- points to ponder
- cross references for further study

Why not place a regular order for *Words of Life*?
Collect each volume and build a lasting resource
for personal or group study. If you require further
information about how you can receive copies of
Words of Life, please contact: The Mail Order Department,
Salvationist Publishing & Supplies, 1 Tiverton Street,
London SE1 6NT, England. Telephone (020) 7367 6580 or
e-mail mail_order@sp-s.co.uk. Alternatively, contact your
territorial Trade Department

If you would like to contact Barbara Sampson,
her e-mail address is:
barbara_sampson@nzf.salvationarmy.org

READER'S NOTES

Ships of the Star Fleet

ONE HUNDRED AND THIRD EDITION
Akyazi-Class Perimeter Action Ships

By Todd Allan Guenther

MASTERCOM DATA CENTER

PUBLISHED BY **MASTERCOM DATA CENTER, POST OFFICE BOX 4990, HOLYOKE, MASSACHUSETTS, 01041-4990**.

DESIGNED, WRITTEN AND ILLUSTRATED BY TODD ALLAN GUENTHER.
ADDITIONAL TEXT BY DAVID NIELSEN.

A CATALOG OF OTHER PUBLICATIONS MAY BE OBTAINED BY WRITING TO MASTERCOM AT THE ABOVE ADDRESS.
VISIT OUR WEB SITE AT **WWW.MASTERCOMDATA.COM**

LIBRARY OF CONGRESS CATALOG CARD NUMBER: 92-114105

ISBN 0-9656016-1-7

PRINTED IN THE UNITED STATES OF AMERICA

FIRST EDITION: DECEMBER 1992
REVISED EDITION: FEBRUARY 1993
CURRENT EDITION: AUGUST 1998

for Honor

"I would lay down my life for America,
but I cannot trifle with my honor."

John Paul Jones
4 September 1777

Contents

Preface

This volume of *Ships of the Star Fleet* illustrates the changing nature of Star Fleet's primary mission over the past ten Earth-years - from a primarily exploratory posture to, unfortunately, a predominantly defensive one. Beginning with the apparent withdrawal of the Organians in the early 2280s and followed by the consolidation of power within the Klingon Empire shortly thereafter, Star Fleet's direction was all but assured when Klingon vessels attacked Federation merchant ships in the Taal Tan region in 2283.

Initiating a combat action that would officially last for more than five months, the Klingonese forces attacked quickly and without warning, all but destroying three merchant convoys while taking 617 lives. Federation response, though swift, was predicated on the attack being an isolated incident. Two days passed before outpost stations received a hyperlink communique indicating that starships *Lafayette* (CH 1720), *Wasp* (CH 1721), and *Tori* (CH 1725) had engaged and defeated the Klingon hunter-killers *K'chss* and *K'utuul* (and a number of lesser craft) at Linze. A full mobilization ensued. Within six days the scope of the Klingon offensive was known, and Star Fleet units were engaging hostile forces all along the disputed Klingon border and at seemingly random spots in subquadrants two south and three south. The hostilities continued until November of 2283; Star Fleet lost 26 Class One starships as well as 5500 personnel and numerous Class Two spacecraft. Klingonese losses were much higher.

During the final week of fighting the heavy frigates *Illustrious* (FH 1863) and *Amiens* (FH 1869) discovered the Romulan outpost Rihanni Tu outside subquadrant four south. Constructed in the middle of an asteroid field, the station had been operational for at least six months. Its clandestine location and relatively small size made it apparent to senior Star Fleet officers and experts in Romulan military history that the sole purpose of the outpost was to collect intelligence information on Star Fleet

strength in the subquadrant four south area. With what would later become known as the Taal Tan Offensive still ongoing, the options available to the Federation at first seemed limited. A cease-fire agreement terminated hostilities with the Klingons four days later, however, and Star Fleet's hand was strengthened considerably. Despite unexpected personnel and spacecraft losses and the need for a continued presence along the Klingon border to maintain the terms of the cease-fire, Class One combat units were now available in larger numbers. While Romulan officials insisted that the station had been established to conduct scientific studies of various stellar phenomena, the Federation demanded that it be abandoned. When the Romulans refused, Star Fleet instituted a blockade of the outpost, severing all supply lines. Romulan representatives engaged in disingenuous politesse for several weeks but finally withdrew without resorting to hostilities.

While the Romulans were somewhat conciliatory, Klingon forces only continued their belligerency. Confrontations continued at an inordinate rate. The Battle of Khatanga and the loss of seven Star Fleet vessels in early 2284; the numerous raids on frontier merchant shipping and the resultant loss of lives and cargo; the Rykla Dagh Incident of 2285 and the loss of the heavy cruiser *Hood* four months later; the destruction and defeat of Klingon vessels by the *Thach* (FR 1949), *Ability* (FR 1953), and *Avenger* (FH 1860) at Pelarsk in 2286; all served to strengthen Federation resolve.

The result of these and other events was a five-year program of significant and somewhat effective Class One fleet rejuvenation presided over by then Federation Commissioner of the Star Fleet Lars-Erik Valdemar. Despite subdued but continued protestations from the pacifist bloc, an impressive 25 classes (totalling approximately 484 hulls) were authorized for construction or refitting during his tenure, most of these in areas requiring much-needed attention. Borderspace operations platforms (perimeter action ships and similar type construction) and the transport arm of Star Fleet (transport and transport/tug classes) received necessary help. Further examination of the classes authorized between 2283 and 2288 reveals that only 154 ships (32%) are of a "non-battle force" nature. This includes 109 new transport/tug hulls but only 38 scout and seven exploratory cruiser hulls. The complete numbers appear below.

NEW CONSTRUCTION AUTHORIZATION 2283-2288

Number of Classes	Number/Type	
1	8	Light Cruisers (CL)
1	20	Frigates (FR)
2	*109	Transport/Tugs (TT)
3	*22	Scouts (ST)
1	26	Destroyers (DD)
1	14	Heavy Cruisers (CH)
1	5	Dreadnoughts (DN)
2	19	Heavy Frigates (FH)
1	3	Battlecruisers (CG)
1	17	Corvettes (CV)
1	*16	Superscouts (SS)
1	19	Fast Frigates (FF)
1	10	Strike Cruisers (CS)
1	5	Command Ships (CO)
1	*7	Large Exploratory Cruisers (CKE)
3	40	Combat Support Ships (SP)
2	133	Perimeter Action Ships (PA)
1	11	Large Perimeter Action Ships (PKA)
25	454	

*Indicates non-combat vessels.

These figures illustrate clearly the aforementioned change in the fleet's primary mission profile. Most of the classes indicated are in either the "building" or "planned" stage (only five classes have completed construction), but all of them have the full support of the Military Staff Committee and all will likely be built. Since Valdemar retired his position in 2288, authorization for new ship construction has slowed somewhat; however, the realization of a 1600-ship Class One fleet (with a minimum of 90% [1440] battle force capable units) is still possible by the 2295 target date.

This volume of *Ships* examines one component of the recent additions to Star Fleet's perimeter defense forces: the *Akyazi*-class perimeter action ships.[1] As with the previous edition, the information in this volume is organized to enable the reader to quickly locate the data desired. The individual vessel listings (which appear in chart form) display a ship's current navigational contact code number, name, builder, date the ship's keel was laid, date the ship was launched, date of commissioning into the Fleet, and current status, respectively. Terran local calendar dates are used where applicable; standard stardates are used in all other instances.

The ship status codes used here have been simplified from the lengthier and more detailed Star Fleet method. The status code **ATAC** indicates a vessel under the operational jurisdiction of TacFleet. Since all perimeter action ships come under this classification, **ATAC** is the only "active" status code used in this volume. The status note "Lost" indicates a vessel lost in the line of duty. Additional notations are "Building" (for ships under construction as of the date of publication), and "Authorized" (for ships that have been approved but have not yet begun building).

The illustrations accompanying the sub-class sections represent the distinctive insignia of those PA sub-classes. (These should not be confused with the creative insignia of individual vessels, which vary from ship to ship and are often designed by members of a particular ship's crew.) The insignia are unique to each starship class (or sub-class) and are accorded "limited approval" status by Star Fleet Command (i.e. they cannot be displayed at official functions or attached to regulation duty uniforms, and they must be deleted from exterior hull surfaces prior to large-scale operations or intelligence assignments).

Unless otherwise noted, all vessel illustrations included in this volume are in the 1:875 scale.

The detailed information on the *Akula* sub-class was prepared by Timothy Farrar and Makita Recamier exclusively for the *Ships* series. A majority of the data was drawn from information made available by Star Fleet; where classification restrictions were encountered, experts in Star Fleet design philosophy were consulted to provide educated conjecture.

The publishers of *Ships of the Star Fleet - Akyazi-Class Perimeter Action Ships* are grateful to many individuals and organizations for providing assistance in its preparation. Among these are Sir Kyle Greenleaf, Dyan Tupir, Jameson Hecht, Huss Randon, and Amye Stalt, all of whom provided invaluable data and insight into the design, operation, and current status of perimeter action ships. Also, vital support and assistance was provided by Carlson Rentee, director of the Defense Forces Institute at Mastercom; Carolann Leviere, superdata coordinator for the Ships series; and Rear Admiral Krisdulas Min Ar (Star Fleet, retired), contributing technical editor and Star Fleet liaison.

Finally, offering essential data and "course correction" were Commodore C. Paul Steele, Tactical Readiness Division, TacFleet; Oson Salingas, Office of Public Relations, TacFleet Command; Donovan Bosch, Temerand Duplicat; Gregory C. Alhaman, Terran Rockwell; Commander Lena P. Everest, Star Station Praeses; Commander Warren Deely, Star Station Tiran; Lt. Commander Erik Y. Tasano, Star Station Dallas; Lt. Commander Justin H. Cates, Starbase 21; Lt. Commander Brenda Shiver, Starbase 27; Lieutenant Femin E. C. Tinghast, Outpost Principale; Lieutenant Dora Redbear, Starbase 15; and Cameron Yelle, director, *Faron* class design team.

The next installment in this series, *Ships of the Star Fleet - Battlecruisers*, is available for datastream download from any authorized technical communications channel. Comments, information, or material may be directed to the headquarters of the Defense Forces Institute at Mastercom Data Center, located at its Bay Colony complex in the United Americas, Earth.

Todd Allan Guenther
March 2290

---

[1] The terms "class," "sub-class," and "group" are used somewhat loosely in Star Fleet parlance. For the purposes of this reference work, "class" refers to the *Akyazi* class as a whole, i.e. including the *Arbiter* and *Akula* designs. "Sub-class" or "group" refers to one of the three design-types individually, as in the *Arbiter* sub-class or *Akula* group.

Ships of the Star Fleet

Akyazi-Class Perimeter Action Ships

Evolution of the *Akyazi* Class

The small but mighty perimeter action ships play an essential role in the realization of modern Federation defense strategies. Based on the concept of "spherical defense" (versus that of "point defense"), these plans provide for complete coverage of the charted perimeter of Federation treaty space. This seemingly impossible task is realized through continuing, detailed probability studies that provide planners with the most advantageous redeployment choices. Patrol combatants (which include those vessels dedicated to spherical defense duty) are deployed in "layers," starting with the outermost reaches of the perimeter where corvettes, clippers, and purpose-built perimeter action ships keep vigil. A second, interior layer providing both fast reinforcement to outer deployments and a second opportunity for initial confrontation consists of perimeter action and large perimeter action ships, strike cruisers, and battlecruisers assigned to outpost protection. Dreadnoughts, destroyers, and heavy destroyers, as well as other starships assigned on an "as needed" basis, patrol the third, innermost layer.

This defensive scheme evolved from lessons learned during the opening stages of the Four Years War, when repeated small-scale Klingon incursions evaded Federation forces concentrated at strategic points. Star Fleet responded by deploying under-utilized corvettes and clippers along front lines to delay such incursions and thus provide additional time for a concentrated response. The success of this plan in preventing further loss of space served as a lesson to defense strategists in the final year of the war. Star Fleet development and procurement strategies were accordingly adapted, and in early 2249 the Military Staff Committee approved purchase of 35 *Kiaga* (PA 820) and 155 *Agilis* (PA 855) class starships. After hostilities ended, however, these vessels were expected to perform a number of tasks in addition to that of first-line defense. With so few starships assigned to the perimeter during that period it was necessary for any deployments to, among other tasks, provide rescue services for

deep space missions, perform frontier police duties, and conduct limited surveys. Long-range exploratory and hostile borderspace scanning (missions still carried out by perimeter action ships to a reduced extent) were among the primary duties.

By the late 2260s, enforcement of the Organian Peace Treaty had rendered Federation-Klingon borderspace relatively quiet. The Romulan Neutral Zone, Gorn and Tholian frontiers, and Kznti borderspace, however, were all active with repeated tests of Federation vigilance. It was with these threats in mind that Star Fleet planners proposed building 178 *Akyazi* (PA 1010)-class perimeter action ships along with five strike cruisers of the *Decatur/Belknap* (CS 2500) design. The *Akyazi* class was to reflect both the advances in propulsion technology afforded by linear warp drive and the changed realities of perimeter defense duty. Many of the auxiliary tasks assumed by this type in the past could now be conducted by outposts, monitor stations, and purpose-built starships and Class Two spacecraft. The mission profile for the *Akyazi* class was thus to focus on maximizing offensive capacities geared solely toward delaying potential adversaries.

The significant cost of undertaking the *Akyazi* program caused great consternation among the members of the Federation Council. Funding postponements forced Star Fleet planners to maintain the aging perimeter action force already in place, in part by reassigning secondary duties to other operations platforms. Put on temporary hold in late 2270, the program was put on indefinite hold in late 2273 as a result of the massive cutbacks and reallocations that followed revelations concerning Star Fleet's role in inciting the Kznti Incursion.

The Klingon Taal Tan Offensive of 2283 undermined support for the pacifist bloc on the Federation Council that had managed for ten Earth-years to prevent reconsideration of funding for the perimeter action program. The obvious weakness of the Star Fleet deterrent in the outer reaches of subquadrants two south and three south forced

TABLE 1-1. PERIMETER DEFENSE PLATFORMS[a]

Type/Class	2245	2250	2255	2260	2265	2270	2275	2280	2285	2290	2295	2300	2305	2310	2315
Various/Strategic[b]	61	55	71	83	67	51	32	30	55	71	57	20	30	40	40
PA 820/*Kiaga* class	—	5[c]	35	35	24[d]	20	18	19	34	35	30	15	6	—	—
PA 855/*Agilis* class	—	11[c]	139	155	83[d]	76	71	70	147	154	123	74	42	24	—
PA 1010/*Akyazi* class	—	—	—	—	—	—	—	—	—	71	102	102	102	102	102
PA 1125/*Engage* class	—	—	—	—	—	—	—	—	—	15	28	28	28	28	28
PKA 1170/*Kirsanov* class	—	—	—	—	—	—	—	—	—	6	11	11	11	11	11
Totals	61	71	245	273	174	147	121	119	236	352	351	250	219	205	181

[a]Figures for 2290 through 2315 are projections.
[b]Includes all vessels stationed to perimeter defense duty (corvettes, clippers, etc.) other than the "perimeter action ship" type.
[c]Numbers reflect vessels lost in action during the Four Years War (2246-2250) and replaced by the Military Staff Committee in subsequent appropriations, thus achieving
 the desired total of 35 *Kiaga* and 155 *Agilis*/class starships.
[d]Many perimeter action ships were cycled in and out of the Star Fleet Reserve Force beginning in 2265 as a result of the Organian Peace Treaty and various other factors.

the issue, and thus one of Federation Commissioner Lars-Erik Valdemar's first recommendations upon taking office was for perimeter action force revitalization.

Valdemar's plan was twofold. On the one hand, corvettes and older perimeter action ships were deployed on the frontier until new vessels could begin entering service. Plans then called for the corvettes to be returned to their previous duties, and for the older PAs to begin retiring. On the other hand, a compromise with the pacifist bloc was reached, and approval was won for construction of 141 perimeter action types, including 105 *Akyazi* class starships. The *Engage* (PA 1125) and *Kirsanov* (PKA 1170) classes were also authorized at this time.

Orders for the *Akyazi* class were placed in three lots over an eighteen month period, with the first lot of 38 ships ordered on 17 August 2283. Each lot reflected a design variation, and design variations also exist reflecting component and design improvements made over the course of building the full complement of each "sub-class." The prospective mission profile, however, is the same for all three sub-classes. "Patience, Vigilance, Endurance" is the motto of the *Akyazi* class and describes well the traits needed for service aboard these starships. Their offensive capacities have been tailored to a multitude of delaying strategies. Many offensive systems have been designed for 100% exhaustion, with the defending starship expending maximum power to repel an attack.[1] Deployment limitations necessitate that one *Akyazi* class vessel be capable of sustaining battle with five *K'teremny*-class battlecruisers for thirty minutes, inflicting twenty percent casualties. Only by realizing these projections will the second sphere of defense avoid being overwhelmed and have adequate response time. Similar estimates hold for other threat force opponents. Under such a scenario, the starship (if it survives) will not have the power to return to base. Lifeboat capacities and survival contingencies are therefore more fully developed as part of the mission profile in these vessels.

The perimeter action ship will continue to play an important role in Star Fleet defense strategy for the forseeable future. Present Commissioner T. Sela Arno has pledged full support for the perimeter action fleet and preliminary designs for at least one additional PA class are already in the development phase *(Faron*/PA 8300). However, the fiscal and political problems inherent in constructing and maintaining such a large force cannot be underestimated. Several members of the Federation Council have stated publicly that they will oppose future PA funding as either unviable, unnecessary, or both. At the same time, intelligence indicates that the Romulan military has made great strides in improving their perimeter fleet units, with indications that some of these developments are not yet fully understood by Star Fleet. With the number of perimeter defense platforms in Star Fleet service about to begin declining, a sensible and impartial discourse is required.

FIGURE 1-1. PERIMETER DEFENSE PLATFORMS 2245-2315

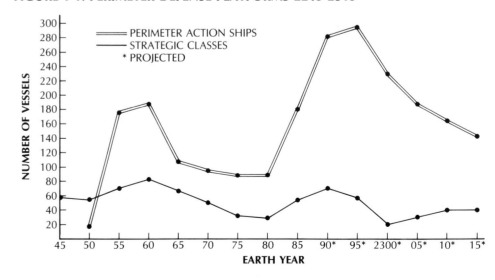

[1]Scans taken by the heavy cruiser *Enterprise* (CH 1701) during an engagement with an Orion suicide craft (see Star Fleet Record, *History of the Coridan Admission,* Babel Conference, 2264) provided information that allowed for the realization of this design philosophy.

Class Deployment

The responsibility of monitoring, patrolling, and defending the more than 3000 perimeter sectors of Federation space is divided among numerous sizes and types of platforms, including outposts, monitor stations, dreadnoughts, corvettes, perimeter action ships, and others. The *Akyazi*-class PAs play a vital role in this mission. On average, each of the 102 individual ships will be responsible for the security of nearly 30 sectors (up from the 29 sectors prior to the loss of three *Akyazi* class ships). These numbers are affected by many factors, however, including the deployment assignments of the other perimeter action ship classes. Also, the deployment of hostile forces at various border areas predetermines Star Fleet strategy in some instances - quadrants two and three receive priority due to the heavy Klingon and Romulan presence adjoining those areas (with subquadrants two south and three south customarily seeing the heaviest PA and strategic platform deployments). Conversely, in areas where no known aggressor force exists, the deployment ratio can range as high as one *Akyazi*-class PA for every 80 perimeter sectors.

Accompanying these different deployments is the need for differing areas of strength on the part of the *Akyazi*-class perimeter action ships. The *Akyazi, Arbiter,* and *Akula* sub-classes differ not only in name and date of construction but in speed, weapons capability, and internal and external design as a result of Star Fleet deployment strategy. Although the objective of the *Akyazi* class as a whole is to move from a posture of spherical defense to one of point defense as quickly as possible when necessary, the mission objectives of the different sub-classes are more clearly defined. Ships of the *Akula* sub-class, for instance, are outfitted with enhanced defensive features and more potent weaponry than their sister ships in the *Akyazi* and *Arbiter* groups; although they possess a slower maximum velocity, they are generally assigned to more dangerous deployments. Ships of the *Akyazi* group, possessing great speed, are often assigned to "sparse" deployments, making them responsible for the security of anywhere from 40

to as many as 80 perimeter sectors. Vessels of the *Arbiter* sub-class receive varying assignments to take advantage of both their speed and weapons capacity.

It must be remembered that perimeter action ships are tactical instruments, commanded by an officer with the rank of lieutenant or lieutenant commander. The *Akyazi* class ships (and other PA classes) are part of an overall strategy; however, their function as individual units is tactical, not strategic. All perimeter action ships currently on station are under the direct jurisdiction of TacFleet Command. (TacFleet was established on 07 June 2251 as a separate, specialized service within Star Fleet.)

Akyazi class ships are often grouped with combat support (SP) and/or intelligence-type vessels when on military or defense assignments. In areas where an aggressor force is less likely to be encountered, they are sometimes deployed with scientific vessels such as exploratory cruisers and other lesser classes. Most often, however, *Akyazi*-class PAs operate individually, far from the nearest bases or outposts and in great seclusion. This isolation contributes to the image of the ships and their crews as rugged, individualistic loners. In reality, the commanders of these PAs possess only situational autonomy. In most instances, their operational scenario falls well within the TacFleet chain of command.

While the operational flexibility of PA commanders and crews may seem limited, they are afforded significant latitude in the outfitting and "embellishing" of their individual vessels. This freedom is permitted in an attempt to offset the demanding and psychologically strenuous aspects of perimeter action ship duty. Various fleet, squadron, and unit affiliations (as well as individual ship bynames) are displayed in the form of customized insignia and descriptive symbols, freely illustrated on the rear of the ships' warp engines (and in the case of the *Akula* sub-class, on the exterior surfaces of the deflector pod support pylons). Also, the "starburst" deflector grid pattern utilized on some Singapore-built *Arbiter* group PAs was designed by the former executive officer of an *Akyazi* group ship; it was later approved by TacFleet for inclusion in the *Arbiter* vessels. Despite these freedoms, however, mission requirements impose certain limitations. Regulations permit a maximum of three tonal variations on a gray color scheme for all insignia that are displayed on exterior hull surfaces. This is necessary so as not to negate the advantages inherent in the ship's black and dark gray opalescent hull finishes. The dark hulls both emit and reflect far less electromagnetic energy than the standard white opalescent finish on most Class One starships, making *Akyazi*-class PAs more difficult to detect.

PERIMETER ACTION SHIP DEPLOYMENT COMPOSITION

Detailed deployment information regarding the *Akyazi*-class perimeter action ships, as with most front-line Star Fleet vessels, is classified. The information in this section is based on a combination of various elements, including port call records, civilian observations, general information made available by Star Fleet, and historical precedent. Only *Akyazi*-class perimeter action ships are included, although the PA groups listed may also include vessels from other perimeter action classes (especially the *Engage* [PA 1125] and *Kirsanov* [PA 1170] classes, now under construction) as well as other vessel types. Also, only those *Akyazi*-class PAs currently in service (or those scheduled to be commissioned before the end of 2290) are included in the listings. The home port for each PA group is listed in the second column. The data on actual PA assignments should be considered conjecture.

TacFleet
Commander, Rear Admiral
FLEET ONE NORTH

Battle Force
PA Group 6	Starbase 25	*Akitsu* (PA 1012)
		Buran (PA 1027)
		Akita (PA 1038)
PA Group 21	Starbase 14	*Brant* (PA 1033)
		Artika (PA 1060)

Patrol and Reconnaissance Force
| PA Group 10 | Star Station Indus | *Eire* (PA 1041) |

TacFleet
Commander, Rear Admiral
FLEET ONE SOUTH

Battle Force
PA Group 5	Starbase 21	*Biisk* (PA 1022)
		Bril (PA 1036)
		Ancylus (PA 1045)
		Aversa (PA 1070)

Patrol and Reconnaissance Force
| PA Group 33 | Star Station Aurora | *Epirus* (PA 1015) |
| | | *Tachira* (PA 1066) |

TacFleet
Commander, Rear Admiral
FLEET TWO NORTH

Battle Force
PA Group 31	Star Station Praeses	*Akyazi* (PA 1010)
		Beuel (PA 1026)
		Armavir (PA 1059)
PA Group 27	Starbase 16	*Accipiter* (PA 1035)
		Athy (PA 1092)

Patrol and Reconnaissance Force
| PA Group 11 | Starbase 29 | *Jico* (PA 1057) |
| | | *Tioga* (PA 1063) |

TacFleet
Commander, Vice Admiral
FLEET TWO SOUTH

Battle Force
PA Group 24	Star Station Tiran	*Astura* (PA 1011)
		Ephesus (PA 1023)
		Apia (PA 1053)
		Sjoto (PA 1098)
PA Group 19	Starbase 12	*Araxes* (PA 1030)
		Ebro (PA 1032)
PA Group 13	Starbase 11	*Kitkun* (PA 1091)
		Krka (PA 1104)

Patrol and Reconnaissance Force
| PA Group 47 | Star Station Tiran | *Jari* (PA 1058) |
| | | *Archer* (PA 1069) |

Tactical Transit Force
| PA Group 50 | Star Station Minsk | *Juist* (PA 1050) |
| | | *Almdes* (PA 1067) |

TacFleet
Commander, Rear Admiral
FLEET THREE NORTH

Battle Force
PA Group 15	Star Station Cepheus	*Braga* (PA 1013)
		Bisbee (PA 1037)
		Echo (PA 1042)
PA Group 18	Starbase 10	*Acerra* (PA 1049)
		Arvika (PA 1093)
		Sybaris (PA 1102)

Patrol and Reconnaissance Force
PA Group 14	Starbase 26	*Thun* (PA 1055)
		Abitibi (PA 1068)
		Jativa (PA 1071)

TacFleet
Commander, Vice Admiral
FLEET THREE SOUTH

Battle Force
PA Group 44	Starbase 9	*Alten* (PA 1019)
		Eiger (PA 1031)
PA Group 26	Outpost Neris	*Atuga* (PA 1028)
		Julin (PA 1065)
		Akula (PA 1090)
PA Group 41	Star Station Yalta	**Kuril* (PA 1094)
		Sandusky (PA 1099)
PA Group 23	Starbase 19	*Atago* (PA 1052)
		Thrace (PA 1064)

Patrol and Reconnaissance Force
PA Group 12	Star Station Brasilia	*Bucke* (PA 1020)
		Acri (PA 1039)
		Atessa (PA 1056)

Tactical Transit Force
PA Group 25	Starbase 27	*Ermont* (PA 1024)
		*Amastra (PA 1046)
PA Group 20	Star Station Yalta	*Arbiter* (PA 1048)
		Talence (PA 1062)

TacFleet
Commander, Rear Admiral
FLEET FOUR NORTH

Battle Force
PA Group 52	Starbase 7	*Ameer* (PA 1014)
		Acavus (PA 1025)
		Bendraze (PA 1040)
PA Group 38	Outpost Principale	*Bengal* (PA 1021)
		*Accra (PA 1047)

Patrol and Reconnaissance Force
PA Group 29	Star Station Dallas	*Amagi* (PA 1016)
		*Aparri (PA 1077)

TacFleet
Commander, Rear Admiral
FLEET FOUR SOUTH

Battle Force
PA Group 17	Starbase 15	*Eleusis* (PA 1018)
		Evian (PA 1043)
		Jelai (PA 1061)
PA Group 28	Outpost Ecija	*Saros* (PA 1096)
		Kern (PA 1100)

Patrol and Reconnaissance Force
PA Group 45	Star Station Eureka	*Avesta* (PA 1034)
		Abila (PA 1044)

Tactical Transit Force
PA Group 30	Star Station Eureka	*Tensas* (PA 1054)

*Scheduled to be commissioned before the end of 2290.

"Patience, Vigilance, Endurance"
Akyazi Class Insignia

The official insignia of the *Akyazi* class consists of many elements. The bottom of the inner circle is dominated by a fiery starburst. This represents the many distant suns on the Frontier, the area of operation for ships of the *Akyazi* class. Likewise, the purple band in the upper portion of the circle represents the energy fluctuations located at certain points along the galactic rim. This is symbolic of the continuing desire to expand Federation space and move the perimeter ever outward.

At the center of the design are white, silver, and gold stylized vectors. These vectors symbolize the three sub-classes (*Akyazi, Arbiter,* and *Akula*) that comprise the *Akyazi* class. (Note that no vector is leading any other in its ascent, indicative of the importance of each sub-class design.) The vectors also honor the achievements and accomplishments of early Terran spaceflight programs, specifically the *Apollo* program of the later twentieth century. (The insignia for *Apollo 15* consisted of three vectors in orbital flight over Luna.) The colors are a reference to the three precious metals of that period — platinum (white), silver, and gold. They also represent purity, duty, and honor, or alternately, the class motto, "Patience, Vigilance, Endurance."

Ship Classifications

Star Fleet ships and small craft are classified by type and by sequence within that type. The list of classifications (by approval of the Federation Commissioner of the Star Fleet) is issued periodically, updating a system that began in Earth-year 2208. Star Fleet's Class One list, considered definitive for Star Fleet Operating Forces at this moment, is indicated below.

The letter 'T' may be used as a suffix with any classification to denote a training vessel. Likewise, the letter 'X' is used unofficially as a suffix to indicate new or experimental designs or classes.

The following classifications are contained on the current list.

Class One Vessels

Cruisers

CH	Heavy Cruiser	Mk IX
CS	Strike Cruiser	Mk XX
CG	Battlecruiser	Mk XIII
CD	Through-Deck Cruiser	Mk XV
CKE	Large Exploratory Cruiser	Mk XXIII
CE	Exploratory Cruiser	Mk XXII
CA	Cruiser	Mk IV
CL	Light Cruiser	Mk III

Frigates

FH	Heavy Frigate	Mk XI
FR	Frigate	Mk V
FF	Fast Frigate	Mk XIX
FS	Small Frigate	Mk XXVII

Destroyers

DH	Heavy Destroyer	Mk XII
DD	Destroyer	Mk VIII

Scouts

SS	Superscout	Mk XVIII
ST	Scout	Mk VII

Patrol Combatants

DN	Dreadnought	Mk X
CO	Command Ship	Mk XXI
PKA	Large Perimeter Action Ship	Mk XXVI
PA	Perimeter Action Ship	Mk XXV
CV	Corvette	Mk XIV
CP	Clipper	Mk II
CR	Corsair	Mk I

Specialized

SC	Shuttlecarrier	Mk XVI
SO	Space Control Ship	Mk XVII

Class One Auxiliaries

Support Ships

TR	Transport	Mk XXIX
TT	Transport/Tug	Mk VI
TE	Tender	Mk XXX
SP	Combat Support Ship	Mk XXIV
ET	Escort	Mk XXVIII

Glossary

ADI a Tellarite acronym for a series of Bzevhistakis-built long-range sensor packages

ARU/SI Active Response Unit/Selective Integrity

ASL an engineering design acronym for a Scarbak emergency impulse drive system, currently installed in *Arbiter* and *Akula* group perimeter action ships (see FORS)

CCE an Andorian acronym for an Orage Ijek impulse engine configuration, currently installed in *Akyazi* group perimeter action ships (see CME)

CIDSS Close-In Deflector Shield System

CME an Andorian acronym for an Orage Ijek impulse engine configuration, currently installed in *Arbiter* and *Akula* group perimeter action ships (see CCE)

DCA/DSA Defense Cloaking Active/Defense Stasis Active countermeasure system

FORS an engineering design acronym for a Scarbak emergency impulse drive system, currently installed in *Akyazi* group perimeter action ships (see ASL)

Hung nawlogh Klingonese language variant, roughly translated as "security squadron"

IPP-1 Internal Perimeter Program One; a long-term research and development program conducted independently by Temerand Duplicat in the early 2280s

ISC Independently Sequenced Control

JAKA an engineering design acronym for an Asakaze Ordnance phaser system

KM kilometer

LIEN Logistical Intercept Encoding Net

LN Manufacturers' standard prefix for linear warp engine model numbers

MCH1 an engineering design acronym for a Cristobal gravity and atmosphere maintenance unit

MCM Motion Control Monitor

MD Multi-Directional, as in the Scarbak FORS MD emergency impulse drive system

MDS a Tellarite acronym for a Kal Achal deflector pod system in the "Bia" series

Mk Mark

Mod Model

MSC Military Staff Committee

NAVCAS Navigational Control And Sequencing

NCC Naval Construction Contract and/or Navigational Contact Code number

Nem Ankh from the Terran Old Egyptian, "Eternal Life"

NPC Navigational Processing Center

PAPE Perimeter Action Platform Experimental; a perimeter action ship development program funded by Star Fleet, active from May 2272 to March 2273

Pls places

P/S port and starboard

PSA Post-Shakedown Availability; refers to a vessel's return to the builder after approximately 6-10 months for systems and performance evaluation

QASR an Alpha Centaurian acronym for a Scarbak particle beam maneuvering thruster system

QEV Quadrillion Electron Volt

RAV/ISHAK a Coridanian acronym for a Tlixis Ramab Warp Celestial Guidance system (see RAV/TENEC)

RAV/TENEC a Coridanian acronym for a Tlixis Ramab Warp Celestial Guidance system, currently being installed in *Arbiter* group perimeter action ships (see RAV/ISHAK)

RCS Reaction Control System

SFD Star Fleet Division shipbuilding subsidiary

STRATAC Strategic and Tactical; sensor net functions independently; also operates in conjunction with holocom room (located immediately above on deck 5) to interpret and decipher incoming signals from dispatched intelligence and reconnaissance drones

TAVITAC a Keindoffer-Klaatsen tactical subsystem, named for its primary designer, Alexander Tavin

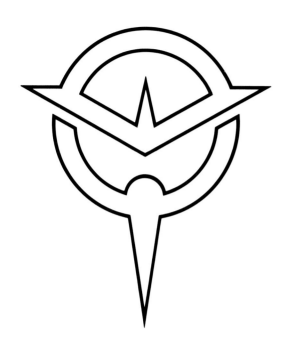

AKYAZI
Group Perimeter Action Ships

The *Akyazi*-class perimeter action ships (including the *Arbiter* and *Akula* sub-classes) are the largest group of Class One starships to be constructed since the *Ariadne* (CP 206)-class clippers were ordered in 2276 (127 vessels). These ships combine various aspects of scouts (speed), destroyers (weapons capacity), and intelligence platforms (sensing, listening, and jamming apparatus) into a single package, making them formidable perimeter defense units.

The *Akyazi* group is the "baseline" design for the *Akyazi* class. The ships' stealth characteristics and design "flexibility" resulted in performance parameters being met or exceeded in every category during acceptance trials. Their developmental history is noted below.

Class: The *Akyazi* class has a long and storied history in Star Fleet program proposals. The class name dates back to 2269 when 178 ships were proposed in the PA 1010 series; the current design, however, bears little resemblance to its aborted predecessors.

February 2269/Stardate 7629.4 -
Responding to an increase in the number of borderspace violations by various threat forces, Procurements Committee recommends Star Fleet Program Proposal No. 34714S - construction of 178 perimeter action platforms in the PA 1010 series and a minimum of four additional strike cruisers of the CS 2500 design.

July 2269 -
Orders for long-lead components for the *Decatur* (CS 2500) Class are placed with subcontractors; PA 1010 class, now dubbed *Akyazi,* enters Category II design phase.

January 2270 -
Star Fleet Requirements Analysis Board issues list of design parameters for the *Akyazi* class. Category III design phase begins and five firms prepare design proposals:

Arias Mastac, Carina, Cosmadyne, Star Fleet Division-Baltic, and Temerand Duplicat.
A Federation Council subcommittee, assembled by Councillor Eso Procuia, questions the need for 178 ships of the perimeter action type and begins an independent investigation.

August 2270 -
TacFleet and Bureau of Spacecraft officials conduct simulation studies on project test articles submitted by the competing firms. The Carina design is the front-runner, benefiting from a low profile and stealth features.

November 2270 -
Councillor Procuia's subcommittee issues its controversial report of findings and, with engineering testimony and data from the publication *Merrel's Fleet Review* adding weight to the "bigger is better" argument, the *Akyazi* program is not only reduced but put on temporary hold altogether.

The Military Staff Committee orders an additional 15 strike cruisers of the *Decatur* design (CS 2501-14, 2519) on 11 November, bringing the total number to 20.

21 October 2271 -
Construction begins on the second ship in the *Decatur* class, U.S.S. *Belknap* (CS 2501), at Cosmadyne's Boston Division shipyards. Numerous improvements are to be incorporated into the design (4½ Earth-years have passed since the commissioning of the lead vessel) and the ships will eventually be redesignated *Belknap* class.

May 2272 -
Star Fleet successfully lobbies for funding of the PAPE (Perimeter Action Platform Experimental) long-term development program on the basis of needing an eventual follow-on to the large numbers of aging and outdated *Kiaga* (PA 826)- and *Agilis*

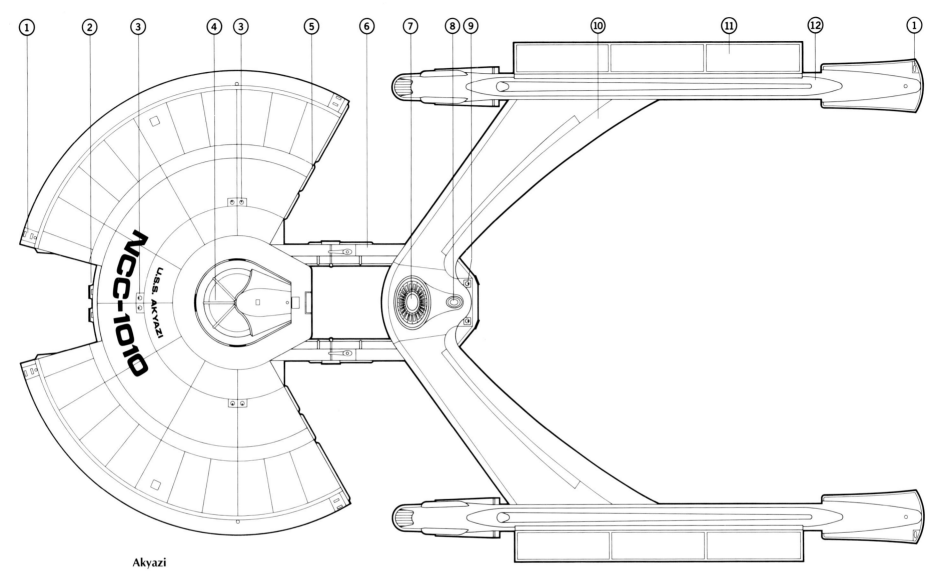

Akyazi

1. Kenelex reaction control system   2. Mk 5 Komati torpedo tubes   3. JAKA-2 phaser banks   4. bridge deflector shield enhancement   5. sensor pallets   6. propulsion section support pylons   7. impulse amplification crystal (primary)   8. impulse amplification crystal (secondary)   9. JAKA-5 phaser banks   10. warp engine support pylons   11. warp field reflector   12. LN-90 Mod 1 warp drive units

(PA 855)-class perimeter action ships. Avondale and Temerand Duplicat begin design programs.

7 August 2272 -

Kzin vessels attack Tau Ceti and begin a six-week offensive action against Federation forces. Star Fleet response is swift, but 11 Class One starships and dozens of Kzin vessels are lost. Kznti forces are finally defeated at Zetar in September.

March 2273 -

Preliminary Evaluation tests are conducted on the 1/3-scale prototypes constructed by Avondale and Temerand. The designs are radically different and neither meets the performance parameters for flight compatibility set down by the Star Fleet Requirements Board. The PAPE program is terminated.

December 2273 -

The Cammell IV revelations concerning Star Fleet's covert operations against the Kzin prior to the Kznti Incursion result in massive cutbacks in Fleet programs. The Federation Council temporarily freezes all Class One starship construction; the *Akyazi* program is put on indefinite hold (where it will remain for nearly ten Earth-years).

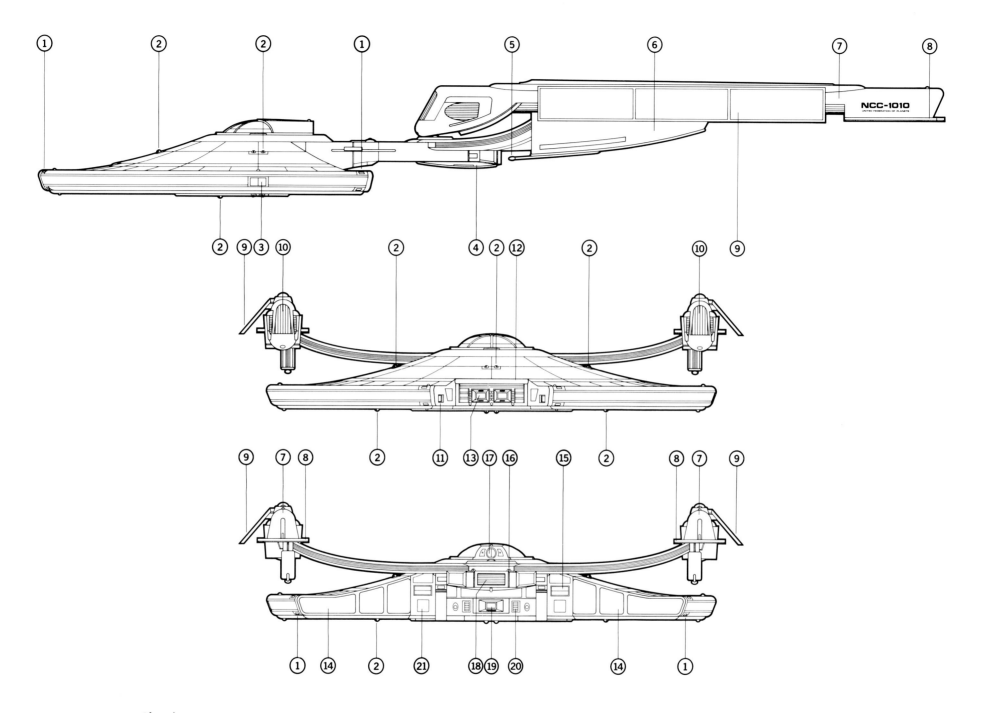

NCC-1010

Akyazi

1. Kenelex reaction control system   2. JAKA-2 phaser banks   3. gangway hatch   4. engineering pod   5. deflector spires   6. deflector spire dissipation assembly   7. LN-90 Mod 1 warp drive units   8. intercooler assembly   9. warp field reflector   10. acquisition vanes
11. QASR maneuvering thrusters   12. Ochu deflector array   13. Mk 5 Komati torpedo tubes   14. sensor pallets   15. workbee stowage
16. JAKA-5 phaser banks   17. bridge docking port   18. CCE impulse engine   19. Mk 9 Boris torpedo tube   20. photon exhaust vanes
21. lifeboat emplacement

Number	Name	Builder	Laid Down	Launched	Commissioned	Status
NCC-1010	Akyazi	Arbing & Lidde Starship Construction, Boston, Earth	16 June 2284	20 Dec 2285	11 Oct 2286	**ATAC**
NCC-1011	Astura	Carina Design & Construction, Tanami Spacebridge, Australia, Earth	05 Sept 2284	19 Feb 2286	22 Nov 2286	**ATAC**
NCC-1012	Akitsu	Arbing & Lidde Starship Construction, Boston, Earth	29 July 2284	04 Jan 2286	17 Oct 2286	**ATAC**
NCC-1013	Braga	Star Fleet Division, Alfras Naval Yards, Deneb V	SD 8520.10	SD 8559.23	SD 8571.15	**ATAC**
NCC-1014	Ameer	Carina Design & Construction, Tanami Spacebridge, Australia, Earth	11 May 2285	21 July 2286	08 Jan 2287	**ATAC**
NCC-1015	Epirus	Rapier Dynamics Group, Melbourne Division, Earth	14 Aug 2284	28 Jan 2286	03 Nov 2286	**ATAC**
NCC-1016	Amagi	Star Fleet Division, Alfras Naval Yards, Deneb V	SD 8611.05	SD 8653.19	SD 8667.21	**ATAC**
NCC-1017	Abreus	Newport News Shipbuilding, Louisiana, Earth	09 July 2284	15 Dec 2285	16 Sept 2286	Lost
NCC-1018	Eleusis	Star Fleet Division, Baltic Yards, Leningrad, Earth	24 Nov 2284	15 Jan 2286	28 Sept 2286	**ATAC**
NCC-1019	Alten	Avondale Group, New Dallas, Rigel IV	SD 7971.21	SD 7999.21	SD 8010.45	**ATAC**
NCC-1020	Bucke	Newport News Shipbuilding, Louisiana, Earth	28 June 2284	11 Dec 2285	30 Aug 2286	**ATAC**
NCC-1021	Bengal	Arbing & Lidde Starship Construction, Boston, Earth	30 Dec 2285	07 Apr 2287	03 Nov 2287	**ATAC**
NCC-1022	Biisk	Carina Design & Construction, Tanami Spacebridge, Australia, Earth	24 Aug 2285	29 Oct 2286	12 May 2287	**ATAC**
NCC-1023	Ephesus	Avondale Group, New Dallas, Rigel IV	SD 7993.61	SD 8022.94	SD 8040.63	**ATAC**
NCC-1024	Ermont	Rapier Dynamics Group, Melbourne Division, Earth	27 Nov 2284	20 Mar 2286	05 Dec 2286	**ATAC**
NCC-1025	Acavus	Star Fleet Division, Baltic Yards, Leningrad, Earth	19 Nov 2284	16 Feb 2286	27 Aug 2286	**ATAC**
NCC-1026	Beuel	Arbing & Lidde Starship Construction, Boston, Earth	13 Jan 2286	29 Apr 2287	25 Oct 2287	**ATAC**
NCC-1027	Buran	Avondale Group, New Dallas, Rigel IV	SD 8035.84	SD 8074.27	SD 8091.10	**ATAC**
NCC-1028	Atuga	Star Fleet Division, Alfras Naval Yards, Deneb V	SD 8654.18	SD 8687.73	SD 8699.44	**ATAC**
NCC-1029	Arauca	Newport News Shipbuilding, Louisiana, Earth	29 Nov 2285	08 Feb 2287	12 Aug 2287	Lost
NCC-1030	Araxes	Carina Design & Construction, Tanami Spacebridge, Australia, Earth	15 Dec 2285	25 Mar 2287	27 Aug 2287	**ATAC**
NCC-1031	Eiger	Star Fleet Division, Alfras Naval Yards, Deneb V	SD 8681.15	SD 8715.42	SD 8729.32	**ATAC**
NCC-1032	Ebro	Star Fleet Division, Baltic Yards, Leningrad, Earth	29 Oct 2285	06 Dec 2286	02 May 2287	**ATAC**
NCC-1033	Brant	Arbing & Lidde Starship Construction, Boston, Earth	17 Nov 2286	03 Jan 2288	19 June 2288	**ATAC**
NCC-1034	Avesta	Arbing & Lidde Starship Construction, Boston, Earth	26 Oct 2286	30 Dec 2287	03 June 2288	**ATAC**
NCC-1035	Accipiter	Rapier Dynamics Group, Melbourne Division, Earth	15 Jan 2285	03 May 2286	29 Nov 2286	**ATAC**
NCC-1036	Bril	Avondale Group, New Dallas, Rigel IV	SD 8071.06	SD 8109.33	SD 8127.93	**ATAC**
NCC-1037	Bisbee	Newport News Shipbuilding, Louisiana, Earth	15 Oct 2286	06 Jan 2288	30 June 2288	**ATAC**
NCC-1038	Akita	Rapier Dynamics Group, Melbourne Division, Earth	20 Nov 2285	21 Jan 2287	11 July 2287	**ATAC**
NCC-1039	Acri	Newport News Shipbuilding, Louisiana, Earth	12 Jan 2287	26 Feb 2288	07 July 2288	**ATAC**
NCC-1040	Bendraze	Star Fleet Division, Baltic Yards, Leningrad, Earth	17 July 2286	05 Sept 2287	25 Feb 2288	**ATAC**
NCC-1041	Eire	Carina Design & Construction, Tanami Spacebridge, Australia, Earth	27 Jan 2287	04 Mar 2288	15 Aug 2288	**ATAC**
NCC-1042	Echo	Carina Design & Construction, Tanami Spacebridge, Australia, Earth	23 May 2287	02 Aug 2288	24 Apr 2289	**ATAC**
NCC-1043	Evian	Arbing & Lidde Starship Construction, Boston, Earth	14 Feb 2288	23 May 2289	02 Nov 2289	**ATAC**
NCC-1044	Abila	Arbing & Lidde Starship Construction, Boston, Earth	05 Apr 2288	17 June 2289	03 Dec 2289	**ATAC**
NCC-1045	Ancylus	Arbing & Lidde Starship Construction, Boston, Earth	21 June 2288	29 Sept 2289		Building
NCC-1046	Amastra	Arbing & Lidde Starship Construction, Boston, Earth	25 Sept 2288	15 Dec 2289		Building
NCC-1047	Accra	Newport News Shipbuilding, Louisiana, Earth	13 Mar 2288	11 July 2289		Building

July 2276-February 2277 -

Recently seated Councillor Arman Thel introduces several plebiscites aimed at re-instituting debate on the validity of a new perimeter action program. Despite promised support from various Council members, the issue is not tabled during any of seven Council sessions.

April 2280 -

Temerand Duplicat funds an internal company design program quietly dubbed IPP-1 (Internal Perimeter Program One). The company's Martian facility begins conducting independent research and development in an effort to produce several PA designs that would be acceptable to Star Fleet should the perimeter action program be reinstated.

30 May 2283 -

The Taal Tan Offensive by Klingon forces shakes the Federation Council; the pacifist bloc falls out of favor. The appointment of Lars-Erik Valdemar as Federation Commissioner on 08 June signifies Council support for a program of Fleet rejuvenation.

July 2283 -

A new Temerand Duplicat design is chosen as the basis for the reinstated Akyazi perimeter action program. The testing phase is accelerated due to the ongoing Taal Tan Offensive and simulation studies reveal few major problems with the basic design.

August 2283 -

The Military Staff Committee authorizes 105 Akyazi (PA 1010)-class perimeter action ships (reduced from the 178 vessels of 2269 proposals) on 02 August. Thirty-eight

MERLIN II DEFLECTOR SYSTEM
OPERATIONAL PARAMETERS

AKYAZI GROUP
Class One - Mk XXV
PORT PERSPECTIVE
BOTTOM PLAN

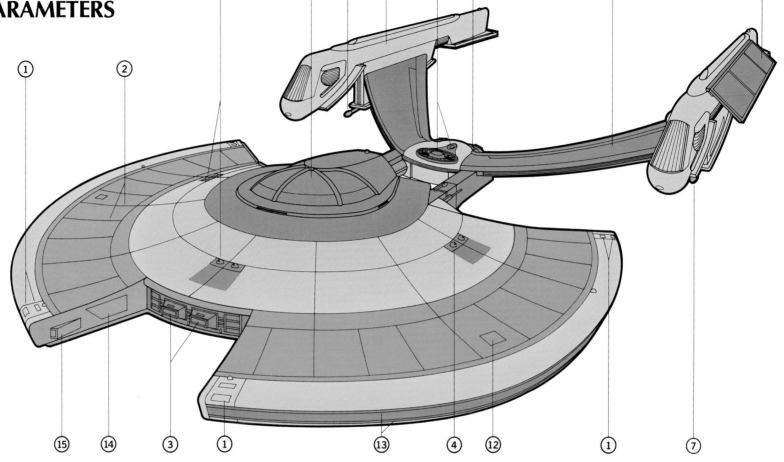

RELATIVE FIELD STRENGTH AT
STANDARD COMBAT PROTOCOL -
Percentage of Assigned Generator Output

▮ PRIMARY 59%

▯ SECONDARY 23%

▮ TERTIARY 18%

1. Kenelex reaction control system   2. defensive systems
grid   3. Mk 5 Komati torpedo tubes   4. JAKA-2 phaser
banks   5. bridge   6. LN-90 Mod 1 warp drive units   7. deflector
spire   8. impulse amplification crystals   9. JAKA-5 phaser
banks   10. warp engine support pylons   11. Kreddick warp field
reflector   12. personnel hatch   13. lateral defensive systems
grid   14. photon torpedo flash shields   15. QASR maneuvering
thrusters

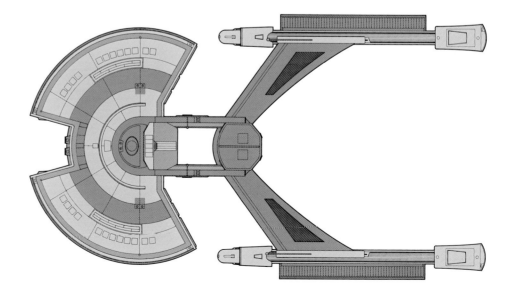

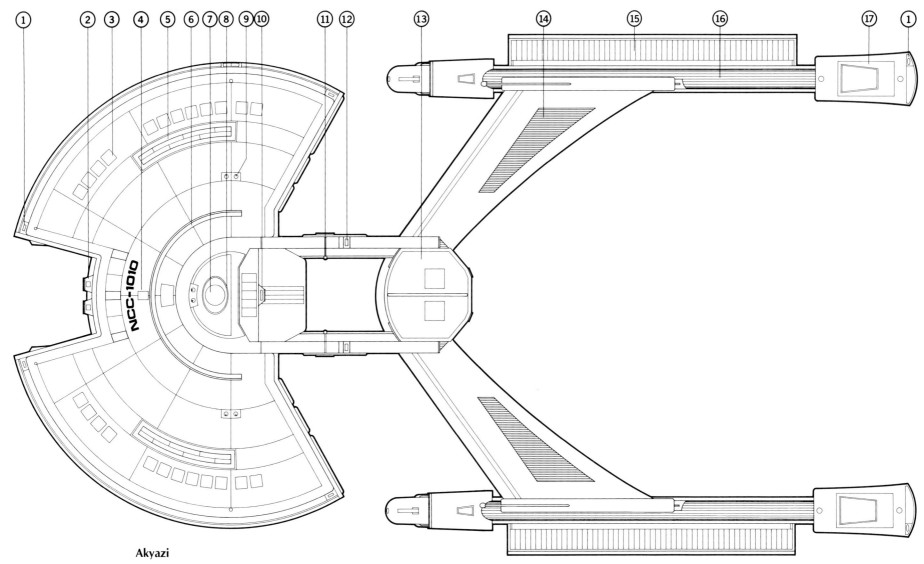

Akyazi

1. Kenelex reaction control system   2. MK 5 Komati torpedo tubes   3. lifeboat emplacements   4. emergency eject (weapons crew)
5. FORS emergency impulse engines   6. Shim sensor assembly   7. McCook primary sensor array   8. tractor beam ring   9. JAKA-2
phaser banks   10. Mk 9 Boris torpedo tube   11. explosive bolt separation   12. QASR maneuvering thrusters   13. engineering
pod   14. emergency flush vents   15. warp field reflector   16. warp field generator assembly   17. intercooler assembly

ships are officially ordered on 17 August; seven construction firms will be contracted.

The MSC and senior TacFleet policymakers issue strict guidelines to the contractors regarding PA mission doctrine and systems compatibility requirements. Among several mandates are the following: "[Akyazi] perimeter action vessels will be the primary focus in Star Fleet's strategic objective of moving from a posture of spherical defense to one of point defense as quickly as possible under anticipated threat force scenarios. As such, all ship systems (communication, propulsion, etc.) will be dedicated to achieving a point defense situation so as to bring defensive weapons to bear with all possible haste."

January 2284 -

Prototype test article evaluations continue on shell prototypes No. 2 and 3 at Temerand. Some changes include: improvement of recognition profile and stealth characteristics by elimination of a sixth deck in the main hull; incorporation of the "Fier" LN-90 warp units into the design, replacing the larger LN-83 system; creation of a "double boom" structure to separate engineering functions from the main hull, resulting in greater warp maneuverability and enhanced safety characteristics.

Prototype No. 1 is loaned to TacFleet for security evaluations.

Current specifications of *Akyazi* sub-class:

Displacement:	68,000 metric tons standard
	(66,800mt light, 69,000mt full load)
	NCC-1043-46: 67,000 metric tons standard
	(66,200mt light, 68,000mt full load)

	Overall	Primary Hull	Nacelles
Length:	216.1m	78.9m	126.7m
Beam:	120.2m	107.6m	16.2m
Draft:	27.5m	18.2m	13.1m

Propulsion:	Two (2) "Fier" LN-90 Mod 1 dilithium-energized antimatter linear warp drive units
	(System contractor: Vickers Engineering Group Ltd., Cumbria, Earth)
	One (1) "Delum" CCE subatomic unified energy impulse unit
	(System contractor: Orage Ijek, Aksajak, Andor)
	Two (2) FORS MD emergency impulse thrust units
	QASR enhanced particle beam maneuvering thrusters
	(Systems contractor: Scarbak Propulsion Systems, Cairo, Earth)
	"Kenelex" pulsed laser reaction control system
	(System contractor: Orage Ijek, Aksajak, Andor)
Velocity:	Warp 8, standard
	Warp 14, maximum
	Warp 21.5, battle maximum
Acceleration:	Rest-Onset Critical Momentum: 2.05 sec
	Onset Critical Momentum-Warp Engage: .68 sec

	Warp 1-Warp 4:	.19 sec
	Warp 4-Warp 8:	.11 sec
	Warp 8-Warp 14:	1.28 sec
	Warp 14-Warp 21.5:	2.01 sec

Duration:	2 Earth years, standard
	3.25 Earth years, maximum
Complement:	84 (8 officers + 76 crew)
	NCC-1033, 1034, 1037, 1039-46: 80 (8 officers + 72 crew)
Embarked craft:	None
Navigation:	NAVCAS Select, Warp Celestial Guidance
	(System contractor: Prinzhenri S.N., Rio de Janeiro, Earth)
Computers:	"Ilorin" Duotronic IV
	(System contractor: Kuchata Pratus Ikyla, Arrasta, Daran V)
	NCC-1013, 1016, 1018, 1025, 1028, 1031, 1032, 1040: Datatac Support Subsystem
	(System contractor: Farranti Mnemonics, Berkshire, Earth)
Phasers:	6 banks of 2 each - JAKA-2 independent twin mount
	2 banks - JAKA-5 single mount
	NCC-1013, 1016, 1018, 1025, 1028, 1031, 1032, 1040: 6 banks of 2 each - JAKA-2 independent twin mount
	(Systems contractor: Asakaze Ordnance Systems Ltd., Honshu-Hamamatsu, Earth)
Photon torpedoes:	2 tubes - Mk 5 "Komati" independent
	1 tube - Mk 9 "Boris" independent
	(Systems contractor: Arvan Toy Conglessum, Binz, Tellar)
Defense:	"Merlin II" primary force field and deflector control system
	NCC-1021, 1026, 1033, 1034, 1043-46: CIDSS (heavy) Deflector Supplement
	"Orissa" cloaking generation and stasis countermeasure system
	(Systems contractor: Prentice-Schafer Inc., Marsport, Mars)
	"Nike" weapon system (enhanced)
	TAVITAC Tactical Subsystem
	(Systems contractor: Keindoffer-Klaatsen DSC, Munich, Earth)
	"Saco Onorvoz" deflector spires
	(System contractor: Kal Achal Conglessum, Takuv, Tellar)
Life support:	MCH1 Modular Gravity and Atmosphere Maintenance Unit
	"Brida" radiation protection package
	(Systems contractor: Cristobal SM/S, Manila, Earth)
	"Lenix" waste regeneration systems
	(System contractor: Jullundur-Lahore Ltd., Bombay, Earth)

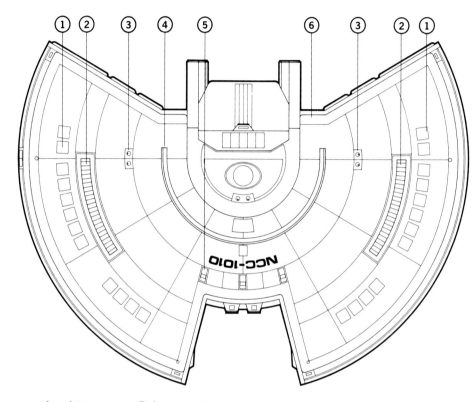

Akyazi (emergency flight posture)

1. lifeboat emplacements   2. FORS emergency impulse engines (minus covers)   3. JAKA-2 phaser banks   4. Shim sensor assembly   5. additional QASR maneuvering thrusters (minus covers)   6. sensor platform

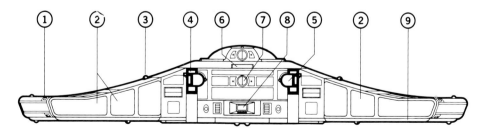

Akyazi (cross-section at pylon bolt, frame 224)

1. Kenelex reaction control system   2. sensor pallets   3. JAKA-2 phaser banks   4. structural bulkheads   5. pylon transfer tube   6. lounge viewport   7. Deck 3 docking port   8. Mk 9 Boris torpedo tube   9. sensor platform

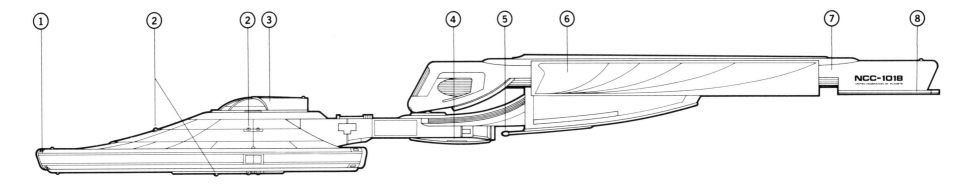

Eleusis

1. Kenelex reaction control system   2. JAKA-2 phaser banks   3. bridge   4. engineering pod   5. deflector spires   6. warp field reflector   7. LN-90 Mod 1 warp drive units   8. intercooler assembly

---

Akyazi Class Performance Characteristics: Planned vs. Realized

The basic *Akyazi* starship design (i.e. those design aspects common to all three sub-classes) is based on 100% power expenditure to achieve stated mission parameters. This design philosophy is a result of Star Fleet's present approach to strategic perimeter defense requirements. Consequently, the *Akyazi* (and *Arbiter*)-class perimeter action ships can achieve higher speeds (for shorter periods of time) than any other Class One starships.

During pre-construction simulation studies it was estimated that the basic *Akyazi* design, under ideal conditions, would be capable of achieving a maximum velocity of warp 12.5-13, and a battle maximum (i.e. limited duration) velocity of approximately warp 19.25-19.75. However, early deployments soon proved these estimates too conservative. On separate occasions, starships *Akyazi* (PA 1010), *Amagi* (PA 1016), *Alten* (PA 1019), *Bengal* (PA 1021), and *Ermont* (PA 1024) all surpassed design velocity limits without exceeding specified safety parameters. (On stardate 8827.3, the *Amagi* achieved warp 23.97 for nearly one minute while in pursuit of Kel family Orion fast attack craft.) Additionally, the PSA schedules of the first ten ships launched (PA 1010-13, 1015-20) revealed fewer initial operational deficiencies than expected.

The lack of excess mass at the centerpoint of the *Akyazi* design (i.e. the "double boom" configuration) resulted in greater "warp flexibility" than anticipated and contributed to the surpassing of various other parameters including acceleration times (estimates exceeded by 11%), post-warp braking (4%), and stress tolerance factors at critical hull points (increasing projected service life by approximately 8-12 Earth-years).

The PSA schedules of those ships involved in combat actions revealed less fatigue in ships weapon systems (particularly the phaser turret assemblies) than had been anticipated. There had been some concern among the designers of the phaser system that its high output capacity (greater than any other Class One starship, albeit in short "bursts") might overload the damping and cancelling ability of the Kyturonium-lined turrets. However, extensive testing of in-port vessels revealed deterioration well within established norms.

March 2284 -

All major design features are finalized and approved by the Requirements Board. The first production ship, the *Akyazi*, will be built by Arbing & Lidde beginning in June. Temerand is informed it will not receive a slot in the construction schedule for the initial order of 38 ships.

Eleven members of a support crew are killed when a temporary bulkhead baffle ruptures on Prototype No. 2 during post-warp stress analysis tests.

16 June 2284 -

Work begins on the *Akyazi* (PA 1010) at Arbing & Lidde Starship Construction, Boston, Earth.

Classification: The *Akyazi* class was ordered under a perimeter action ship (PA) classification in August 2283; the *Akyazi* sub-class was officially ordered as PA 1010 through PA 1047.

Design: Virtually all of the evaluation studies and "final fit" systems testing for this sub-class was performed on the *Akyazi* (the Temerand-built test articles were configured to somewhat different warp geometries and utilized numerous different sub-systems). The *Bucke* (PA 1020) was the first ship of the class to be launched and participated in warp field propagation tests before and immediately after her commissioning.

The later Arbing & Lidde ships (PA 1043-46) have lower displacement figures due to the elimination of redundant reinforcement features within the "twin boom" support pylons.

All ships of the *Akyazi* sub-class possess multiple stealth characteristics, foremost among these the "Orissa" cloaking generation system. However, it should also be noted that from the outset the design team was instructed to create a hull form that was both psychologically challenging to potential humanoid adversaries as well as superior in its ability to deceive enemy sensing and scanning systems. This was partially achieved by the incorporation of a "low recognition profile" in the *Akyazi* (and *Arbiter*) sub-classes, i.e. the ships have a very low draft (approximately 28 meters). Further, while scanning any ship at warp speed can be difficult, scanning an *Akyazi*

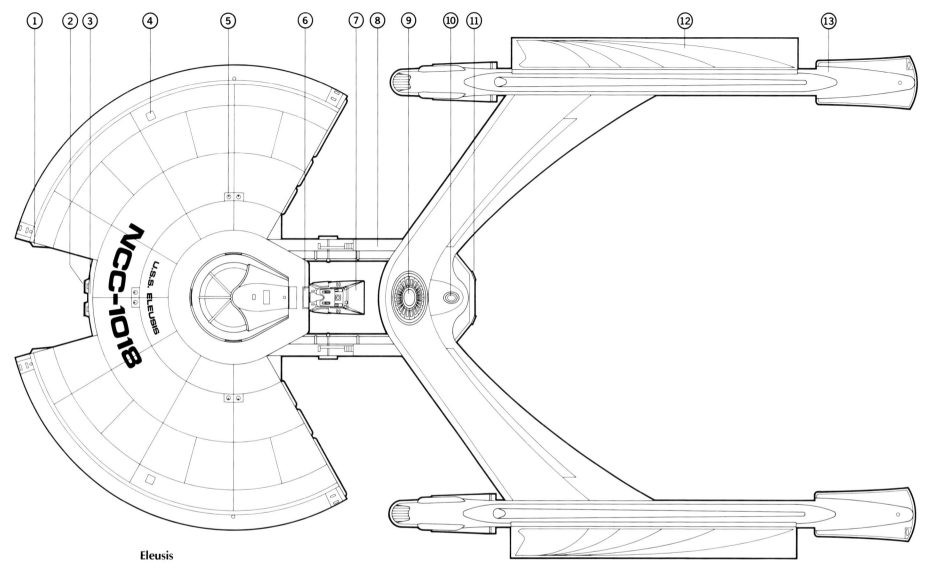

Eleusis

1. QASR maneuvering thrusters   2. Mk 5 Komati torpedo tubes   3. Ochu deflector array   4. personnel hatch   5. JAKA-2 phaser banks   6. lounge viewport   7. Star Fleet standard shuttlecraft   8. propulsion section support pylons   9. impulse amplification crystal (primary)   10. impulse amplification crystal (secondary)   11. impulse drive fusion reactor covers   12. warp field reflector   13. LN-90 Mod 1 warp drive units

class vessel is an even more formidable task because of its very negligible "subspace signature." The resulting warp bubble creates an almost insignificant turbulence reading on threat force sensor systems. Additional stealth advantages are achieved by the inclusion of a countermeasures subsystem within the ships' respective cloaking systems - the "Orissa" units in the *Akyazi* group and the DCA/DSA configuration in the *Arbiter* sub-class. These subsystems provide the PAs with the ability to produce false sensor images, multiple sensor echoes, and/or contradictory recognition readings in an attempt to further confuse and deceive threat force detection systems and their operators. This array of features helps make the *Akyazi*-class perimeter action ships

more difficult to detect than other Class One starships of similar size.

These ships are fitted with the NAVCAS Select primary navigation suite. This is a modified and downsized version of the system currently in use aboard *Cyane* (FH 1890)-class heavy frigates.

The Kuchata-built "Ilorin" Duotronic computer system is supplemented by the Datatac subsystem in the SFD-built ships only. The Datatac support units were provided to more efficiently augment those ships' phaser systems, since all of the other vessels in this sub-class carry an additional pair of single mount phaser banks (see *Weapons*).

Engineering: The "Fier" LN-90 warp units are fitted in all ships. These engines are the progenitors of the later LN-91 and (to a slightly lesser extent) LN-94 models (see *Arbiter* and *Akula* sub-classes). Vickers Engineering was awarded the contract to design the units specifically for this class.

The FORS emergency impulse units were incorporated into the *Akyazi* sub-class late in the design stage. There was much debate and disagreement among senior members of the design team and Star Fleet officials about the need for the units. In the end, however, the survival of the ship and crew were deemed paramount and the FORS units were incorporated into the bottom of the primary hull. In the event they are needed (primary hull integrity must be maintained and the entire propulsion package must be abandoned), the ship's RCS system must first flight-correct the hull to its destination coordinates. After the covers are blown, the emergency impulse units can be engaged with both the enhanced QASR units and the RCS system providing in-flight adjustment. The FORS system has its own fuel supply (30 cells, 15 for each unit) and can be fired continuously at full power for approximately 260 hours. This provides the ship and its surviving crew with the potential ability to reach a nearby outpost, deep space station, or, at the very least, access a communications lane to relay a rescue signal if the ship's own communication system has failed.

Weapons: The JAKA series phaser banks are fitted in the *Akyazi* class. This is a high-output phaser system with the capability of delivering a more powerful phaser discharge (in brief salvos) than any other system currently in use aboard Class One starships. A total of eight banks (including two on the impulse platform) are fitted in all but the SFD-built ships, which have six.

The *Akyazi* sub-class utilizes a three-tube photon torpedo system - two "Komati" bow units and one "Boris" stern unit. Both the photon torpedo assemblies and the JAKA phaser units are directed by the enhanced "Nike" weapon system, which was developed by Keindoffer-Klaatsen especially for the *Akyazi* class. The later Arbing & Lidde ships, beginning with the *Bengal* (PA 1021), have the "Merlin II" unit supplemented by the CIDSS (heavy) Deflector Supplement, which is more powerful than the standard CIDSS configuration.

Operational: The *Eleusis* (PA 1018) and *Acavus* (PA 1025) engaged Orion vessels near the Klingon border on 11 January 2287. The four Orion craft were surveilled by intelligence units for several stardates and were known to be engaged in smuggling operations. After a brief skirmish, all four ships were rendered threat-negative when their propulsion systems were neutralized by torpedo salvos from *Eleusis* and *Acavus*. This marked the first battle action involving *Akyazi*-class perimeter action ships.

The first encounter with Klingon forces occurred on 27 April 2287. In an unmistakable attempt to gain information on PA performance characteristics, the battle skiffs *K'trk* and *K'lss* ventured more than seven parsecs into Federation territory. The *Akitsu* (PA 1012) was forced to challenge the ships near Korta Fe. The Klingons responded with disruptor fire and the initiation of a predetermined attack maneuver. The *Akitsu* jumped to warp and in less than two minutes had eliminated the offensive capability of *K'trk* and forced the retreat of a badly damaged *K'lss*.

Two members of the *Akyazi* sub-class were not as fortunate as their aforementioned sister ships. On 03 April 2289, the *Abreus* (PA 1017) responded to a distress call from what was believed to be a TacFleet intelligence ship. Upon arriving at the confirmed coordinates in the three south area, however, the *Abreus* was ambushed by no fewer than seven hostile vessels. Debris analysis revealed the weaponry to be of Romulan origin, but Star Fleet intelligence experts believe units of a Klingon *Hung nawlogh* (perhaps utilizing Romulan vessels) were responsible.

The *Arauca* (PA 1029) encountered heavily-armed, unidentified spacecraft at the subquadrant four north perimeter on stardate 8922.6. Due to deployment limitations in the area, the *Arauca* was forced to "shadow" the unidentified units in an attempt to gain information and stall for time. After a period of several hours the *Arauca* was informed by an area command ship that Star Fleet contact specialists were too far distant to provide immediate assistance. With the alien vessels moving closer to sensitive installations and deeper into Federation space, the *Arauca* was forced to confront the ships on 8922.79. After transmitting linguacode friendship messages and attempting to communicate by other methods, the *Arauca* engaged the unidentified spacecraft after being fired upon three times. The ensuing battle saw the *Arauca* destroyed after inflicting significant amounts of damage on several of the unidentified units, as indicated by the ship's recorder marker. Second tier perimeter units arrived too late to provide assistance. The alien ships are believed to have withdrawn beyond Treaty territory; additional Fleet units were assigned to the area and Star Fleet's investigation is continuing.

Nomenclature: All of the perimeter action ships in the *Akyazi* sub-class have names that begin with the letter 'A,' 'B,' or 'E.'

ypes after *Akyazi* design finalization
ovement tests for the *Arbiter* design
oorated into later ships of the *Akyazi*
all completed between early-March
iation studies.

bles simultaneous evaluations to be
:elerating the *Akyazi* and *Arbiter* test
ire conducted beginning 17 May,
haracteristics, task force capability,
Assignment of the prototype PAs to
:signations are announced:

configuration per TacFleet require-
o *Akyazi* specifications.

structural stress analyzation testing.
and engine height above centerline

al and like-systems integration on a
ondary and redundant units. Sched-
and reliability demonstrations and

mpulse ship," assigned to sub-light
iltiple-redundant studies of the ASL

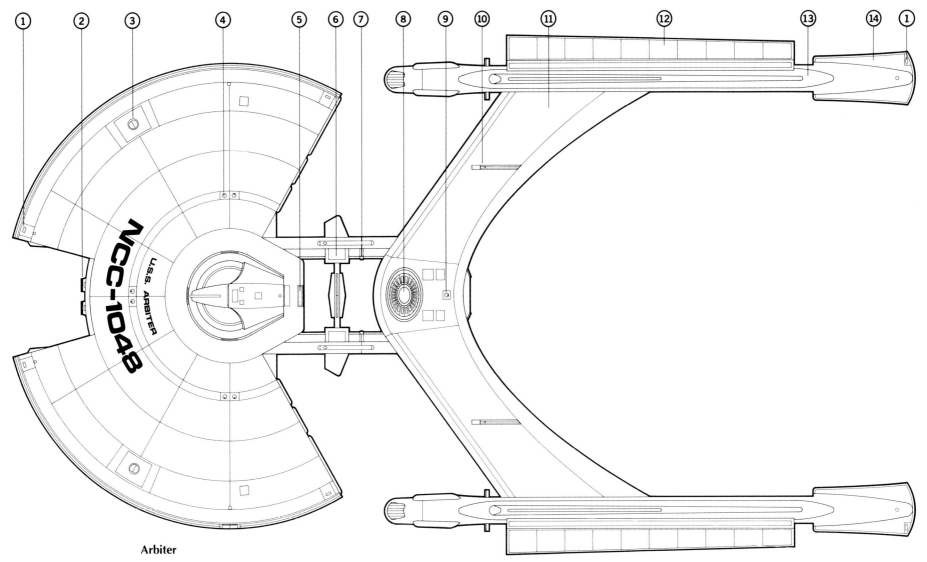

Arbiter

1. Kenelex reaction control system   2. Mk 20 Teviot torpedo tubes   3. topside docking ports   4. JAKA-2 phaser banks   5. lounge viewport   6. Iulus Protective Envelope generator   7. explosive bolt separation   8. impulse amplification crystal   9. JAKA-5 phaser bank   10. sensor emplacement   11. warp engine support pylons   12. warp field reflector   13. LN-91 Mod 1 warp drive units   14. intercooler assembly

Prototype No. 5 (Star Fleet) - Loaned to Prentice-Schafer for incorporation and evaluation of the "Iulus" Protective Envelope deflector system. Additional (experimental) defensive units tested, including the "Portico" sectional deflector system and "Jort" series deflector spires.

Prototype No. 6 (Star Fleet) - Assigned to Starbase 6 for evaluation of the "Nike" (enhanced) weapon system and related subsystems. Operational (live-fire) phaser and photon torpedo systems installed and activated for evaluation with the "Nike" unit.

Prototype No. 7 (Star Fleet) - Assigned to Starbase 8 for testing of task force compatibility and capacity to interface with established Class One Fleet units in a variety of multi-ship scenarios.

Prototypes No. 8, 9, 10 (Star Fleet) - Designated flight training craft for command crew compatibility and familiarity evaluations. Those senior officers that have been assigned to *Akyazi* class command crews begin rotation to these fully-outfitted prototypes for "operational familiarity" deployments of limited duration. Crew assignment and mix is based on the present availability of the officers who are called. Rotations begin out of Starbase 2.

ARBITER
Group Perimeter Action Ships

Like their earlier sister ships, vessels of the *Arbiter* sub-class were designed to be fast, stealthy, and well-armed. These 41 ships (the *Arashi* [PA 1051] was lost on 17 February 2288) represent the intermediate construction group, bearing much greater resemblance to the *Akyazi* sub-class than to the later *Akula* ships. Building on the basic *Akyazi* design, they are augmented with the "Iulus" Protective Envelope system and an additional rear-firing torpedo tube. Construction of this sub-class was delayed to take advantage of both the "Iulus" system and the ASL series emergency impulse units, neither of which was available when the *Akyazi* sub-class began building in 2284.

Class: These ships were officially ordered on 02 October 2284, almost 14 months after the *Akyazi* sub-class. There was some debate as to how many ships to include in this group and how many to build to the substantially different *Akula* design. Long-range deployment scenarios required a minimum of 20 ships of the *Akula* design. By increasing the number of *Arbiter*-type ships from 35 to 42 vessels, Star Fleet was still able to meet its minimum requirement for *Akula*-type construction. The number and frequency of threat force aggressive actions during this period was a factor in this decision, as was the more expensive per-unit cost of the *Akula* PA design.

March 2284/Stardate 8315.6 -

Temerand design teams, working closely with the designers of the "Iulus" Protective Envelope system and the ASL emergency impulse package, develop modifications to the basic *Akyazi* design which allow for the incorporation of these units.

April 2284 -

TacFleet returns Prototype No. 1 after concluding security evaluation tests on the basic *Akyazi* design. Seventeen modifications are required, including improvement of long-range sensor capability and relocation of the internal security area.

Star Fleet clears access to the No. 2 and 3 prototypes after *Akyazi* design finalization is completed. Temerand begins substructure improvement tests for the *Arbiter* design (some of the resulting improvements will be incorporated into later ships of the *Akyazi* sub-class). Temerand's prototypes 4 through 11, all completed between early-March and mid-April, are activated for testing and evaluation studies.

May 2284 -

The April delivery of additional prototypes enables simultaneous evaluations to be conducted by Temerand and Star Fleet, further accelerating the *Akyazi* and *Arbiter* test programs. Fleet Performance Evaluation trials are conducted beginning 17 May, analyzing various factors including warp flight characteristics, task force capability, humanoid dynamics, and operational reliability. Assignment of the prototype PAs to the manufacturer or the Fleet and their testing designations are announced:

Prototype No. 1 (Temerand) - Undergoing reconfiguration per TacFleet requirements. Devoted to internal structural buildup to *Akyazi* specifications.

Prototype No. 2 (Temerand) - Assigned to warp structural stress analyzation testing. Warp engine pylon "sweep angle" is increased and engine height above centerline is adjusted.

Prototype No. 3 (Temerand) - Devoted to actual and like-systems integration on a complex (near-operational) scale, including secondary and redundant units. Scheduled to conduct the majority of maintenance and reliability demonstrations and testing.

Prototype No. 4 (Temerand) - Known as the "impulse ship," assigned to sub-light propulsion testing and evaluation, including multiple-redundant studies of the ASL emergency thrust units.

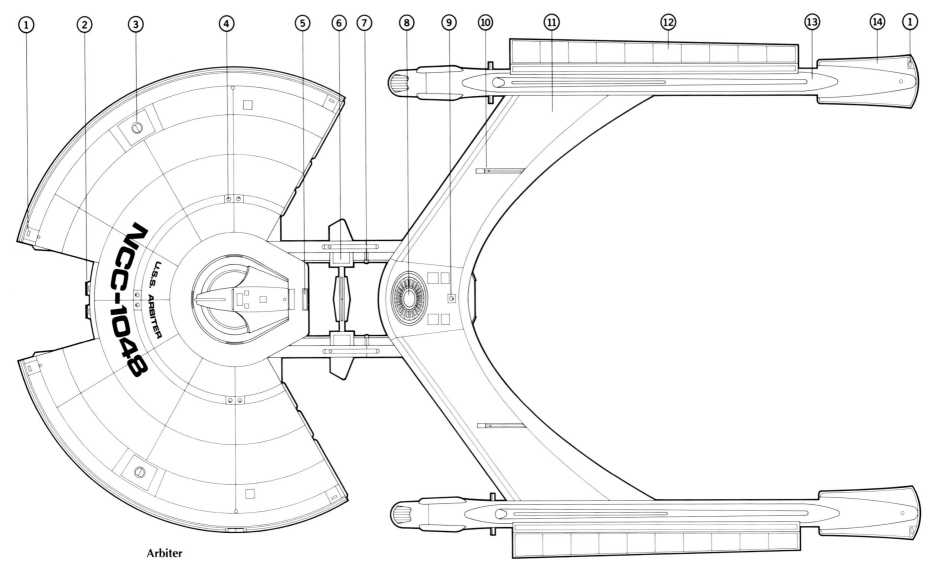

Arbiter

1. Kenelex reaction control system   2. Mk 20 Teviot torpedo tubes   3. topside docking ports   4. JAKA-2 phaser banks   5. lounge viewport   6. Iulus Protective Envelope generator   7. explosive bolt separation   8. impulse amplification crystal   9. JAKA-5 phaser bank   10. sensor emplacement   11. warp engine support pylons   12. warp field reflector   13. LN-91 Mod 1 warp drive units   14. intercooler assembly

Prototype No. 5 (Star Fleet) - Loaned to Prentice-Schafer for incorporation and evaluation of the "Iulus" Protective Envelope deflector system. Additional (experimental) defensive units tested, including the "Portico" sectional deflector system and "Jort" series deflector spires.

Prototype No. 6 (Star Fleet) - Assigned to Starbase 6 for evaluation of the "Nike" (enhanced) weapon system and related subsystems. Operational (live-fire) phaser and photon torpedo systems installed and activated for evaluation with the "Nike" unit.

Prototype No. 7 (Star Fleet) - Assigned to Starbase 8 for testing of task force compatibility and capacity to interface with established Class One Fleet units in a variety of multi-ship scenarios.

Prototypes No. 8, 9, 10 (Star Fleet) - Designated flight training craft for command crew compatibility and familiarity evaluations. Those senior officers that have been assigned to *Akyazi* class command crews begin rotation to these fully-outfitted prototypes for "operational familiarity" deployments of limited duration. Crew assignment and mix is based on the present availability of the officers who are called. Rotations begin out of Starbase 2.

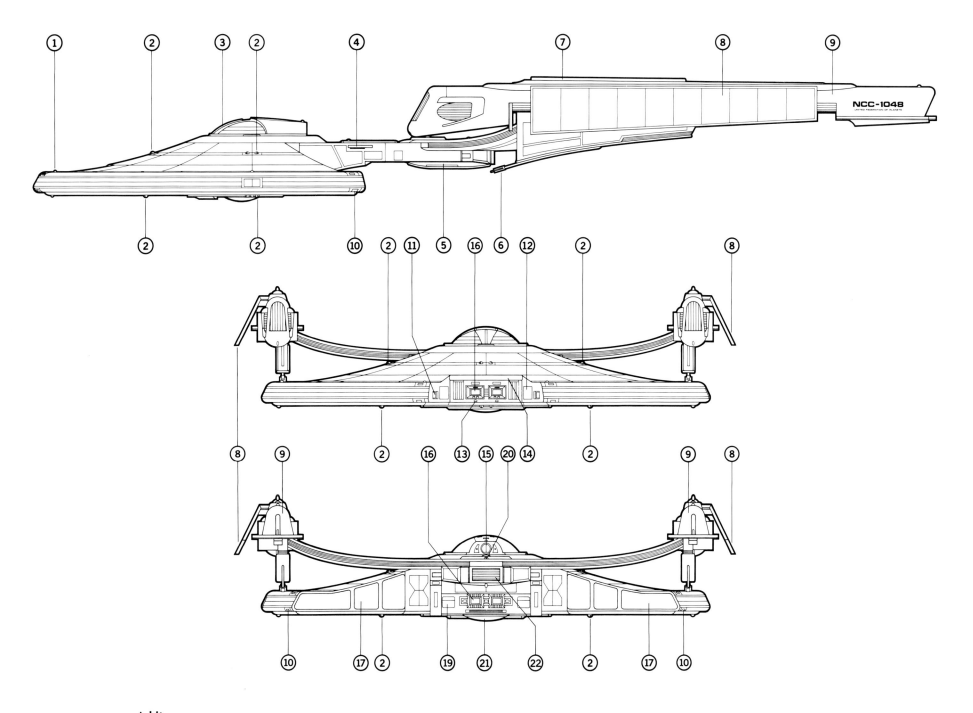

Arbiter

1. bow light 2. JAKA-2 phaser banks 3. bridge deflector shield enhancement 4. Iulus generator vanes 5. engineering pod 6. deflector spires 7. sensor emplacement 8. warp field reflector 9. LN-91 Mod 1 warp drive units 10. Kenelex reaction control system 11. QASR maneuvering thrusters 12. photon torpedo flash shields 13. probe launch tubes 14. Ochu II deflector array 15. bridge docking port 16. Mk 20 Teviot torpedo tubes 17. sensor pallets 18. ASL emergency impulse engines 19. workbee stowage 20. JAKA-5 phaser bank 21. Efiro primary sensor array 22. CME impulse engine

Number	Name	Builder	Laid Down	Launched	Commissioned	Status
NCC-1048	Arbiter	Rodriquez Ingenieria, Lima, Earth	24 July 2285	21 Aug 2286	09 Apr 2287	**ATAC**
NCC-1049	Acerra	Rodriquez Ingenieria, Lima, Earth	21 Sept 2285	02 Nov 2286	10 May 2287	**ATAC**
NCC-1050	Juist	Star Fleet Division, Puget Sound Yards, Earth	15 Aug 2285	22 Oct 2286	02 Apr 2287	**ATAC**
NCC-1051	Arashi	Singapore Shipbuilding & Engineering Co. Ltd., Singapore, Earth	23 Nov 2285	11 Jan 2287	27 June 2287	Lost
NCC-1052	Atago	Rodriquez Ingenieria, Lima, Earth	14 Dec 2285	05 Mar 2287	15 Sept 2287	**ATAC**
NCC-1053	Apia	Sy Ris Abagon, New Aberdeen Naval Yards, Aldebaran	SD 7922.17	SD 7962.45	SD 7979.83	**ATAC**
NCC-1054	Tensas	Sy Ris Abagon, New Aberdeen Naval Yards, Aldebaran	SD 7964.28	SD 7993.51	SD 8012.91	**ATAC**
NCC-1055	Thun	Singapore Shipbuilding & Engineering Co. Ltd., Singapore, Earth	09 Dec 2286	19 Feb 2288	12 Aug 2288	**ATAC**
NCC-1056	Atessa	Star Fleet Division, Puget Sound Yards, Earth	22 July 2286	18 Oct 2287	04 Apr 2288	**ATAC**
NCC-1057	Jico	Star Fleet Division, Puget Sound Yards, Earth	08 Sept 2286	30 Dec 2287	15 July 2288	**ATAC**
NCC-1058	Jari	Sy Ris Abagon, New Aberdeen Naval Yards, Aldebaran	SD 7987.64	SD 8024.47	SD 8038.36	**ATAC**
NCC-1059	Armavir	Rodriquez Ingenieria, Lima, Earth	17 Aug 2286	05 Sept 2287	20 Feb 2288	**ATAC**
NCC-1060	Artika	Rodriquez Ingenieria, Lima, Earth	21 Jan 2287	27 Mar 2288	29 Aug 2288	**ATAC**
NCC-1061	Jelai	Sy Ris Abagon, New Aberdeen Naval Yards, Aldebaran	SD 8030.40	SD 8062.51	SD 8074.76	**ATAC**
NCC-1062	Talence	Singapore Shipbuilding & Engineering Co. Ltd., Singapore, Earth	12 Apr 2287	28 Apr 2288	10 Sept 2288	**ATAC**
NCC-1063	Tioga	Singapore Shipbuilding & Engineering Co. Ltd., Singapore, Earth	27 Feb 2288	04 May 2289	01 Nov 2289	**ATAC**
NCC-1064	Thrace	Singapore Shipbuilding & Engineering Co. Ltd., Singapore, Earth	19 May 2288	15 June 2289	13 Dec 2289	**ATAC**
NCC-1065	Julin	Seskon Trella (Starcraft Design Section), Chagala, Tellar	SD 7721.50	SD 7765.24	SD 7777.35	**ATAC**
NCC-1066	Tachira	Seskon Trella (Starcraft Design Section), Chagala, Tellar	SD 7914.62	SD 7950.81	SD 7969.07	**ATAC**
NCC-1067	Almdes	Star Fleet Division, Puget Sound Yards, Earth	24 July 2287	13 Oct 2288	09 Mar 2289	**ATAC**
NCC-1068	Abitibi	Star Fleet Division, Puget Sound Yards, Earth	01 May 2288	17 July 2289		Building
NCC-1069	Archer	Seskon Trella (Starcraft Design Section), Chagala, Tellar	SD 8075.32	SD 8104.55		Building
NCC-1070	Aversa	Rodriquez Ingenieria, Lima, Earth	26 May 2287	17 July 2288	06 Jan 2289	**ATAC**
NCC-1071	Jativa	Rodriquez Ingenieria, Lima, Earth	18 Apr 2288	27 June 2289		Building
NCC-1072	Jersey	Sy Ris Abagon, New Aberdeen Naval Yards, Aldebaran	SD 8115.74	SD 8152.19		Building
NCC-1073	Tuira	Sy Ris Abagon, New Aberdeen Naval Yards, Aldebaran	SD 8153.22	SD 8183.25		Building
NCC-1074	Azusa	Temerand Duplicat, Calabay City, Mars	SD 8475.90			Building
NCC-1075	Trigarta	Rodriquez Ingenieria, Lima, Earth	30 Jan 2289			Building
NCC-1076	Arques	Singapore Shipbuilding & Engineering Co. Ltd., Singapore, Earth	10 Jan 2289			Building
NCC-1077	Aparri	Star Fleet Division, Puget Sound Yards, Earth	24 Aug 2288	30 Oct 2289		Building
NCC-1078	Argus	Star Fleet Division, Puget Sound Yards, Earth	13 Oct 2289			Building
NCC-1079	Tanaga	Singapore Shipbuilding & Engineering Co. Ltd., Singapore, Earth	15 Aug 2289			Building
NCC-1080	Timis	Singapore Shipbuilding & Engineering Co. Ltd., Singapore, Earth	28 Dec 2289			Building
NCC-1081	Alava	Temerand Duplicat, Calabay City, Mars	SD 8500.10			Building
NCC-1082	Agtekerk	Temerand Duplicat, Calabay City, Mars	SD 8502.37			Building
NCC-1083	Ashiya	Rodriquez Ingenieria, Lima, Earth	11 Nov 2289			Building
NCC-1084	Jaro	Temerand Duplicat, Calabay City, Mars	SD 8691.49			Building
NCC-1085	Tinian	Sy Ris Abagon, New Aberdeen Naval Yards, Aldebaran	SD 8179.34			Building
NCC-1086	Antibes	Temerand Duplicat, Calabay City, Mars	SD 8722.40			Building
NCC-1087	Arban	Temerand Duplicat, Calabay City, Mars				Authorized
NCC-1088	Apure	Temerand Duplicat, Calabay City, Mars				Authorized
NCC-1089	Aulon	Star Fleet Division, Puget Sound Yards, Earth				Authorized

Prototype No. 11 (Temerand) - Scheduled to become the operational prototype for the *Akula* design, with LN-94 warp drive units and the "Zelus" cloaking system to be evaluated.

July 2284 -

Temerand and Jeffries Transdimensional Dynamics announce they have developed a new "bottle containment" apparatus for the dilithium gas piping and antimatter conduit system. This development is the result of tests that revealed the formation of fissures in the propulsion shaft coupling units. These fissures were caused by an overtaxing of the coupling units during high-velocity (above warp 20) warp maneuvering of Prototype No. 2, resulting in a partial or complete loss of the impulse amplification crystal. This necessitated the addition of a second, back-up amplification crystal to the *Akyazi* design. The containment apparatus will be perfected in time for inclusion in the *Arbiter* sub-class.

August 2284 -

Prototype No. 7 is shifted to TacFleet for evaluation of acceleration rates, warp braking, warp and sub-light maneuverability and "dead-weapon" war games

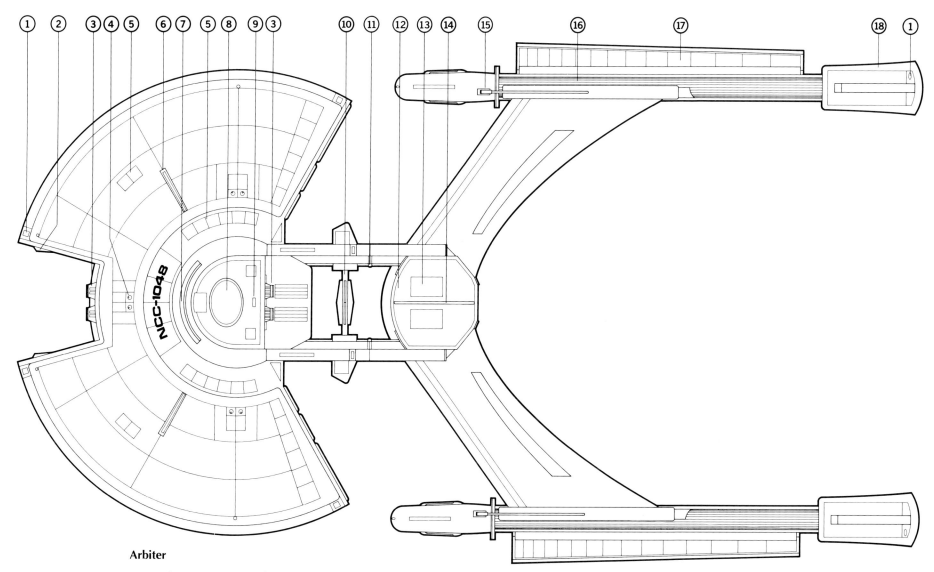

Arbiter

1. Kenelex reaction control system   2. QASR maneuvering thrusters   3. Mk 20 Teviot torpedo tubes   4. JAKA-2 phaser banks   5. lifeboat emplacements   6. sensor array   7. Shim sensor assembly   8. Efiro primary sensor array   9. tractor beam   10. Iulus Protective Envelope generator   11. explosive bolt separation   12. engineering pod   13. antimatter eject covers   14. engineering pod deflector vane   15. deflector spires   16. warp field generator assembly   17. warp field reflector   18. intercooler assembly

scenarios. Several classified intelligence systems are installed for testing purposes. The No. 7 ship will be "hunted" by as many as nine TacFleet adversaries in some exercises.

September 2284 -

The various design improvements and alterations to the *Arbiter* sub-class prototypes are individually evaluated. All successful adaptations are incorporated into Prototype No. 6 in order to achieve a fully operational testbed.

02 October 2284 -

Forty-two ships of the *Arbiter* design are officially ordered by Star Fleet on this date.

Though refinements to some systems continue, the basic external design is nearly identical to the *Akyazi* sub-class.

16 January 2285 -

A series of failures in both the antimatter conduit system and integrated coupling units during high-warp battle maneuvers leads to the loss of Prototype No. 8. None of the test vessels have been equipped with the Jeffries containment system which was completed and approved in early December 2284. The nine-member command crew escaped safely after jettisoning the entire bridge/lifeboat assembly; all five crew members in the engineering pod were killed.

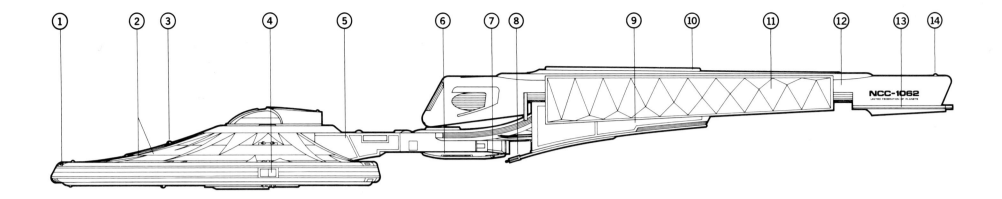

Talence

1. Kenelex reaction control system   2. deflector grid   3. JAKA-2 phaser banks   4. gangway hatch   5. propulsion section support pylons   6. engineering pod   7. JAKA-7D phaser banks   8. deflector spires   9. deflector spire dissipation assembly   10. sensor emplacement   11. warp field reflector   12. LN-91 Mod 1 warp drive units   13. intercooler assembly   14. formation light.

Current specifications of *Arbiter* sub-class:

Displacement:	69,250 metric tons standard		
	(67,000mt light, 70,300mt full load)		
	NCC-1065, 1066, 1069, 1074, 1081, 1082, 1084, 1086-88: 68,700 metric tons standard		
	(66,900mt light, 70,000mt full load)		
	Overall	Primary Hull	Nacelles
Length:	215.8m	78.9m	126.7m
Beam:	120.2m	107.6m	16.2m
Draft:	28.6m	19.3m	13.7m
Propulsion:	Two (2) "Skade" LN-91 Mod 1 dilithium-energized antimatter linear warp drive units		
	(System contractor: Vickers Engineering Group Ltd., Cumbria, Earth)		
	One (1) "Delum" CME subatomic unified energy impulse unit		
	(System contractor: Orage Ijek, Aksajak, Andor)		
	Two (2) ASL-3 emergency impulse thrust units		
	QASR enhanced particle beam maneuvering thrusters		
	(Systems contractor: Scarbak Propulsion Systems, Cairo, Earth)		
	"Kenelex" pulsed laser reaction control system		
	(System contractor: Orage Ijek, Aksajak, Andor)		
Velocity:	Warp 8, standard		
	Warp 15, maximum		
	Warp 22, battle maximum		
Acceleration:	Rest-Onset Critical Momentum: 1.98 sec		
	Onset Critical Momentum-Warp Engage: .72 sec		
	Warp 1-Warp 4:	.19 sec	
	Warp 4-Warp 8:	.10 sec	
	Warp 8-Warp 15:	1.38 sec	
	Warp 15-Warp 22:	2.06 sec	
Duration:	2 Earth years, standard		
	3.25 Earth years, maximum		

Complement:	77 (7 officers + 70 crew)
	NCC-1053, 1054, 1058, 1061, 1072, 1073, 1085: 80 (8 officers + 72 crew)
Embarked craft:	None
Navigation:	RAV/TENEC Warp Celestial Guidance
	(System contractor: Tlixis Ramab RRB, Balikan, Coridan III)
Computers:	"Ilorin" Duotronic IV; "Krasnysulyn" Subsystem
	(Systems contractor: Kuchata Pratus Ikyla, Arrasta, Daran V)
Phasers:	6 banks of 2 each - JAKA-2 independent twin mount
	1 bank - JAKA-5 single mount
	NCC-1050, 1051, 1055-57, 1062-64, 1067, 1068, 1076-80, 1089:
	6 banks of 2 each - JAKA-2 independent twin mount
	2 banks - JAKA-7D single mount
	(Systems contractor: Asakaze Ordnance Systems Ltd., Honshu-Hamamatsu, Earth)
Photon torpedoes:	4 tubes - Mk 20 "Teviot" independent
	(System contractor: Arvan Toy Conglessum, Binz, Tellar)
Defense:	"Merlin II" primary force field and deflector control system
	DCA/DSA cloaking generation and stasis countermeasure system
	"Iulus" Protective Envelope system
	(Systems contractor: Prentice-Schafer Inc., Marsport, Mars)
	"Nike" weapon system (enhanced)
	TAVITAC Tactical Subsystem
	(Systems contractor: Keindoffer-Klaatsen DSC, Munich, Earth)
	"Podi Aschura" deflector spires
	(System contractor: Kal Achal Conglessum, Takuv, Tellar)
Life support:	MCH1 Modular Gravity and Atmosphere Maintenance Unit
	(System contractor: Cristobal SM/S, Manila, Earth)
	ARU/SI radiation protection systems
	(System contractor: Kym Lan Den Terra, New Kyoto, Earth)
	"Lenix-B" waste regeneration systems
	(System contractor: Jullundur-Lahore Ltd., Bombay, Earth)

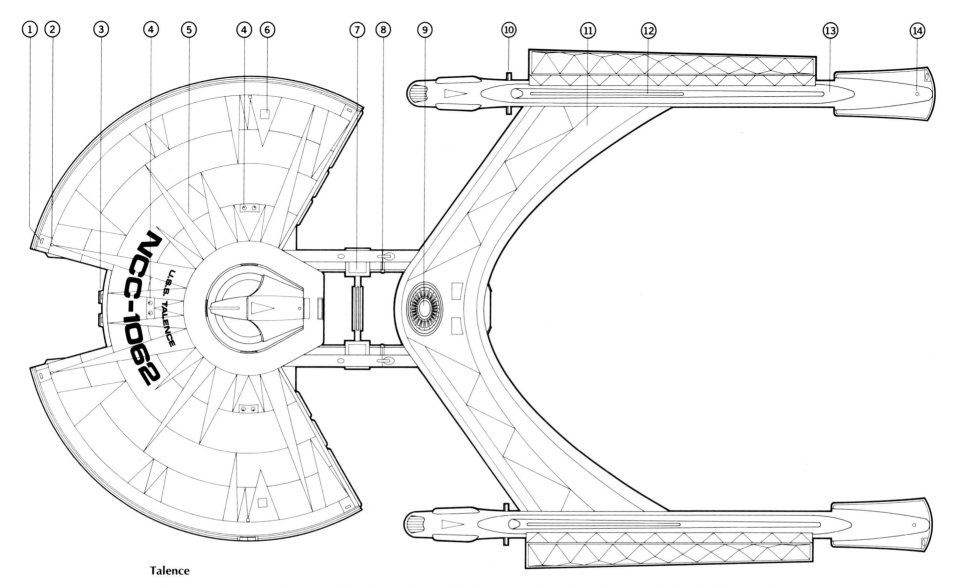

Talence

1. Kenelex reaction control system   2. bow lights   3. Mk 20 Teviot torpedo tubes   4. JAKA-2 phaser banks   5. deflector grid   6. personnel hatch   7. Iulus Protective Envelope generator   8. explosive bolt separation   9. impulse amplification crystal   10. primary flow sensor   11. warp engine support pylons   12. sensor emplacement   13. LN-91 Mod 1 warp drive units   14. formation light

March 2285 -

Construction on the *Akyazi* (PA 1010) and *Akitsu* (PA 1012) is delayed at Arbing & Lidde to allow for the incorporation of various design improvements, including modification and reinforcement of the bridge/lifeboat configuration and minor rear-rangement of the internal bracing within the double boom structure. These changes are the result of improvements made to the prototypes during the *Arbiter* test program.

24 July 2285 -

Work begins on the *Arbiter* (PA 1048) at Rodriquez Ingenieria, Lima, Earth.

Classification: The *Arbiter* sub-class was ordered as the middle construction group of the *Akyazi*-class perimeter action ships, reflecting various design improvements within the same hull form. This group includes hull numbers 1048 through 1089, inclusive.

Design: These ships, like their sisters in the *Akyazi* sub-class, are much more "steal-thy" than had been anticipated when they were originally conceived. They benefit from the same hull form but are slightly faster and carry greater firepower. The *Juist* (PA 1050) was the first ship commissioned and was delivered with only 28 contract deficiencies; the *Arbiter* (PA 1048) was launched on 21 August 2286, six days before

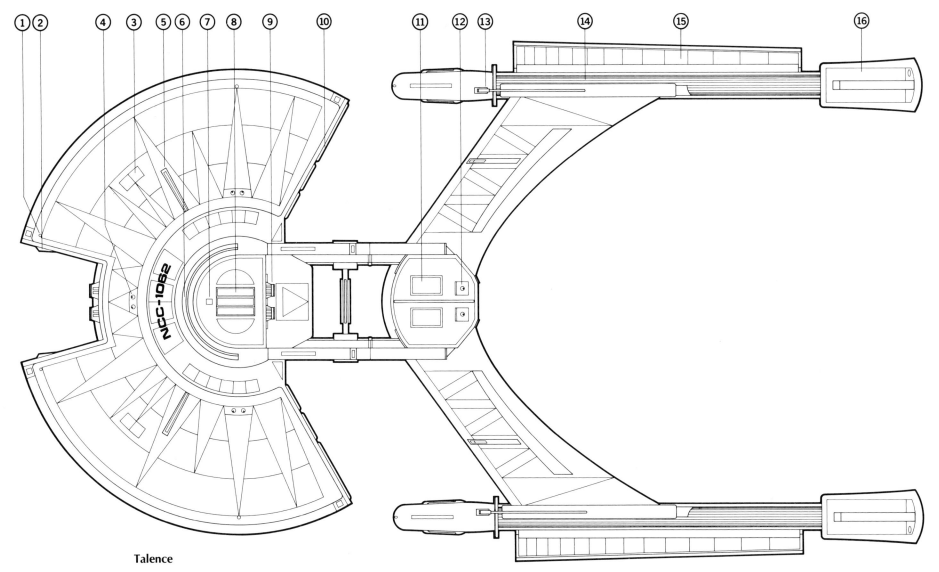

Talence

1. bow light   2. QASR maneuvering thrusters   3. lifeboat emplacements   4. JAKA-2 phaser banks   5. sensor emplacements   6. Shim sensor assembly   7. tractor beam   8. Tirpit primary sensor array   9. Mk 20 Teviot torpedo tubes   10. sensor pallets   11. antimatter eject covers   12. JAKA-7D phaser banks   13. deflector spires   14. warp field generator assembly   15. warp field reflector   16. intercooler assembly

the first ship of the *Akyazi* group (*Acavus* [PA 1025]) was commissioned.

The exterior angle of the primary hull leading edge was inverted in the *Arbiter* design (and in the last nine ships of the *Akyazi* sub-class) after warp field formation and propagation tests conducted on Prototype No. 2 revealed enhanced warp handling characteristics with the new design. The primary deflector array is located immediately above the forward photon torpedo assembly (as in the *Akyazi* sub-class); it has been upgraded from the standard "Ochu" units in the *Akyazi* ships and provides the forward torpedo tubes (and the entire ship) with even greater protection. The flash shields were also enlarged to provide more protective coverage.

Several ships of this group were provided with three docking ports - one at the 01 bridge level and two additional ports on the primary hull topside. After construction of the sub-class had begun, it was decided that the two primary hull docking port locations would be a potential weak point in battle situations (despite structural reinforcement) and the topside ports were deleted in all but the early ships (PA 1048-52, 1055, 1056). Because of the location of the "Iulus" Protective Envelope generator, this leaves a majority of the *Arbiter* group vessels with only one docking port (at the 01 level).

The RAV/TENEC navigation suite is a defensive refinement of the Tlixis-built RAV/

ISHAK navigation unit currently being installed in the uprated *Enterprise* (CH-1701)-class heavy cruisers.

A mandate by TacFleet early in the design stage required all ships of the *Akyazi* class to be able to function as mobile borderspace "listening posts" if required. As a result, all *Akyazi*-class PAs (including the *Arbiter* group) are equipped with a multitude of listening devices and highly sensitive scanning apparatus, located at strategic points on the ships' hulls. Among those units mounted are the Gufurdi long-range pallet, ADI 95000 series capaldic imager, and Shim combined field sensor system.

Most of these ships are fitted with the Efiro primary sensor array, located on the bottom of the primary hull. However, the ships constructed by Singapore Shipbuilding are equipped with the Tirpit sequenced primary sensor unit. They also carry three additional personnel in the standard crew complement due to internal arrangement variations.

Engineering: Like their *Akyazi* sister ships, the warp drive system for the *Arbiter* sub-class was designed and built by Vickers Engineering Group. However, these ships are equipped with the slightly more powerful "Skade" LN-91 warp units in place of the "Fier" system of the earlier ships. As with the LN-90 configuration (and the "Kratos" system - see *Akula* sub-class), the "Skade" engines utilize a warp reflector assembly to "bounce" or reflect the transmissive warp energies between the two engines, passing the warp field underneath the ship in the process. This method of warp field manipulation greatly enhances the maneuverability of all *Akyazi*-class PAs and is a key element in their ability to achieve such high warp velocities.

The "Delum" CME impulse engine represents a one-model improvement over the CCE units of the *Akyazi* group. The CME system is slightly more powerful.

The FORS emergency impulse units of the *Akyazi* group were deleted in the *Arbiter* design in favor of the more conventional ASL system. Like the FORS system, the ASL-3 units carry a total of 30 fuel cells. They can be fired continuously at 100% power expenditure for approximately 230 hours, achieving .29c in the process.

The shape of the warp engine support pylon assembly has been changed and its overall structural configuration improved from the original design (see *Akyazi* sub-class).

Weapons: The defensive suite of the *Arbiter* group is identical for all of the ships in the sub-class. As in the *Akyazi* group, the peripheral systems are centered around the performance characteristics of the enhanced "Nike" weapon system. "Podi Aschura" deflector spires replace the "Saco Onorvoz" units of the earlier ships.

The "Iulus" Protective Envelope system acts as a secondary unit to the "Merlin II" primary configuration. The "Iulus" system can be engaged in critical situations, providing superior protection at the expense of greater power consumption.

The majority of the *Arbiter* group ships have a single JAKA-5 phaser bank mounted on the warp engine support pylon (above the impulse deck). This is in addition to the standard six banks mounted on the primary hull. The SFD- and Singapore-built ships replace the JAKA-5 unit with two single mount JAKA-7D phaser banks mounted on the underside of the engineering pod. The Mk-20 "Teviot" photon torpedo system is fitted in all ships, with two tubes forward and two tubes aft.

Operational: Among the many readiness exercises conducted during the early operational service lives of the *Akyazi* class, several are notable for a variety of reasons. Foremost among these is the Makus Fleet Maneuver, conducted in the vicinity of that frontier planet in February 2288. The PAs *Amagi* (PA 1016), *Bucke* (PA 1020), *Eiger*

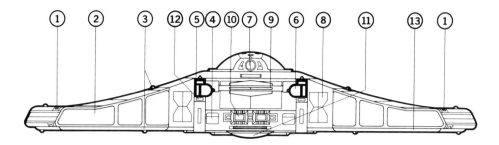

Arbiter (cross-section at pylon bolt, frame 251)

1. Kenelex reaction control system 2. sensor pallets 3. JAKA-2 phaser banks
4. workbee stowage 5. structural bulkheads 6. pylon transfer tube
7. docking port 8. ASL emergency impulse engines 9. Iulus Protective
Envelope generator 10. Mk 20 Teviot torpedo tubes 11. Efiro primary
sensor array 12. QASR maneuvering thrusters 13. sensor platform

(PA 1031), *Arashi* (PA 1051), and *Apia* (PA 1053) were allied against a force of three heavy frigates and the heavy cruiser *Monitor* (CH 1713). For the first three hours of the exercise the PA force was limited to minor scoring in the dead-weapon scenario. At +3.42, the *Eiger* and *Arashi* entered warp while in pursuit of the *Monitor*. When the captain of the *Monitor* turned his ship to engage the PAs, the two ships executed a standard crossover maneuver, passing over the heavy cruiser at warp 15 and initiating their "turn-to-target" while simultaneously beginning warp braking. However, an apparent miscalculation by the *Arashi* helmsman in programming the maneuver caused the two ships to make contact at the moment of subspace termination. The *Arashi*'s starboard "Skade" engine struck the portside primary hull of *Eiger*. The impact, combined with the ships' velocity, overloaded the primary force field and deflector systems and tore away a large section of *Eiger*'s primary hull. Twelve of her crew were killed. The *Arashi* was destroyed approximately 2.6 seconds later when her collapsed warp unit caused an antimatter containment rupture; she carried a crew of 63. The *Eiger* suffered additional structural damage from the explosion.

The *Talence* (PA 1062) and *Thrace* (PA 1064) exceeded velocity maneuvering records while on Fleet trials with the heavy cruiser *Alkaid* (CH 1829) in April 2290. The ships regularly outscored the heavy cruiser, rendering her offensive capability ineffectual during multiple engagements.

During the Primmin's Hunt Exercise of August 2290 (commanded by Admiral Joseph Primmin, Special Operations, TacFleet), the *Acerra* (PA 1049), *Jico* (PA 1057), and *Armavir* (PA 1059) were tracked into separate areas of operation by three individual task force units. Their orders were to avoid their respective group of "hunters" (each consisting of one heavy cruiser and one fast frigate) while remaining within their assigned areas of space. After six days of attempts only the *Acerra* had been located by her assigned search task force. The PAs had been instructed to utilize all of the elements at their disposal, including their speed, maneuverability, cloaking systems, and overall stealth characteristics.

Nomenclature: All of the perimeter action ships in the *Arbiter* sub-class have names that begin with the letter 'A,' 'J,' or 'T.' PA 1050 was originally named *Atende*; was renamed *Juist* on 11 April 2285. PA 1069 was originally named *Jenk*; was renamed *Archer* on 21 April 2285.

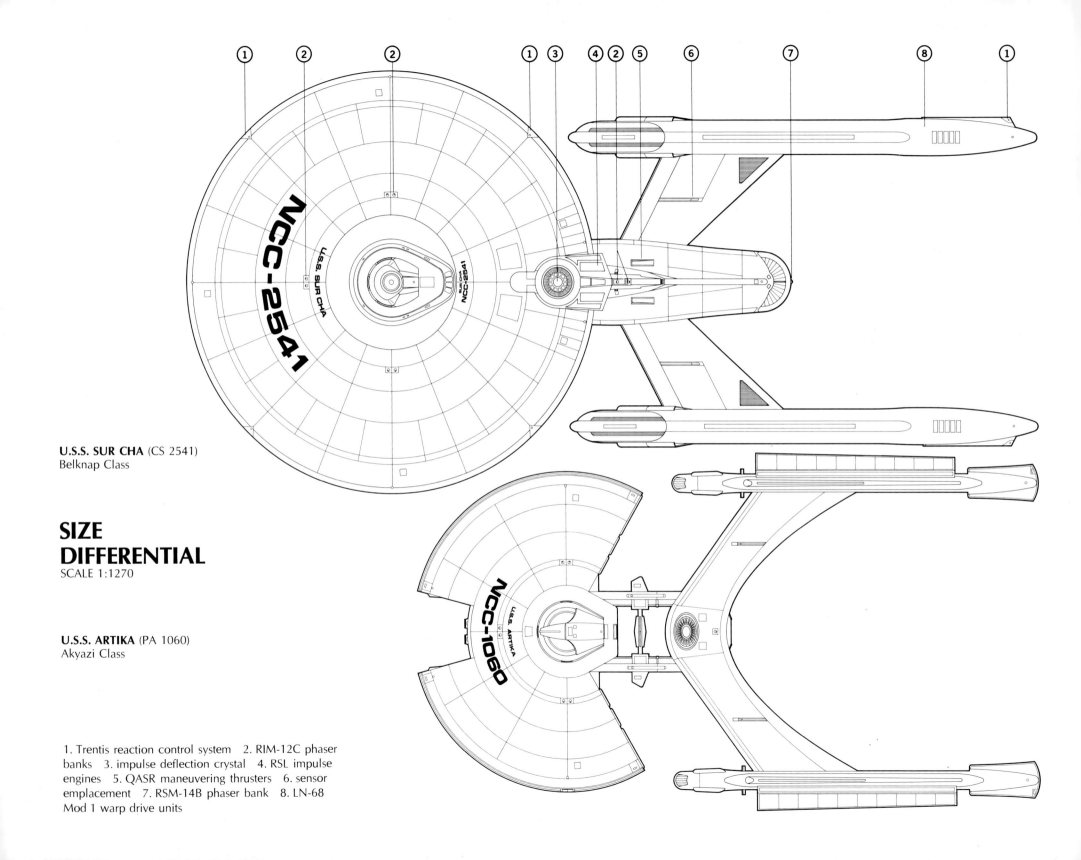

U.S.S. SUR CHA (CS 2541)
Belknap Class

SIZE DIFFERENTIAL
SCALE 1:1270

U.S.S. ARTIKA (PA 1060)
Akyazi Class

1. Trentis reaction control system   2. RIM-12C phaser banks   3. impulse deflection crystal   4. RSL impulse engines   5. QASR maneuvering thrusters   6. sensor emplacement   7. RSM-14B phaser bank   8. LN-68 Mod 1 warp drive units

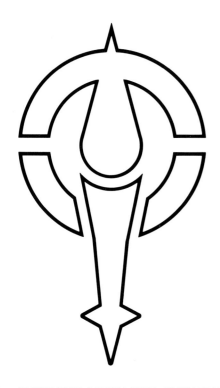

AKULA
Group Perimeter Action Ships

8 + 17 PERIMETER ACTION SHIPS: "AKYAZI/AKULA" CLASS

Number	Name	Builder	Laid Down	Launched	Commissioned	Status
NCC-1090	Akula	Terran Rockwell (Spacecraft Division), Pedersen Spaceport, Earth	30 May 2286	24 Aug 2287	03 Mar 2288	**ATAC**
NCC-1091	Kitkun	Terran Rockwell (Spacecraft Division), Pedersen, Spaceport, Earth	22 Sept 2286	29 Nov 2287	18 June 2288	**ATAC**
NCC-1092	Athy	Vickers Shipbuilding Group Ltd., Arcadia Lake, Mars	SD 8225.40	SD 8261.75	SD 8290.38	**ATAC**
NCC-1093	Arvika	Axaanivus Celesco Starcraft, Bedi Plains, Alpha Centauri V	SD 7993.42			Building
NCC-1094	Kuril	Terran Rockwell (Spacecraft Division), Pedersen Spaceport, Earth	15 Nov 2288			Building
NCC-1095	Atami	Avondale Group, Ferrata Docks, Rigellum, Rigel II	SD 8155.06			Building
NCC-1096	Saros	Vickers Shipbuilding Group Ltd., Arcadia Lake, Mars	SD 8384.52	SD 8421.19	SD 8437.05	**ATAC**
NCC-1097	Avaricum	Vickers Shipbuilding Group Ltd., Arcadia Lake, Mars	SD 8617.70			Building
NCC-1098	Sjoto	Axaanivus Celesco Starcraft, Bedi Plains, Alpha Centauri V	SD 7697.83	SD 7739.24		Building
NCC-1099	Sandusky	Vickers Shipbuilding Group Ltd., Arcadia Lake, Mars	SD 8305.93	SD 8352.71	SD 8369.36	**ATAC**
NCC-1100	Kern	Terran Rockwell (Spacecraft Division), Pedersen Spaceport, Earth	12 Nov 2287	05 Jan 2289	14 July 2289	**ATAC**
NCC-1101	Atyra	Axaanivus Celesco Starcraft, Bedi Plains, Alpha Centauri V	SD 8000.57			Building
NCC-1102	Sybaris	Terran Rockwell (Spacecraft Division), Pedersen Spaceport, Earth	28 Mar 2287	15 May 2288	23 Nov 2288	**ATAC**
NCC-1103	Kuei	Terran Rockwell (Spacecraft Division), Pedersen Spaceport, Earth	27 Oct 2289			Building
NCC-1104	Krka	Terran Rockwell (Spacecraft Division), Pedersen Spaceport, Earth	29 Apr 2287	03 May 2288	16 Sept 2288	**ATAC**
NCC-1105	Akuri	Avondale Group, Ferrata Docks, Rigellum, Rigel II	SD 8071.60			Building
NCC-1106	Shirante	Avondale Group, Ferrata Docks, Rigellum, Rigel II	SD 8254.38			Building
NCC-1107	Samakov	Vickers Shipbuilding Group Ltd., Arcadia Lake, Mars	SD 8639.31			Building
NCC-1108	Sitka	Axaanivus Celesco Starcraft, Bedi Plains, Alpha Centauri V	SD 7963.80			Building
NCC-1109	Ajanta	Avondale Group, Ferrata Docks, Rigellum, Rigel II				Authorized
NCC-1110	Kalinin	Avondale Group, Ferrata Docks, Rigellum, Rigel II				Authorized
NCC-1111	Kutaisi	Terran Rockwell (Spacecraft Division), Pedersen Spaceport, Earth	03 Dec 2289			Building
NCC-1112	Sangamon	Axaanivus Celesco Starcraft, Bedi Plains, Alpha Centauri V				Authorized
NCC-1113	Kelkit	Vickers Shipbuilding Group Ltd., Arcadia Lake, Mars				Authorized
NCC-1114	Anaiza	Avondale Group, Ferrata Docks, Rigellum, Rigel II				Authorized

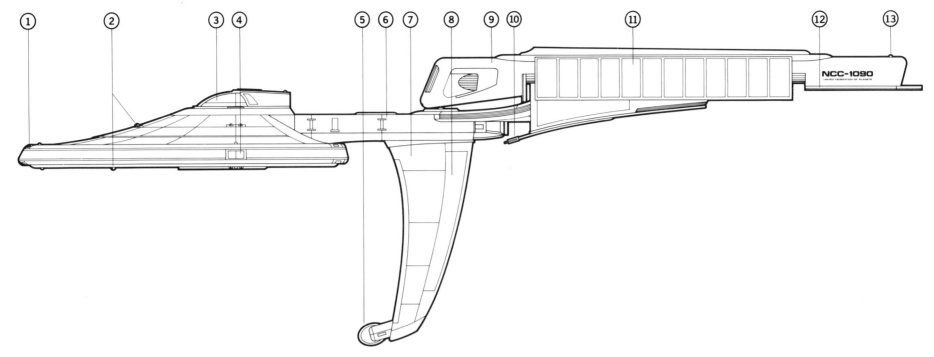

Akula

1. Shilka reaction control system 2. JAKA-2 phaser banks 3. bridge 4. gangway hatch 5. Bia deflector pod 6. propulsion section support pylons 7. deflector pod support pylons 8. deflector pod dissipation vanes 9. LN-94 Mod 1 warp drive units 10. deflector spires 11. warp field reflector 12. intercooler assembly 13. formation light

The ships of the *Akula* sub-class comprise the final construction group of the *Akyazi*-class perimeter action ships. This sub-class is also the smallest - it will consist of 25 vessels when construction is completed. The *Akula* ships are (or will be) assigned to high-threat areas because of their enhanced defensive capabilities. PA 1109, 1110, and 1112-14 have been authorized but have not yet begun building.

Class: Although all 105 *Akyazi* class ships were authorized at the same time (02 August 2283), three individual sub-classes were envisioned from the outset, and the *Akula* design was last due to the extensive testing and evaluation necessary on the "Bia" deflector pod assembly. The "Bia" unit contributes heavily to the visually distinctive *Akula* design, creating an almost unmistakable sensor signature and recognition profile. Star Fleet officially ordered the *Akula* sub-class nine months after ordering the *Arbiter* group (and 17 days before the *Arbiter* [PA 1048] was laid down).

16 May 2284/Stardate 8321.4 -
   Temerand installs LN-94 warp units on Prototype No. 11 at the Symmons T. Bodio dockyard complex. Warp engine activation tests will be conducted over the next three weeks, with the ship scheduled to leave the dockyard facility under its own power on 09 June.

July 2284 -
   Refinements to the *Akula* prototype configuration are necessary after poor results following warp field stability tests with the "Kratos" engines. Modifications include

reconfiguration of the internal flux chillers, expansion of the intake vents, and new alignments for the support pylon propulsion shafts.

October 2284 -
   Prototype No. 6 is shifted to the *Akula* test program after Star Fleet concludes weapons evaluations on the "Teviot" torpedo and JAKA phaser systems in the *Arbiter* operational mode. The "Bia" deflector unit and a support pylon assembly will be fitted to evaluate the "Bia" MDS system and the Flocon-designed Tuch compact phaser mounts. Tests with the system installed in Prototype No. 11 have resulted in an overloading of the Tuch phaser system whenever the deflector unit successfully absorbs and dissipates a significant amount of offensive energy.

16-19 February 2285 -
   Prototype No. 11 performs flawlessly under the direction of Lieutenant Commander Sori Descanta and the command crew that will be assigned to the *Kitkun* (PA 1091) when that ship is completed. The prototype was put through a series of complicated maneuvers, readiness inspections, and war games exercises during the four-day Admiralty Inspection event at Starbase 20. Eight vessels participated, with the prototype garnering a second-place scoring finish overall (surpassed by only the *Engage* [PA 1125]).

June 2285 -
   Prototype No. 5 shifts to the *Akula* test program. She will perform the majority of

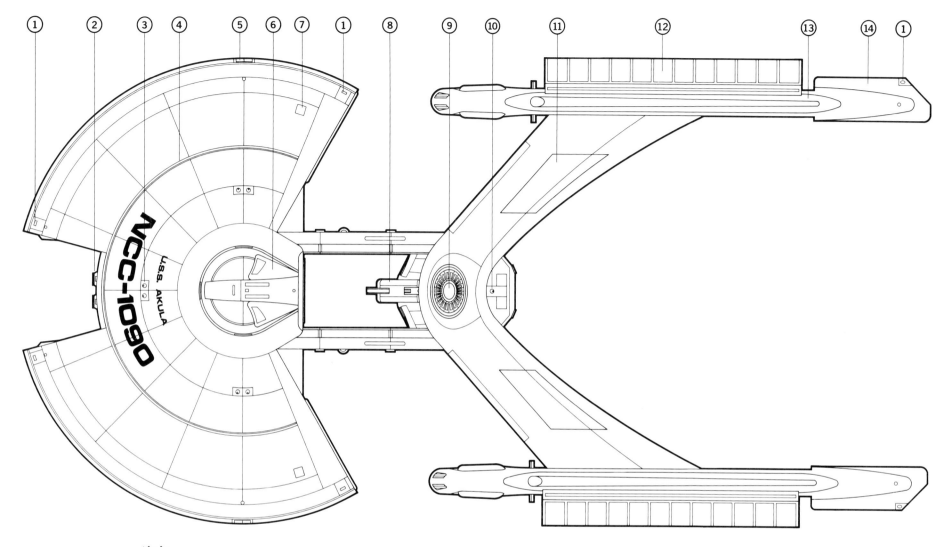

Akula

1. Shilka reaction control system   2. Mk 5 Komati torpedo tubes   3. JAKA-2 phaser banks   4. sensor emplacement   5. gangway hatch   6. bridge magnetic drive units   7. personnel hatch   8. Bia deflector pod   9. impulse amplification crystal   10. JAKA-5 phaser bank   11. emergency flush vents   12. warp field reflector   13. LN-94 Mod 1 warp drive units   14. intercooler assembly

testing and evaluation on a "B" version of the *Akula* design after it is announced by Star Fleet that Axaanivus Celesco and Avondale Group will construct 11 ships closer in configuration to the *Akyazi/Arbiter* design. These ships will be equipped with the "Skade" LN-91 warp units of the *Arbiter* group and will have the "Kenelex" reaction control system in place of the newer "Shilka" units. Most of the other primary operating systems, however, will remain the same. Long-range manufacturing proposals submitted by the two primary contractors indicate that the less-sophisticated "B" variants will have lower procurement costs, while requiring less construction time and smaller reserve parts stockpiles. A subsequent review of the proposal by TacFleet finds that performance characteristics will be reduced by less than 8%.

All operational design characteristics regarding the "Bia" deflector unit and its support pylon assembly are finalized as Prototype No. 6 ends its *Akula* design weapons evaluation phase. The initial tests on the different shape of the *Akula* design, including the deflector pod assembly, revealed that warp field formation and warp handling characteristics were negatively affected because the deflector unit was positioned too near the main body of the ship. As a result, the support pylons were lengthened (and the deflector pod lowered), thereby improving the warp geometry of the design. An additional bonus of this modification is that incoming enemy fire (which is absorbed and dissipated by the deflector pod) remains a greater distance from the primary hull.

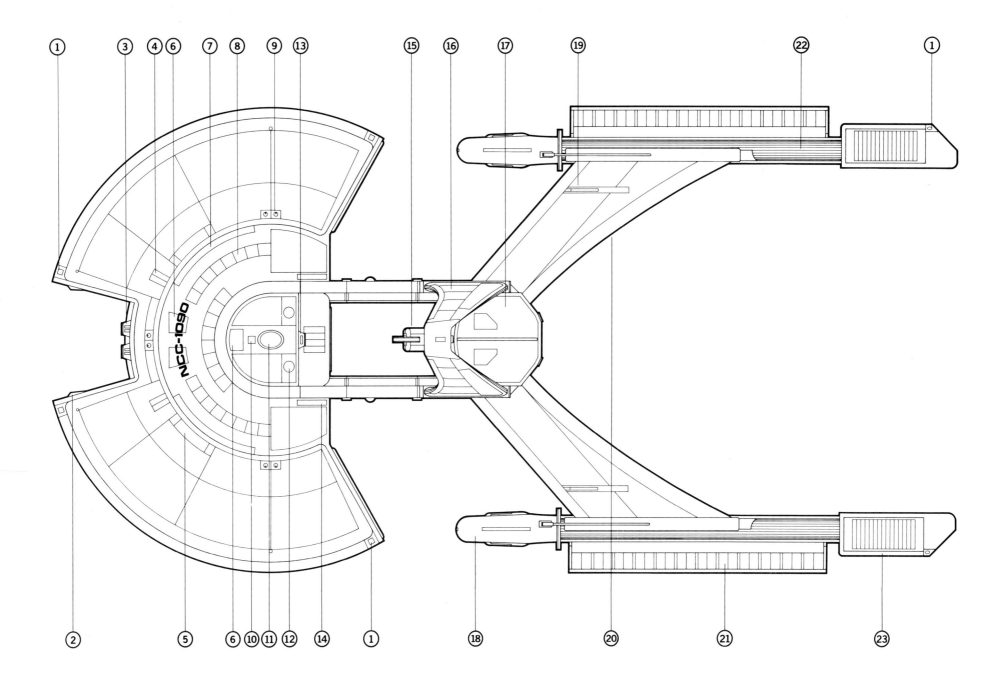

Akula

1. Shilka reaction control system   2. QASR maneuvering thrusters   3. Mk 5 Komati torpedo tubes   4. workbee bay doors   5. intelligence drone launch covers   6. photon torpedo containment chamber eject   7. secondary power core emergency jettison   8. lifeboat emplacements   9. JAKA-2 phaser banks   10. tractor beam   11. Dugoyne primary sensor array   12. turbolift jettison   13. Mk 9 Boris torpedo tube   14. ASL emergency impulse engine fuel dump   15. Bia deflector pod   16. deflector pod support pylons   17. engineering pod   18. LN-94 Mod 1 warp drive units   19. sensor emplacements   20. emergency flush vents   21. warp field reflector   22. warp field generator assembly   23. intercooler assembly

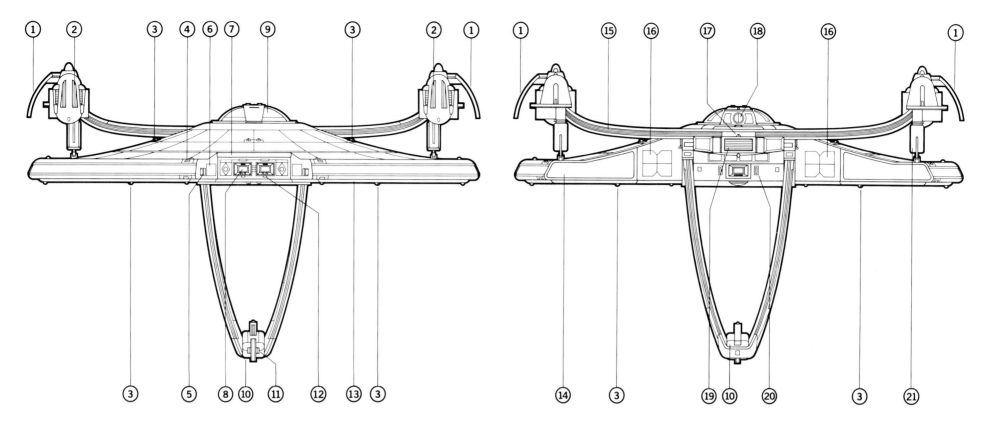

Akula

1. warp field reflector   2. acquisition vanes   3. JAKA-2 phaser banks   4. Shilka reaction control system   5. QASR maneuvering thrusters   6. photon torpedo flash shields   7. Tyme-Wilcox deflector array   8. Mk 5 Komati torpedo tubes   9. bridge   10. Bia deflector pod   11. Tuch phaser bank covers   12. probe launch tubes   13. sensor platform   14. sensor pallet   15. emergency flush vents   16. ASL emergency impulse engines   17. JAKA-5 phaser bank   18. bridge docking port   19. CME impulse engine   20. photon exhaust ports   21. sensor emplacement

7 July 2285 -

Star Fleet places the order for 25 ships of the *Akula* design, bringing the total number of *Akyazi*-class perimeter action ships to 105 (as authorized by the Military Staff Committee on 02 August 2283).

September 2285 -

TacFleet deployment requirements for the *Akula* sub-class necessitate the inclusion of numerous back-up systems and many redundant subsystems in the ships' design. The *Akula*s will be assigned to volatile areas of Federation space where the PA/adversary ratio will be inordinately high.

Prototype No. 7, which was shifted to the *Akula* program in August, will be the full-systems prototype for the *Akula* design; Prototype No. 5 will serve the same function for the "B" variant.

November 2285 -

A standard periodic examination reveals microscopic stress fractures and mild fatigue at certain points along the propulsion package support pylon assembly of Prototype No. 11. The cause is determined to be the different warp geometries created by the inclusion of the "Bia" deflector unit and its pylon assembly in the *Akula* design. The increased distance from the primary hull to the engineering pod and the corresponding increase in length of the propulsion pylons is also a factor. The other ships in the prototype fleet will be examined and a program implemented to redesign the structural reinforcement features of the propulsion support pylon assembly.

11 December 2285 -

The first ship of the *Akyazi* class, the U.S.S. *Bucke* (PA 1020), is launched at Earth.

March 2286 -

Several TacFleet officials announce they are displeased with the velocity limitations of the basic *Akula* design. Feasibility studies conducted early in the *Akula* program indicated that the ships' probable "battle maximum" would be in the vicinity of warp 20, making them comparable to the *Akyazi* and *Arbiter* sub-classes in that regard. However, the entirely different warp characteristics of the *Akula* design (the inclusion of the deflector pod assembly resulting in a bisecting of the warp field along the Z-axis)

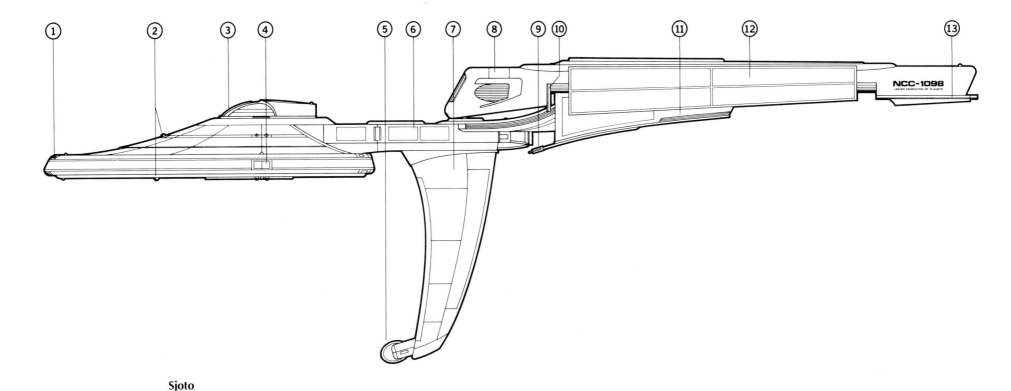

Sjoto

1. Kenelex reaction control system   2. JAKA-2 phaser banks   3. bridge deflector shield enhancement   4. gangway hatch   5. Bia deflector pod   6. propulsion section support pylons   7. deflector pod support pylons   8. LN-91 Mod 1 warp drive units   9. deflector spire   10. primary flow sensor   11. deflector spire dissipation assembly   12. warp field reflector   13. intercooler assembly

limit the ships' velocity capabilities more than originally anticipated. TacFleet later states that it is "satisfied with the combination of the enhanced defensive capabilities of the *Akula*s and their attainable maximum velocity" of warp 18.5 (see *Weapons*).

April 2286 -

Star Fleet directs that additional crew safeguards be added to the *Akula* design, including the addition of a shuttle/escape craft in the Avondale-built ships. Also, the three-person lifeboats in the primary hull of the *Akula*s will have improved "sleeper" qualities.

30 May 2286 -

Work begins on the *Akula* (PA 1090) at Terran Rockwell's Pedersen Spaceport, Earth.

Classification: The *Akula* sub-class was ordered as the final construction group of the *Akyazi*-class perimeter action ships, displaying multiple design differences due to Star Fleet deployment requirements. This sub-class includes hull numbers 1090 through 1114, inclusive.

Design: The ships of the *Akula* sub-class will be assigned to high-threat areas of Federation space. They carry additional defensive systems and more powerful weaponry than their earlier sister ships, enabling them to better fulfill their deployment requirements. The *Akula* (PA 1090) was the first ship launched, and within three weeks of her first deployment (17 May 2288) she had already engaged and defeated

Orion fast attack craft in the vicinity of Kat II. The first of the "B" variant ships, the *Sjoto* (PA 1098), will be commissioned in June of 2290.

As in all *Akyazi* class ships, the *Akula*s possess no "viewing ports" or environmental system reactors of any kind, the exception being those on deck four at the ships' lounge location. (Two small observation ports are located on deck five in the aft weapons section.) This is a safety feature necessitated by mission requirements.

The 01 level bridge of these ships was designed as a more functional lifeboat assembly than the bridge configurations of the *Akyazi* and *Arbiter* groups. The bridge assembly contains a complete thruster package as well as magnetic drive units mounted on the rear port and starboard bulkheads. (These units are similar to those mounted on Star Fleet shuttlecraft.) The internal bridge arrangement of the vessels built by Terran Rockwell differs slightly from the layout of the Vickers-built ships. The bridge configuration of the "B" variant ships (those built by Axaanivus Celesco and Avondale Group) is similar to the bridge design of the *Arbiter* sub-class, with minor variations.

All ships in the *Akula* group possess two holocom rooms, located on deck five. These facilities serve the dual purpose of improving crew morale and well-being and providing intelligence data interpretation. In non-operational situations, each holocom room can be utilized as a holographic entertainment facility, providing stress reduction and relaxation benefits for individual crew members. The mind-link provisions of the holocom facility (more advanced than Star Fleet's senceiver-type

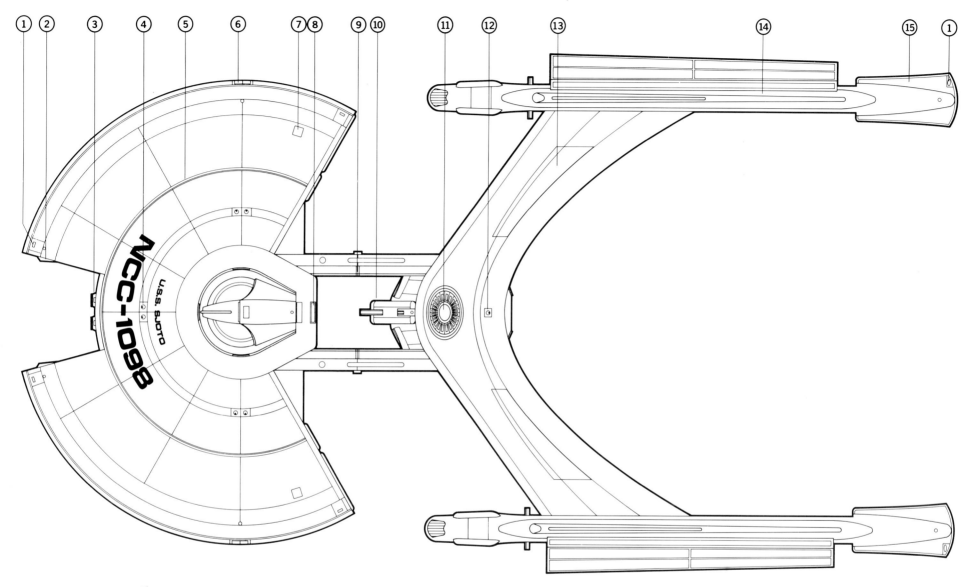

Sjoto

1. Kenelex reaction control system   2. QASR maneuvering thrusters   3. Mk 5 Komati torpedo tubes   4. JAKA-2 phaser banks   5. sensor emplacement   6. gangway hatch   7. personnel hatch   8. lounge viewport   9. explosive bolt separation   10. Bia deflector pod   11. impulse amplification crystal   12. JAKA-5 phaser bank   13. emergency flush vents   14. LN-91 Mod 1 warp drive units   15. intercooler assembly

implants) enable crew members to experience more realistic ''visualizations'' of selected activities. During intelligence operations, information from intelligence drones is transmitted back to the ship and can be analyzed at this location. The holocom apparatus provides a direct link to the user's cerebral cortex, permitting detailed, first-person data analysis and interpretation. Actual visual information from the drone is displayed within the entire area of each holocom room in two- and three-dimensional form, allowing senior officers to interpret incoming data as well. Crew members assigned to interpret holocom images have received specialized training in raw data interpretation and mind-link techniques.

Like the ships of the *Akyazi* group, the *Akula*s are equipped with three-person lifeboats (24 units for a 72-person capacity); all are located on deck five and can be ejected from the bottom of the primary hull in the event of an emergency. (Likewise,

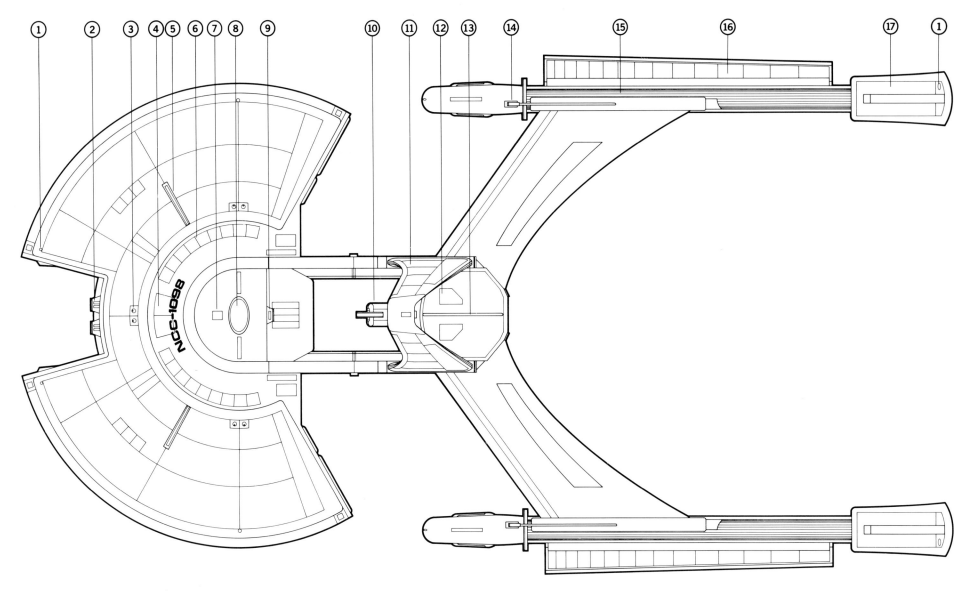

Sjoto

1. bow light   2. Mk 5 Komati torpedo tubes   3. JAKA-2 phaser banks   4. intelligence drone launch covers   5. sensor emplacement   6. lifeboat emplacements   7. tractor beam   8. Lusurre primary sensor array   9. Mk 9 Boris torpedo tube   10. Bia deflector pod   11. deflector pod support pylons   12. antimatter eject covers   13. engineering pod deflector vane   14. deflector spire   15. warp field generator assembly   16. warp field reflector   17. intercooler assembly

the *Akyazi* ships carry 24 lifeboats mounted on the primary hull underside, but also have two additional units at the deck five rear location, giving them a 78-person total capacity. The *Arbiter* ships have 16 individual lifeboat units, each slightly more sophisticated and with a five-person maximum per unit.) All of these lifeboats, supplied by Vorasseur Industries, have advanced sleeper qualities and life support sufficient to sustain their occupants (in ''sleep'' mode) for anywhere from seven to ten

months. A homing beacon detectable by Federation vessels is emitted to aid rescue ships in locating active lifeboats. TacFleet ethic requires that all lifeboats with survivors aboard be retrieved at any cost.

The distance between the warp drive units in the *Akula* ''B'' design is greater than in the other ships of the sub-class due to the inclusion of the ''Skade'' LN-91 warp system in those vessels. Other ''B'' variations include subtle differences in hull forms and

Current specifications of *Akula* sub-class:

Displacement:	74,500 metric tons standard		
	(72,500mt light, 75,750mt full load)		
	NCC-1093, 1095, 1098, 1101, 1105, 1106, 1108-10, 1112, 1114:		
	77,200 metric tons standard		
	(76,000mt light, 78,500mt full load)		
	Overall	Primary Hull	Nacelles
Length:	215.5m	78.9m	119.1m
Beam:	108.0m	107.6m	14.7m
Draft:	68.7m	18.4m	13.8m
	NCC-1093, 1095, 1098, 1101, 1105, 1106, 1108-10, 1112, 1114:		
Length:	222.4m	78.9m	126.7m
Beam:	119.9m	107.6m	16.2m
Draft:	70.4m	18.4m	13.8m

Propulsion: Two (2) "Kratos" LN-94 Mod 1 dilithium-energized antimatter linear warp drive units
 (System contractor: Vickers Engineering Group Ltd., Cumbria, Earth)
NCC-1093, 1095, 1098, 1101, 1105, 1106, 1108-10, 1112, 1114:
Two (2) "Skade" LN-91 Mod 1 dilithium-energized antimatter linear warp drive units
 (System contractor: Vickers Engineering Group Ltd., Cumbria, Earth)
One (1) "Delum" CME-A subatomic unified energy impulse unit
 (System contractor: Orage Ijek, Aksajak, Andor)
Two (2) ASL-5A emergency impulse thrust units
QASR enhanced particle beam maneuvering thrusters
 (Systems contractor: Scarbak Propulsion Systems, Cairo, Earth)
"Shilka" pulsed laser reaction control system
 (System contractor: Vickers Engineering Group Ltd., Cumbria, Earth)
NCC-1093, 1095, 1098, 1101, 1105, 1106, 1108-10, 1112, 1114:
"Kenelex" pulsed laser reaction control system
 (System contractor: Orage Ijek, Aksajak, Andor)

Velocity: Warp 8, standard
Warp 12, maximum
Warp 18.5, battle maximum

Acceleration:	Rest-Onset Critical Momentum: 2.27 sec	
	Onset Critical Momentum-Warp Engage: .93 sec	
	Warp 1-Warp 4:	.28 sec
	Warp 4-Warp 8:	.19 sec
	Warp 8-Warp 12:	1.05 sec
	Warp 12-Warp 18.5:	2.36 sec

Duration: 2 Earth years, standard
3 Earth years, maximum
Complement: 75 (7 officers + 68 crew)
NCC-1093, 1095, 1098, 1101, 1105, 1106, 1108-10, 1112, 1114:
81 (7 officers + 74 crew)
Embarked craft: None
NCC-1095, 1105, 1106, 1109, 1110, 1114: 1
Navigation: "Owl's Eye" Warp Celestial Guidance
 (System contractor: Valdemar NCS Inc., Copenhagen, Earth)
Computers: "Perim" Duotronic IV; "Okios Atur" Logic Subsystem
 (Systems contractor: Kuchata Pratus Ikyla, Arrasta, Daran V)
NCC-1093, 1095, 1098, 1101, 1105, 1106, 1108-10, 1112, 1114:
"Perim" Duotronic IV
 (System contractor: Kuchata Pratus Ikyla, Arrasta, Daran V)
Datatac Support Subsystem
 (System contractor: Farranti Mnemonics, Berkshire, Earth)

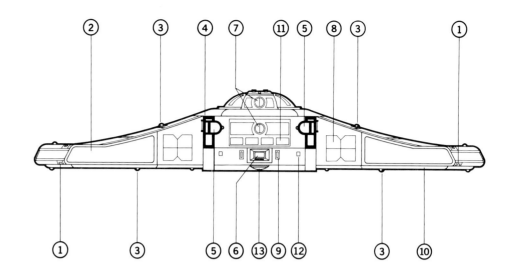

Akula (cross-section at pylon bolt #1, frame 209)

1. Kenelex reaction control system   2. sensor pallets   3. JAKA-2 phaser banks   4. structural bulkheads   5. pylon transfer tube   6. Mk 9 Boris torpedo tube   7. docking ports   8. ASL emergency impulse engines   9. photon exhaust   10. sensor platform   11. lounge viewports   12. viewports   13. Dugoyne primary sensor array

Phasers: 6 banks of 2 each - JAKA-2 independent twin mount
1 bank - JAKA-5 single mount
 (Systems contractor: Asakaze Ordnance Systems Ltd., Honshu-Hamamatsu, Earth)
2 banks - Tuch ISC compact single mount
 (System contractor: Flocon Fleet Defense Systems, Great Lakes, Earth)
Photon torpedoes: 2 tubes - Mk 5 "Komati" independent
1 tube - Mk 9 "Boris" independent
 (Systems contractor: Arvan Toy Conglessum, Binz, Tellar)
Defense: "Merlin II" primary force field and deflector control system
"Zelus" cloaking generation and stasis countermeasure system
 (Systems contractor: Prentice-Schafer Inc., Marsport, Mars)
"Nike" weapon system (enhanced)
TAVITAC Tactical Subsystem
 (Systems contractor: Keindoffer-Klaatsen DSC, Munich, Earth)
"Podi Aschura" deflector spires
"Bia" MDS deflector pod
 (Systems contractor: Kal Achal Conglessum, Takuv, Tellar)
Life support: MCH1 Modular Gravity and Atmosphere Maintenance Unit
 (System contractor: Cristobal SM/S, Manila, Earth)
ARU/SI radiation protection systems
 (System contractor: Kym Lan Den Terra, New Kyoto, Earth)
"Lenix-B" waste regeneration systems
 (System contractor: Jullundur-Lahore Ltd., Bombay, Earth)

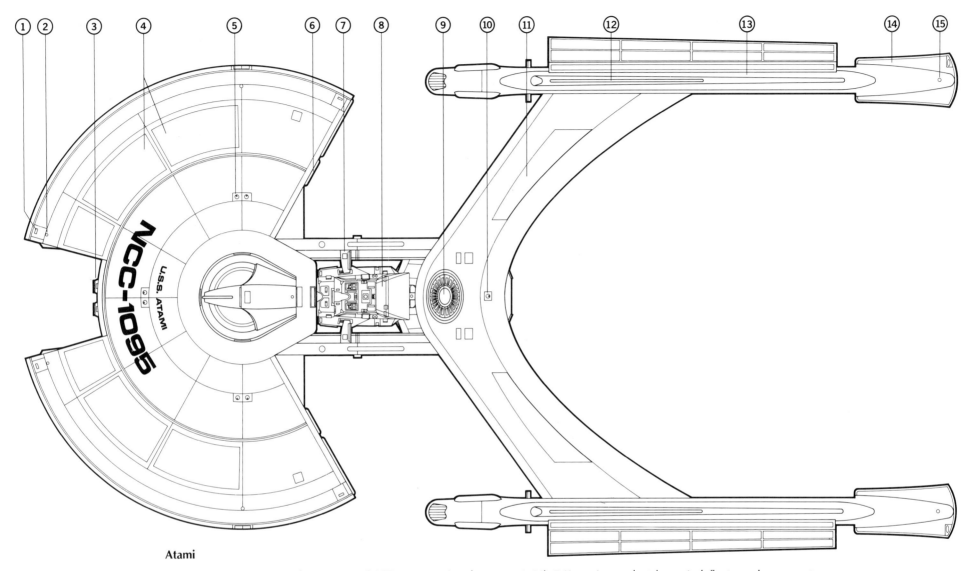

Atami

1. Kenelex reaction control system   2. QASR maneuvering thrusters   3. Mk 5 Komati torpedo tubes   4. deflector enhancement grids   5. JAKA-2 phaser banks   6. sensor pallets   7. docking contact points   8. Mk K (special) warp shuttle   9. impulse amplification crystal   10. JAKA-5 phaser bank   11. emergency flush vents   12. sensor emplacement   13. LN-91 Mod 1 warp drive units   14. intercooler assembly   15. formation light

STAR FLEET STANDARD SHUTTLE

LENGTH:	13.8M	CAPACITY: 6 + 2 CREW
BEAM:	7.8M	MAXIMUM
DRAFT:	3.5M	VELOCITY: SUBLIGHT

STAR FLEET LONG-RANGE SHUTTLE

LENGTH:	18.7M	CAPACITY: 14 + 4 CREW
BEAM:	11.1M	MAXIMUM
DRAFT:	4.4M	VELOCITY: SUBLIGHT

STAR FLEET WARP SHUTTLE MK K (SPECIAL)

LENGTH:	22.8M	CAPACITY: 26 + 3 CREW
BEAM:	14.2M	MAXIMUM
DRAFT:	5.4M	VELOCITY: WARP 2

different dimension figures (see "Specifications" section), as well as the change in bridge configuration mentioned earlier. Additionally, the Avondale-built "B" vessels have deflector enhancement grids on their primary hull topsides and they embark a single, limited-warp escape craft for emergency situations (mounted between the propulsion package support pylons and docked at the deck three docking port location). With minor in-flight modifications this escape craft can be utilized as a limited-duty shuttlecraft in planetfall and other situations.

Engineering: The "Kratos" LN-94 warp units are fitted in most of these ships (the "Skade" units in the "B" variants). The warp reflectors on the "Kratos" engines are curved, increasing their efficiency at capturing the warp field and reflecting it between each engine. Also, as in all *Akyazi* class ships, the warp reflector assemblies act as defensive "shields" for the warp units, protecting them from enemy fire.

The CME-A impulse units are fitted in all ships of the *Akula* sub-class. They are a modification of the CME system in the *Arbiter* group. The ASL-5A emergency impulse system was specifically modified from the basic ASL configuration to operate effectively with the *Akula* design. In the event of propulsion system loss or failure, the units can be fired continuously for approximately 240 hours.

Power for both the deflector spires and the "Bia" deflector pod in these ships is provided by the warp engines. (The deflector spires in the *Akyazi* and *Arbiter* sub-classes also draw power directly from the warp drive system.) In the event of warp unit failure, the CME-A impulse system can provide limited power to the deflector pod, while the spires can be supplied by the secondary power core located on deck five.

Weapons: The *Akula*s mount the JAKA-2 and JAKA-5 phaser systems; all ships (including the "B" variants) are fitted with seven banks (13 emplacements). The Tuch compact phaser system is fitted within the deflector pod assembly - one bank on either side of the deflector unit's generating disk. These units are concealed and are generally used in situations where a tactical advantage is desired.

A retractable phaser system for the *Akula* sub-class was considered early in the design phase. However, the system's development was delayed and it was eventually considered impractical based on PA mission requirements.

The photon torpedo suite is identical to the configuration in the *Akyazi* sub-class - two "Komati" Mk 5 tubes forward and one "Boris" Mk 9 tube aft. At one point, TacFleet had directed that two rear-firing tubes be incorporated into the *Akula* design to further offset the ships' lack of speed. However, the proximity of the deflector pod support pylons to the rear torpedo firing line forced the installation of the single "Boris" rear-firing unit.

The "Bia" series deflector pod operates on the same principle as the ships' deflector spires. Acting as a "lightning rod" during battle, the pod absorbs and dissipates incoming enemy fire (through a series of dissipation vanes located in its support pylon assembly), thereby lessening the strain on the ship's deflector shield system. The pod's successful "attract" rate (the percentage of incoming fire it will successfully "capture" and neutralize) is between 28% and 41%, depending on various factors. (This compares to an 18% to 22% attract rate for each "Podi Aschura" deflector spire.) The deflector pod's tolerance and overload capacities are classified. The "Bia" units have never been tested in actual combat.

Operational: On 04 June 2288 the *Akula* (PA 1090), operating in conjunction with the *Atago* (PA 1052), was challenged by Pryn family Orion fast attack craft at the outskirts of the Kat system. In the mistaken belief that the *Akula* was in the area to close down their latest smuggling route, the Pryn family cited the independence of the Kat system as evidence of Star Fleet's lack of jurisdiction in the area. After being informed of the request for Federation protection by the Conservator of Kat II, the three Pryn vessels ceased communication and opened fire on the *Akula*. After relaying her status to the *Atago* (which was four parsecs distant), the *Akula* quickly neutralized two of the ships by eliminating their warp drive capabilities with photon torpedo volleys directed at their main engines. The third vessel was intercepted two hours later by the *Atago*. The *Akula* suffered minor damage to her port deflector spire and aft RCS system.

Nomenclature: All of the perimeter action ships in the *Akula* sub-class have names that begin with the letter 'A,' 'K,' or 'S.'